# SCIENCE FUSION

**fusion** [FYOO • zhuhn] a combination of two
or more things that releases energy

**This Write-In Student Edition belongs to**

_____

**Teacher/Room**

_____

 HOUGHTON MIFFLIN HARCOURT

HOUGHTON MIFFLIN HARCOURT

**Front Cover:** *stingray* ©Jeffrey L. Rotman/Corbis; *moth* ©Millard H. Sharp/Photo Researchers, Inc.; *astronaut* ©NASA; *thermometer* ©StockImages/Alamy; *robotic arm* ©Garry Gay/The Image Bank/Getty Images.

**Back Cover:** *rowers* ©Stockbyte/Getty Images; *beaker* ©Gregor Schuster/Getty Images; *tree frog* ©DLILLC/Corbis; *Great Basin National Park* ©Frans Lanting/Corbis.

Printed in the U.S.A.

ISBN   978-0-547-58875-9

13   0868   20 19
4500785567   CDEFG

# Consulting Authors

**Michael A. DiSpezio**
*Global Educator*
North Falmouth, Massachusetts

**Marjorie Frank**
*Science Writer and Content-Area Reading Specialist*
Brooklyn, New York

**Michael R. Heithaus**
*Director, School of Environment and Society*
*Associate Professor, Department of Biological Sciences*
Florida International University
North Miami, Florida

**Donna M. Ogle**
*Professor of Reading and Language*
National-Louis University
Chicago, Illinois

# Program Advisors

**Paul D. Asimow**
*Professor of Geology and Geochemistry*
California Institute of Technology
Pasadena, California

**Bobby Jeanpierre**
*Associate Professor of Science Education*
University of Central Florida
Orlando, Florida

**Gerald H. Krockover**
*Professor of Earth and Atmospheric Science Education*
Purdue University
West Lafayette, Indiana

**Rose Pringle**
*Associate Professor*
School of Teaching and Learning
College of Education
University of Florida
Gainesville, Florida

**Carolyn Staudt**
*Curriculum Designer for Technology*
KidSolve, Inc.
The Concord Consortium
Concord, Massachusetts

**Larry Stookey**
*Science Department*
Antigo High School
Antigo, Wisconsin

**Carol J. Valenta**
*Associate Director of the Museum and Senior Vice President*
Saint Louis Science Center
St. Louis, Missouri

**Barry A. Van Deman**
*President and CEO*
Museum of Life and Science
Durham, North Carolina

# Power Up with Science Fusion!

Your program fuses . . .

**e-Learning & Virtual Labs**

**Labs & Explorations**

**Write-In Student Edition**

. . . to generate new science energy for today's science learner—*you.*

# Write-In Student Edition

Be an active reader and make this book your own!

### escribe

use all the words you see here to
You can use your senses to find an
color, taste, size, shape, odor, or te

**tive _____ing** As you read these two pages, circle words
hrases t___ _eal a detail about physical properties.

Write your ideas, answer questions, make notes, and record activity results right on these pages.

### ardness

hard. The grapes
cribes how easily
d or dent.

### Textur
feels li
texture

### Co_____
e words we use for ___ _escribe
e way light bounces ___ object.
at colors do you see ____?

### Taste
ckers are salty. Candy can taste
t or sour. Can you think of
so___hing that tastes bitter?

### These sh
has a nic
you if mi

Learn science concepts and skills by interacting with every page.

# Labs & Activities

Science is all about doing.

Exciting investigations for every lesson.

Ask questions and test your ideas.

Draw conclusions and share what you learn.

## How Can You Model a School?

There are many types of models: mental models, two-dimensional, three-dimensional, and computer models. In this activity, you'll model a part of your school in two ways.

With a team, choose a part of your school to model. It may be a single room, a floor, or a whole building.

Next, choose two types of models to make. Get permission from your teacher to carry out your plans.

With your team, choose the materials you will use. Make any measurements you need, and record them carefully.

Make the two models, and compare them to those of other teams.

# e-Learning & Virtual Labs

Digital lessons and virtual labs provide e-learning options for every lesson of *ScienceFusion*.

Do it!

Initial speed (m/s)
1 2 3 4 5 6 7 8 9 1

1 2 3 4 5 6 7 8 9 10 11 12

Unit 6 Lesson 1 : What Are Some Forms of Energy?

Sound is a form of energy made by vibrations.
Click the first bar on the instrument to see how sound travels.

1 2 3 4 5 6 7 8 9

On your own or with a group, explore science concepts in a digital world.

360° of Inquiry

# Contents

Track Your Progress

LIFE SCIENCE

# Studying Science

## Big Idea

Scientists answer questions about the world around us by carrying out careful investigations.

## I Wonder Why

Why is the work of a scientist doing field research like the work of a scientist doing research in a laboratory? *Turn the page to find out.*

**Here's Why** All scientists ask questions, answer them with investigations, and communicate their results to other scientists.

In this unit, you will explore the Big Idea, the Essential Questions, and the Investigations on the Inquiry Flipchart.

**Levels of Inquiry Key** ■ DIRECTED ■ GUIDED ■ INDEPENDENT

Track Your Progress

**Big Idea** Scientists answer questions about the world around us by carrying out careful investigations.

## Essential Questions

Now I Get the Big Idea!

**Science Notebook**

Before you begin each lesson, be sure to write your thoughts about the Essential Question.

**Essential Question**

# What Do Scientists Do?

##  Engage Your Brain!

Find the answer to the following question in this lesson and record it here.

Biologists make observations about living things. What are some observations you can make about lizards?

_____

_____

_____

_____

_____

## Active Reading

### Lesson Vocabulary

List the terms. As you learn about each one, make notes in the Interactive Glossary.

_____  _____

_____  _____

_____  _____

### Main Ideas

In this lesson, you'll read about how scientists do their work. Active readers look for main ideas before they read to give their reading a purpose. Often, the headings in a lesson state its main ideas. Preview the headings in this lesson to give your reading a purpose.

# The Role of Scientists

It's career day for Mr. Green's fourth-grade class! Mr. Green invited a scientist named Dr. Sims to talk to the class. The students are ready, and they have many questions to ask.

**Active Reading** As you read these two pages, turn the heading into a question in your mind. Then underline the sentence that answers the question.

What do scientists do?

▶ Write a question you would ask a scientist.

_____

_____

_____

_____

"Thank you for inviting me to your school! My name is Dr. Sims, and I am a scientist. A **scientist** asks questions about the natural world. There are many kinds of scientists and many questions to ask!

**Science** is the study of the natural world. Earth scientists study things like rocks, weather, and the planets. Physical scientists study matter and energy. Life scientists, like me, study living things. I am a wildlife biologist, which means I study animals in the wild.

Scientists work alone and in teams. Sometimes, I travel alone on long hikes to watch animals. At other times, I ask other biologists to go with me. I share ideas with other scientists every day.

Science is hard work but fun, too. I like being outdoors. Discovering something new is exciting. The best part, for me, is helping animals. The best way to explain what a scientist does is to show you."

▶ For each area of science, write a question a scientist might ask.

Earth Science

_____

_____

_____

Life Science

_____

_____

_____

Physical Science

_____

_____

_____

Do you work all by yourself?

Is it fun to be a scientist?

# Making Observations and Asking Questions

Dr. Sims looks around the classroom. She observes everything for a few moments. Then she asks questions about what she sees.

> How does that plant produce offspring?

> Does the lizard's skin ever change colors?

> Does the goldfish spend more time near the top of the tank or the bottom of the tank?

▶ Ask your own question about the classroom in the photo.

_____

_____

_____

▶ Name five things you observe in this classroom.

_____

_____

_____

_____

Scientists make observations about the world around them. An **observation** is information collected by using the five senses.

Scientists ask questions about their observations. Notice that Dr. Sims' questions are about the living things in the classroom. That's because she is a wildlife biologist. Your questions might be different if you observed different things than she did.

Dr. Sims asks, "How would you find an answer to my question about the goldfish?" She and the students talk about watching the fish. Someone suggests writing observations in a notebook. Someone else says a stopwatch can help.

Dr. Sims says, "I could do all these things in an investigation." Scientists conduct an **investigation** to answer questions. The steps of an investigation may include asking questions, making observations, reading or talking to experts, drawing conclusions, and sharing what you learn.

# Experiments

Dr. Sims seems very excited to talk about investigations. She says, "Describing what you see is one kind of investigation. Other investigations include doing an experiment."

**Active Reading** As you read these two pages, circle the lesson vocabulary word each time it is used.

## A Fair Test

An *experiment* is a fair test. It can show that one thing causes another thing to happen. In each test, you change only one factor, or *variable*. To be fair and accurate, you conduct the experiment multiple times.

To test something else, you must start a new experiment. Being creative and working in teams can help scientists conduct experiments.

Carlos is conducting an experiment. He gives the lizard fruit and crickets to see which will be eaten. The food is the only variable that is changed. Each day, the lizard gets two different types of food at the same time and in the same amounts.

# Scientific Methods

Scientific investigations use scientific methods. Scientific methods may include the following activities:

- make observations

- ask a question

- form a hypothesis

- plan and conduct an experiment

- record and analyze results

- draw conclusions

- communicate results

Sometimes, these steps are done in this order. At other times, they're not.

A **hypothesis** is an idea or explanation that can be tested with an investigation. Dr. Sims gives the students an example from their classroom. She says, "I hypothesize that this lizard eats more insects than fruit."

▶ Talk with other students in your class. Then write a hypothesis to explain what makes the lizard in the photo change color.

_____

_____

_____

_____

_____

_____

# Other Kinds of Investigations

Dr. Sims smiles. She says, "I hope this doesn't confuse anyone, but doing an experiment isn't always possible."

**Active Reading** As you read these two pages, circle the clue words or phrases that signal a detail such as an example or an added fact.

Many science questions cannot be answered by doing an experiment. Here's one question: What kind of lizard have I found? This question can be answered by using an identification guide. Here's another question: What causes the sun to seem to rise and set? This question can be answered by making and using a model of Earth and the sun. Here's another: At what time of year does a state get the most rain? This question can be answered by looking for patterns through many years of rainfall records. Here's another: How did people who lived 100 years ago describe Mars? This question can be answered with research. Research includes reading what others have written and asking experts.

What is the surface of Mars like? This question is hard to answer with an experiment. NASA scientists sent robot spacecraft to Mars. Cameras on these spacecraft take pictures of the planet for scientists to observe.

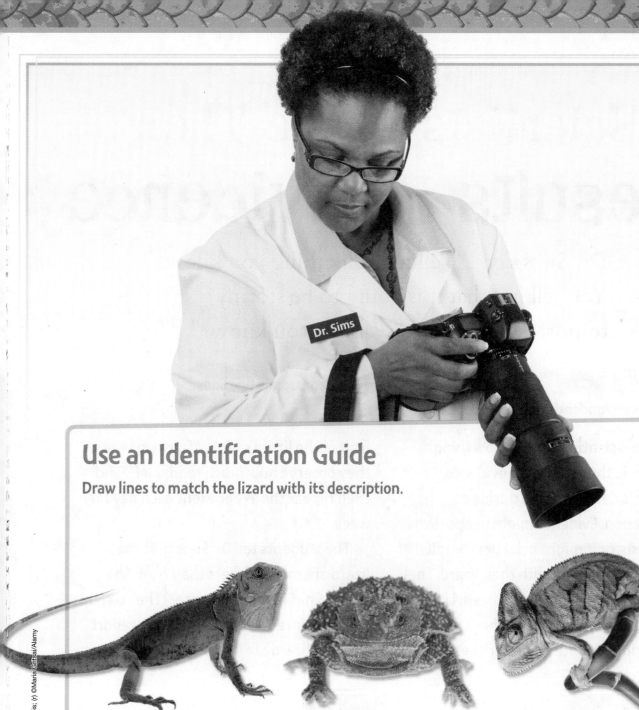

## Use an Identification Guide

Draw lines to match the lizard with its description.

### Texas Horned Lizard

- Colors: brownish
- Body: wider and flatter than other lizards
- Tail: straight and shorter than the body
- Spines: several short horns on head, spiny scales on sides of body

### Common Chameleon

- Colors: green, yellow, gray, or brown
- Eyes: big and bulge out from side of head
- Body: tall and flat, a ridge of scales along the backbone
- Tail: curls for grasping branches

### Common Iguana

- Colors: green, gray, brown, blue, lavender, or black
- Spines: along center of back and tail
- Body: Large flap of skin under the chin

# Scientists Share Their Results as Evidence

Dr. Sims says, "Tell me something you know." You tell her that it is going to be stormy tomorrow. She says, "*How* do you know?"

**Active Reading** As you read these two pages, draw two lines under the main idea.

When scientists explain how things work, they must give evidence. *Evidence* is data gathered during an investigation. Evidence might support your hypothesis, or it might not. For example, think about the class with their lizard. The students tell Dr. Sims a hypothesis: Lizards eat more insects than fruit. They carry out an experiment, putting tiny crickets and fruit in the lizard's tank. After two hours, they observe how much food is left, and then repeat the experiment each day for a week.

The students tell Dr. Sims that their lizard ate more crickets than fruit. She says, "What is your evidence?" The students share their recorded results. They report that the lizard ate 13 crickets and no fruit.

# Science Notebook

A *conclusion* is an explanation that is based on evidence. Write conclusions for the evidence given below.

### Evidence

We used thermometers and found that when the air temperature changed by 5 degrees, a chameleon's skin color changed.

### Conclusion

_____

_____

_____

_____

### Evidence

We measured the temperature at the same time each morning and afternoon for one month. Each day, the air temperature was higher in the afternoon than in the morning.

### Conclusion

_____

_____

_____

_____

_____

### Evidence

| Paper Airplane Wingspan (cm) | Time in the Air (sec) |
|---|---|
| 5 | 7 |
| 10 | 12 |
| 15 | 21 |
| 20 | 28 |

### Conclusion

_____

_____

_____

_____

# Sum It Up!

When you're done, use the answer key to check and revise your work.

**Fill in the missing words to tell what scientists do.**

## Summarize

Mr. Brown's fourth-grade class wants a pet in their classroom. Their teacher says they have to think like a (1) _____ to care for animals. The students know that means (2) _____ about the natural world. The class wonders what kinds of animals make good classroom pets. They decide to do an (3) _____ to find out. They go to the library and use books and websites to (4) _____ pets.

The class concludes that guinea pigs are the best pets for their classroom. Mr. Brown asks them what (5) _____ they have to support their conclusion. The students explain that guinea pigs are quiet and gentle. They are also active in the daytime and sleep at night.

Once the guinea pigs are in the classroom, the students watch and listen. They keep a science journal and list all their (6) _____. Then, students ask (7) _____ based on what they observe. One is: What does it mean when the guinea pigs make squeaking sounds? Two students have a (8) _____ : guinea pigs make that noise when they want to be fed.

Mr. Brown suggests that the students record the time when they hear the sound and write down what they are doing at the same time. After a few days, the students see that their guinea pigs make that noise just as the zippered bag that holds the fresh vegetables is opened. So, what do you think the sound means? (9) _____

_____

Answer Key: 1. scientist, 2. asking questions, 3. investigation, 4. research, 5. evidence, 6. observations, 7. questions, 8. hypothesis, 9. It means they want to eat the vegetables right away.

Name _____

## Word Play

**1** Use the words in the box to complete the puzzle.

### Across

5. An explanation based on evidence
7. Scientists do one of these to answer questions

### Down

1. An idea or explanation that can be tested with an investigation
2. To share the results of investigations
3. A person who asks questions about the natural world
4. You ask this
6. A kind of investigation that is a fair test

| communicate | conclusion | experiment* | hypothesis* |
| investigation* | question | scientist* | |

\* Key Lesson Vocabulary

# Apply Concepts

**2** Choose an object to observe. List some observations. Then ask some questions related to your observations.

Name of Object: _____    Questions: _____

Observations: _____    _____

_____    _____

_____    _____

_____    _____

**3** Your family uses steel wool soap pads for cleaning pots and pans. Often they get rusty after use. What could you do to stop the pads from rusting? Write a hypothesis you could test. _____

_____

**4** The graph shows the results of a national online poll in which students were asked to name their favorite lunch food. What conclusions can you draw? _____

_____

_____

_____

_____

_____

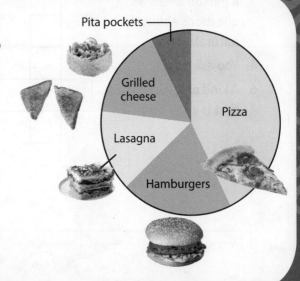

Pita pockets

Grilled cheese

Pizza

Lasagna

Hamburgers

**Take It Home!** You can think like a scientist at home, too. Which window cleaner leaves fewer streaks? What kind of bird did I see outside my window? Make a list of questions with your family. Investigate them together.

# What Skills Do Scientists Use?

Essential Question

© Houghton Mifflin Harcourt Publishing Company  ©Richard H Johnston/Getty Images

## Engage Your Brain!

Find the answer to the following question in the lesson and record it here.

Splash it. Pour it. Freeze it. Make bubbles in it. What skills might a scientist use to test how water behaves?

_____

_____

_____

_____

## Active Reading

### Lesson Vocabulary

List the terms. As you learn about each one, make notes in the interactive Glossary.

_____

_____

_____

_____

### Visual Aids

In this lesson, you'll see large graphics with labels. The labels call attention to important details. Active readers preview a lesson's graphics and decide how the information in them provides details about the main idea.

# Everyday Science Skills

Do you ask questions about the world around you? If so, you use these science skills all day, every day—just like a scientist!

**Active Reading** As you read the next four pages, circle the names of nine science skills.

As you read about scientists, think → **"Hey, I can do this, too!"**

## Infer

Scientists *infer* how things work by thinking about their observations. A biologist may infer that the color patterns of fish enable them to blend in and avoid predators.

## Observe

Scientists may *observe* many things, such as changes in color, temperature, and bubbling.

Scientists use inquiry skills every day—and so do you. When you observe, you use your five senses to get information. Let's say you smell cheese, bread, and spicy odors. You *infer* "I think we are having pizza for lunch today!" An **inference** is a statement that explains an observation.

When you think about how things are the same and different, you *compare* them. For example, your family wants to adopt a new kitten. You compare different kittens, looking for one that is playful and friendly. When you decide which kitten is the best, you *communicate* that decision to your family. You can communicate by speaking, writing, and by using pictures or models.

## Compare

Scientists *compare* objects and things that happen.

▶ Practice the skill of *comparing*. List ways these two fish are similar and different.

Powder-Blue Tang          Porcupinefish

| Similarities | Differences |
|---|---|
|  |  |
|  |  |
|  |  |
|  |  |
|  |  |

## Communicate

▶ Scientists *communicate*, or share, their results and inferences with other scientists. What did you communicate today?

_____

_____

_____

19

# Think Like a
# Scientist

Scientists use these skills every day in their investigations. Find out what they are and when you might use them.

## Predict

Scientists use their observations and existing research to make predictions about what will happen in the future. For example, a meteorologist uses weather patterns to determine whether it will rain over the weekend.

## Use Variables

When scientists plan experiments, they think, "What is the one thing I will change?" That one thing is a variable. Let's say you want to find out how cold a freezer has to be to make fruit pops. The variable that you will change is the temperature inside the freezer.

Some science skills are part of doing science investigations, including experiments. They may sound unfamiliar to you. But when you read about these skills, you might realize that you already use them.

## Plan and Conduct Investigations

Scientists plan and conduct investigations that will answer science questions. Say you want to know how salty water must be to make an egg float. First, you think about the steps you'll take to find the answer. Next, you gather the materials you'll use. Then, you test the amount of salt.

▶ You are a marine biologist. You study living things in the ocean. What is one investigation you might plan?

_____

_____

_____

Predict what a marine biologist might look for on a dive.

_____

_____

## Hypothesize

Scientists hypothesize when they think of a testable statement that tries to explain an observation. Suppose you notice that water seems to evaporate at different rates from containers with different shapes. What would you hypothesize is a cause?

## Draw Conclusions

Scientists draw conclusions when they use evidence to evaluate a hypothesis. If you investigate how the size of a sail affects how quickly a toy boat moves, you might conclude that boats with larger sails move faster because larger sails collect more wind.

# Math and Science Skills

Using rulers and balances. Putting things in order. Measuring the speed of a car. Making tables and graphs. Sounds like math, but it's science, too!

**Active Reading** As you read this page, turn the heading into a question in your mind. Then underline the parts of the text that answer the question.

Every scientist uses math. Let's say you are a marine biologist who studies whales. You *classify* whales by how much they weigh or how long they are from head to tail. You put them in *order* when you arrange them by length from smallest to largest. You *use numbers* to tell how many are alive today. You *use time and space relationships* to investigate when and where they migrate each year. You *measure* how long they are and how much food they eat. You *record and display* the results of your investigations in writing and in tables, graphs, and maps.

## Classify and Order

You classify things when you put them into groups. To put things in order, you may make a list in which position matters, such as ordering bird species by how fast they fly or move.

## Measure

In science and math, you measure by using tools to find length, width, height, mass, weight, volume, and elapsed time.

## Use Numbers

You use numbers when you observe by counting or measuring. You also use numbers to compare and order. And, you use numbers to describe speed and force.

# Do the Math!

## Compare Numbers

Some of the world's biggest mammals live under the oceans' waves. The table gives the names of several kinds of whales and the number that scientists estimate are alive today.

| Kind of Whale | Population |
|---|---|
| Beluga whale | 200,000 |
| Blue whale | 14,000 |
| Fin whale | 55,000 |
| Humpback whale | 40,000 |
| Minke whale | 1,000,000 |
| Pilot whale | 1,200,000 |
| Sei whale | 54,000 |
| Sperm whale | |

1. Which two kinds of whales have the closest number alive?

_____

2. How many more Pilot whales are there than Minke whales?

_____

3. Scientists estimate there are about three hundred and sixty thousand sperm whales alive today. Write that number, using numerals, in the table.

## Use Time and Space Relationships

You use stopwatches and clocks to tell the time. You can predict when it will be high tide or low tide. You can also determine how the planets move in space.

## Record and Display Data

You record observations on clipboards, in notebooks, and on computers. You display, or show, data so that it's easy to understand by making tables, graphs, or diagrams.

# Sum It Up!

When you're done, use the answer key to check and revise your work.

**Fill in the missing skills in the column where they belong.**

## Summarize

### Scientists Use Skills

| Everyday Science Skills | Science Investigation Skills | Math and Science Skills |
|---|---|---|
| 1. _____ | 5. _____ | 10. _____ |
| 2. _____ | 6. _____ | 11. _____ |
| 3. _____ | 7. _____ | 12. _____ |
| 4. _____ | 8. _____ | 13. _____ |
| | 9. _____ | 14. _____ |

Answer Key: 1–4. infer, communicate, compare, observe; 5–9. predict, use variables, plan and conduct investigations, draw conclusions, hypothesize; 10–14. measure, classify and order, record and display data, use time and space relationships, use numbers

Name _____

## Word Play

**1** It's easy to get tongue-tied describing what scientists do. Look at the statements below. Switch the red words around until each statement about inquiry skills makes sense.

In order to sort his beakers and other tools, Dr. Mallory hypothesizes each object by size and shape. _____

Gabriella measures that her dog will want his favorite food for dinner, because she has observed him eat it quickly many times before. _____

Kim predicts when planning an experiment with her older brother. She keeps everything the same during their procedure, except for the one factor being tested. _____

After completing an experiment and summarizing her findings, Dr. Garcia classifies what she has learned with other scientists. _____

Dr. Jefferson studies the age of rocks and fossils. She uses variables to tell how old each specimen is. _____

Before conducting his experiment for the science fair, Derrick uses time and space relationships about which sample of fertilizer will make his tomato plant grow the fastest.

_____

To find out how long it takes Deshawn to ride his bike 100 m, Jessica communicates the time with a stopwatch. _____

# Apply Concepts

**2** Write how you would use numbers to investigate each object.

_____      _____      _____

_____      _____      _____

_____      _____      _____

_____      _____      _____

**3** For each one, what kinds of observations could you record on a calendar?

_____      _____      _____

_____      _____      _____

_____      _____      _____

_____      _____      _____

**Take It Home!**

There are many books in the library about scientists and how they think about the world around them. Pick a book with a family member. Find examples of the skills you learned about and make a list.

Essential Question

# How Do Scientists Collect and Use Data?

**Engage Your Brain!**

Find the answer to the following question in this lesson and record it here.

Are the ladybugs on this tree identical to each other? How would you investigate this question?

_____

_____

_____

_____

## Active Reading

### Lesson Vocabulary

List the terms. As you learn about each one, make notes in the Interactive Glossary.

_____

_____

_____

_____

### Main Idea and Details

Details give information about a topic. The information may be examples, features, or characteristics. Active readers stay focused on the topic when they ask, What facts or information do these details add to the topic?

# Research Is the Key

Tiny insects fly and flash on a summer night. Are you curious about them? Do you wonder how to find out what they are and how they light up? Do some research!

Often scientists ask themselves, "What do other scientists know about this?" To find out, they do *research*. When you research, you use reference materials and talk to experts to learn what is known. So, if you want to learn what scientists know about fireflies, you can do these things:

- Use an encyclopedia.

- Read a book.

- Read science articles.

- Visit a museum.

- E-mail a scientist.

- Visit science websites.

These kinds of resources may have plenty of information about fireflies. But you will still have questions they do not answer. That's when you conduct your own investigations.

Natural history museums have insect collections as well as scientists who can answer questions about them.

## Do the Research!

You just saw bees flying in and out of a hole in an old tree. You know it's not a good idea to get too close. So, how can you find out what bees do inside a tree? What research resource would you go to first? Explain why.

_____

_____

_____

_____

# Science Tools

What comes to mind when you hear the word *tools*? Hammers, saws, and screwdrivers? How about computers and calculators? Both of these are science tools.

**Active Reading** As you read these two pages, circle the lesson vocabulary each time it is used.

Scientists use all kinds of tools. Many turn the five senses into "super-senses." Tools enable scientists to see things that are far away, to smell faint odors, to hear quiet sounds, and to feel vibrations their bodies can't.

Let's say you want to observe craters on the moon. A telescope, which makes faraway objects look closer, will turn your sense of sight into "super-vision."

An ant looks larger in a magnifying box or with a hand lens.

What if you're interested in studying tiny critters, such as leaf cutter ants? Take along a hand lens. Hand lenses make small objects look bigger. Is the ant crawling away too fast to see it with the hand lens? Try gently placing the ant in a magnifying box. The top of the box has a lens in it.

Wondering what the ant's bite marks look like? Place a tiny piece of a cut leaf under a microscope. A **microscope** is a tool for looking at objects that cannot be seen with the eye alone.

▶ Predict how the ant would look using a microscope. Make a drawing and add labels.

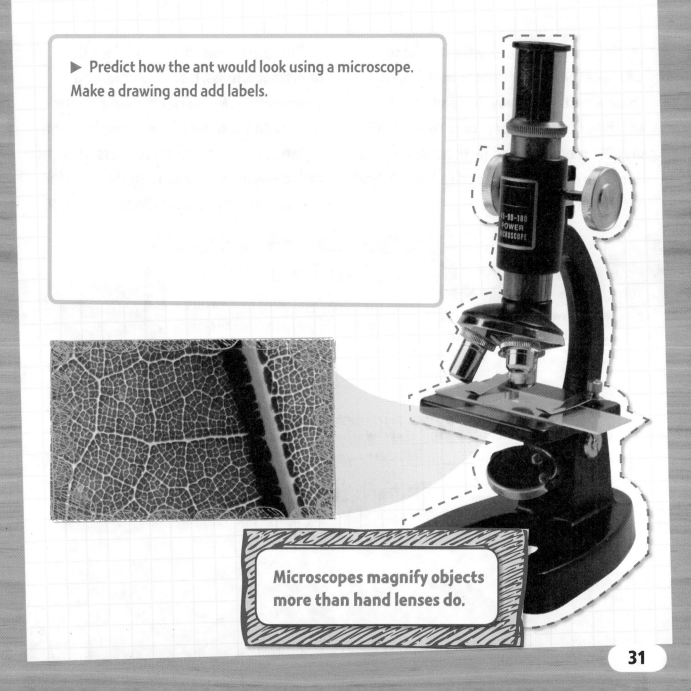

Microscopes magnify objects more than hand lenses do.

# Measurement Tools

What's the biggest bug in the world? How far can a grasshopper hop? How long can a butterfly fly? How do scientists find exact answers?

Scientists use measurement tools to make their observations more exact. Think about it this way. You and your friend watch two grasshoppers hop. Your friend says, "This one jumped farther." But you think the other one jumped farther. To find out for sure, you need to measure.

There are tools to measure length or distance, mass, force, volume, and temperature. Most scientists use metric units with these tools. For example, a **pan balance** is used to measure mass with units called grams (g). A **spring scale** is used to measure force in units called newtons (N).

## Pan Balance

Place the object you want to measure on one pan. Add gram masses to the other pan until the two pans balance. Add the masses together to find the total in grams (g).

# Tape Measure

This tool is used to measure length in millimeters (mm), centimeters (cm), and meters (m).

# Spring Scale

Hang an object from the hook. As the spring stretches, the marker will show the size of the force in newtons (N). What could you measure with a spring scale?

_____

_____

# Thermometer

Used to measure temperature, this tool has two sets of units: degrees Celsius (°C) and degrees Fahrenheit (°F).

## Do the Math!
### Make Measurements

You've found a stick insect! Use the ruler to find the length of its body. Write the number and units.

_____

_____

_____

Find an object in your classroom to measure with a spring scale. Write the name of the object and number of units.

_____

_____

_____

Look at the thermometer on this page. Write the temperature in degrees Celsius (°C) and degrees Fahrenheit (°F).

_____

_____

_____

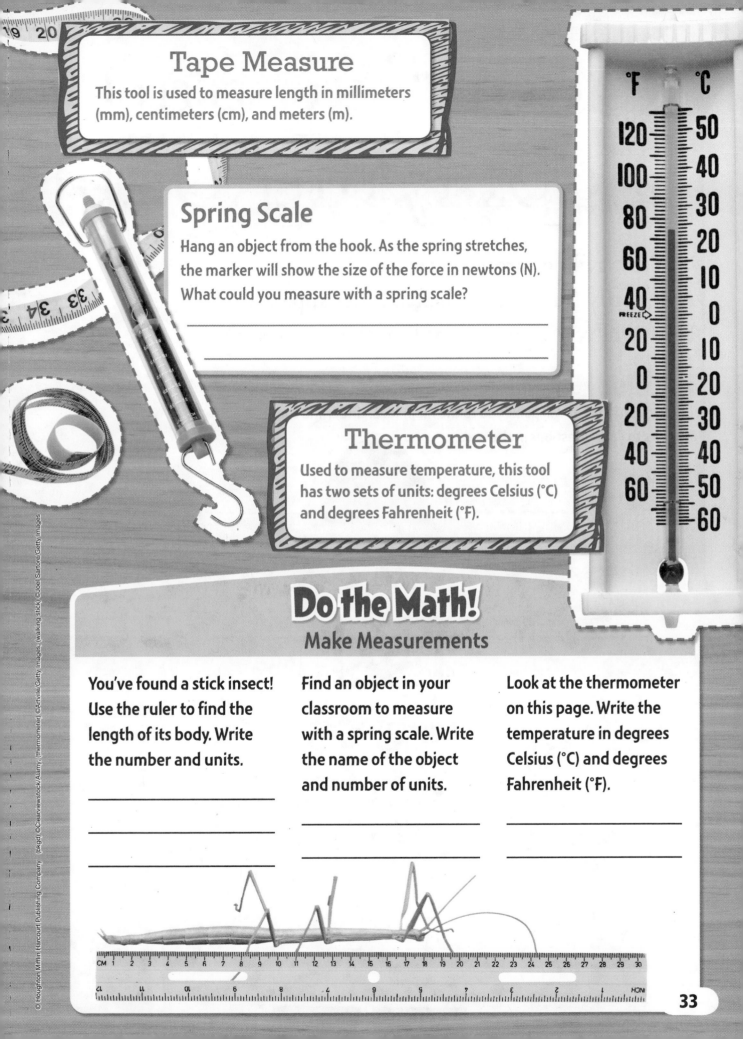

# Recording and Displaying Data

You're crawling through a tropical jungle.
A butterfly flutters by. Then another appears.
How will you keep track of how many you see?

A poster is one way to display data.

# Recording Data

**T**he bits of information you observe are called **data**. Some data are in the form of numbers. For example, the number of butterflies you see in an hour is a piece of data. Other data are in the form of descriptions. Examples include written notes, diagrams, audio recordings, and photographs.

Only observations are data. So when you think, "There are more butterflies here than in Canada," that's a guess, not data.

# Displaying Data

The data you record as you investigate may be correct, but not easy to understand. Later, you can decide how to display the data. For example, you might use your scribbled notes from the jungle to draw a map showing where you saw each butterfly. You might compare the number of each kind of butterfly you found in a circle graph. You might use a bar graph to show the number of butterflies you saw each hour.

## Data Two Ways

The table on the left lists six butterflies and the number of wing flaps each one made as it passed by an observer. The bar graph on the right can display the same data. Use the data in the table to complete the graph.

| Individual Butterfly | Number of Wing Flaps in a Row |
|---|---|
| A | 3 |
| B | 9 |
| C | 4 |
| D | 3 |
| E | 3 |
| F | 10 |

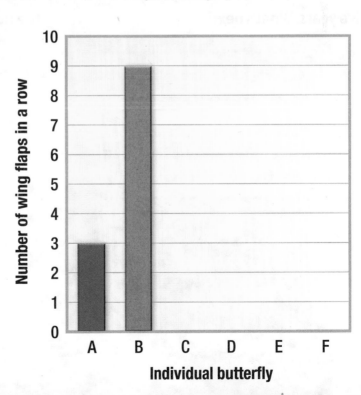

# Using Data

You see on the news that the number of honeybees in the United States is decreasing. What is happening to them? How do scientists use data to solve problems and share information?

## Drawing Conclusions

You've recorded your data. You've displayed it in a way that is easy to understand. Your next step is to analyze, or look for patterns in, the data. You might identify a trend, or a direction in the data over time. For example, you might conclude that the number of honeybees in your hometown has decreased by 30% in the last five years. What's next?

## Communicating

Scientists communicate in many ways. They may work together to collect data. They compare their data with other scientists doing similar investigations. They report their results and conclusions by giving talks and writing reports. Conclusions often lead to new questions to investigate. Scientists are still studying why the number of honeybees is decreasing.

Scientists can share data as they make observations by using electronic devices.

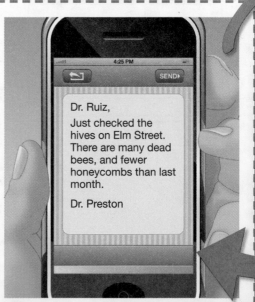

4:25 PM

SEND

Dr. Ruiz,

Just checked the hives on Elm Street. There are many dead bees, and fewer honeycombs than last month.

Dr. Preston

Scientists may work alone or in teams to analyze data and draw conclusions.

▶ A database is a collection of information or objects. Databases are organized so they are easy to search—like a search website. How would you search a database of insect facts to see what others have learned about the decrease in the number of honeybees?

_____

_____

_____

_____

Museums often have large collections of specimens, so scientists can compare what they have found to what's in a museum.

When you're done, use the answer key to check and revise your work.

**The outline below is a summary of the lesson. Complete the outline.**

## Summarize

I. Research Is the Key

    A. Scientists do research to find out what others know.

    B. Reference sources you can use:

        1. encyclopedias

        2. _____

        3. _____

        4. _____

        5. _____

        6. _____

II. Science Tools

    A. Scientists use tools to make the senses more powerful.

    B. Tools that aid the sense of sight:

        1. telescope

        2. _____

        3. _____

        4. _____

III. _____

    A. pan balance

    B. spring scale

    C. tape measure/ruler

    D. _____

IV. Recording and Displaying Data

    A. Data are the bits of information you observe.

    B. Ways to display data:

        1. tables

        2. _____

        3. _____

## Word Play

**1** Put the mixed-up letters in order to spell a science term from the box.

tada ⬡⬡⬡⬡

eama supteer ⬡⬡⬡⬡ ⬡⬡⬡⬡⬡⬡

crasheer ⬡⬡⬡⬡⬡⬡⬡⬡

priclg harce ⬡⬡⬡⬡⬡ ⬡⬡⬡⬡⬡

croopsmice ⬡⬡⬡⬡⬡⬡⬡⬡⬡⬡

gripes clans ⬡⬡⬡⬡⬡ ⬡⬡⬡⬡⬡⬡

montumceica ⬡⬡⬡⬡⬡⬡⬡⬡⬡⬡⬡

axingbynim fog ⬡⬡⬡⬡⬡⬡⬡⬡⬡ ⬡⬡⬡

metermother ⬡⬡⬡⬡⬡⬡⬡⬡⬡⬡⬡

lap cannaeb ⬡⬡⬡ ⬡⬡⬡⬡⬡⬡⬡

| circle graph | communicate | data* | magnifying box | microscope* |
| pan balance* | research | spring scale* | tape measure | thermometer |

* Key Lesson Vocabulary

# Apply Concepts

**2** Someone gives you an object. You think it's a rock, but you aren't sure. Write how you could use each resource to do research.

encyclopedia

websites

books

_____

_____

_____

_____

_____

_____

contact a scientist

museum

_____

_____

_____

_____

**3** Draw lines to match the tool to its use.

pan balance      to measure force

spring scale      to look closely at insects outdoors

thermometer      to measure mass

microscope      to find temperature

hand lens      to view objects too small to be seen with the eye alone

**Take It Home!** Tell your family about the measurement tools scientists use. Discuss ways your family measures at home. Find and learn to use these tools. Hint: Does your kitchen have tools for measuring foods?

Name _____

Essential Question

# Why Do Scientists Compare Results?

## Set a Purpose
What will you learn from this investigation?

_____

_____

_____

## Think About the Procedure
Which tool will you use to measure mass?

_____

_____

_____

_____

Which units of length will your group use?
Explain your choice.

_____

_____

_____

_____

## Record Your Data
In the space below, make a table in which you record your measurements.

## Draw Conclusions

Of the three measurement tools you used, which did you find the easiest to use? Which was the hardest? Explain.

_____

_____

_____

_____

## Analyze and Extend

1. Why is it helpful to compare results with others?

_____

_____

_____

2. What should you do if you find out that your measurements are very different than those of other teams?

_____

_____

_____

3. What other characteristics of the object can you measure?

_____

_____

_____

_____

4. The picture shows two more measurement tools. Write about what you could measure with each one.

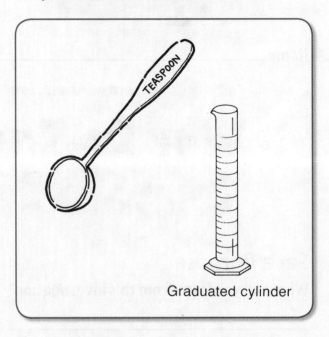

Graduated cylinder

_____

_____

_____

5. What other questions would you like to ask about science tools?

_____

_____

_____

_____

42

## John Diebold

Dr. John Diebold spent much of his life studying Earth's oceans. He worked in the lab and in the field. He studied volcanoes, ancient ice sheets, and faults that cause earthquakes under water. Dr. Diebold improved the design of the *air gun*, a tool used to make underwater sound waves. Then he used these sound waves to make 3-D pictures of the ocean floor.

Much of Earth's oceans are too deep to study directly. John Diebold used many tools like this air gun to help people study the ocean floor from the surface.

# Meet the Inventors

These gears are many times smaller than a millimeter! Dr. Culpepper's tools can be used to assemble objects this small.

## Martin Culpepper

Dr. Martin Culpepper is a mechanical engineer. He invents tools that work with machines so small you cannot see them with a regular light microscope. These machines are many times smaller than the thickness of a human hair! One day these tiny machines could be used to find cancer cells. Unlike Dr. Diebold, Dr. Culpepper does most of his research in a lab. His lab has to be dust-free; a tiny bit of dust could ruin the results of his investigations.

# Field Versus Lab

**In the Field** Scientists often work in the field, or the world outside of labs. What did Dr. Diebold learn from his studies in the field?

_____
_____
_____

Research done by Dr. Diebold and others in the field led to the development of maps like this one. The map shows rock and sediment layers beneath the ocean floor.

This tool is a tiny lifter! It moves and sets into position the incredibly small parts of tiny machines.

**In the Lab** Why do you think Dr. Culpepper builds machines in a lab? Why would he not build them in the field?

_____
_____
_____
_____

## Think About It!

How might a scientist's work be both in the field and in a lab? Think of an example.

_____
_____
_____

**Essential Question**

# What Kinds of Models Do Scientists Use?

## Engage Your Brain!

Find the answer to the following question in this lesson and record it here.

This is a scale model of the moon. What can scientists learn by studying it?

_____

_____

_____

_____

## Active Reading

### Lesson Vocabulary

List the terms. As you learn about each one, make notes in the Interactive Glossary.

_____

_____

_____

_____

### Signal Words: Comparisons

Signal phrases show connections between ideas. Words that signal comparisons, or similarities, include *like, better than, also, alike, as close as,* and *stands for.* Active readers remember what they read because they are alert to signal phrases that identify comparisons.

Two-dimensional model
of the solar system

# Models and Science

Native Americans had mental models for the sun, moon, and planets. Several tribes in North America tell stories of the beginning of time, when Earth did not exist. All of the animals applied mud to the shell of a turtle. Earth was born when the mud became thick and large on the turtle's back.

## Make a Two-dimensional Model!

Good models are as close to the real thing as possible. Draw a floor plan of a room in your home. Show the doorways and windows. Show the objects that sit on the floor. Add labels. Be as accurate as you can!

A toy car. A doll's house. A person who shows off clothes on a runway. These are all models. But what is a model in science?

As you read these two pages, draw a star next to what you think is the most important sentence. Be ready to explain why.

Scientists make models to investigate questions and explain conclusions. In science, a **model** represents something real that is too big, too small, or has too many parts to investigate directly. For example, our solar system is too big to see all the parts at once. So, scientists make models of the solar system. They use models to investigate the motion and positions of planets and moons. They can use the models to predict when a comet or asteroid will pass close to Earth.

Models can take many forms. A *mental model* is a picture you create in your mind. One good thing about this kind of model is that you always have it with you! A **two-dimensional model** has length and width. It can be a drawing, a diagram, or a map.

# Other Models Scientists Use

## Do the Math!
### Use Fractions

You plan to make a model of the solar system. You make the tiniest ball of clay you can for Mercury. The ball is 4 mm across. If Mercury were that size, the chart shows how big all the other objects in your model would be.

| Object | Diameter (mm) |
|--------|---------------|
| Sun | 1,100 |
| Mercury | 4 |
| Venus | 9 |
| Earth | 10 |
| Mars | 5 |
| Jupiter | 110 |
| Saturn | 92 |
| Uranus | 37 |
| Neptune | 36 |

1. What fraction tells how the size of Mars compares to Earth?

_____

2. Which object is about 1/4 the diameter of Neptune?

_____

3. Which object is about 1/9 the diameter of Saturn?

_____

You see thousands of stars in the night sky. You point to a very bright star. Suddenly, you are zooming through space. As you get closer, the star gets bigger and brighter. Your trip isn't real, but it feels like it is. It's another kind of model!

**Active Reading** As you read these two pages, draw boxes around a clue word or phrase that signal things are being compared.

## Three-Dimensional Models

The more a model is like the real thing, the better it is. If the object you want to model has length, width, and height, a **three-dimensional model** is useful. Such a model can show the positions of planets, moons, and the sun better than a two-dimensional model can.

If you want to compare sizes and distances in a model, then you make a *scale model.* The scale tells how much smaller or bigger the model is than the real thing. For example, a model railroad may have a scale of 1 to 48. This means each one inch on the model stands for 48 inches on the real train.

## Computer Models

What if you want to understand how asteroids move through the solar system? You'd use a computer model. A **computer model** is a computer program that models an event or object. Some computer models make you feel like you are moving through the solar system!

# Weather Models Save Lives

Dangerous weather can happen suddenly. Hurricanes, tornadoes, floods, and winter storms can harm people, pets, and homes. How can models save lives?

FLORIDA

## Data from Space

Satellites circle Earth 24 hours each day. Images and other weather data are beamed back to Earth. It's called *real-time* data because scientists see the pictures almost as soon as they are taken. In this image, a hurricane sits along the coast of Florida. The colors are not real. Scientists choose them to show differences in wind speeds, heights of clouds, and other factors.

## Using Models

Meteorologists use satellite data to make computer models of weather. They model hurricanes, tornadoes, and thunderstorms. The models are used to predict how and where storms will get started.

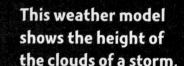
This weather model shows the height of the clouds of a storm.

## Getting the Word Out

Weather reporters also use models. They make two-dimensional maps for TV and Internet viewers to see. The maps can change to show how fast and where bad weather will be.

## What Can We Do?

You can use models to help your family be prepared for dangerous weather. Draw a diagram of your home in your Science Notebook. Label the exits. Does your family have a safe place to meet in an emergency? Where is it?

_____

_____

_____

_____

How can your model help you in an emergency?

_____

_____

_____

_____

# Sum It Up!

When you're done, use the answer key to check and revise your work.

**Use information from the summary to complete the graphic organizer in your own words.**

## Summarize

For scientists, a model represents something real that is too big, too small, or has too many parts to investigate directly. Scientists use models to investigate and understand the real thing. Several kinds of models are used in science. Two-dimensional models, such as drawings, diagrams, and maps, have length and width. Three-dimensional models have length, width, and height. Computer models are computer programs that behave like the real thing. Some models, such as models of storms, can be used to save lives.

**Main Idea:** Models in science are like real things and are used to understand real things.

**Detail:** Two-dimensional models are flat, like a map or a diagram.

**Detail:** _____ _____ _____

**Detail:** _____ _____ _____ _____

**Answer Key: 1.** Three-dimensional models have length, width, and height. **2.** Computer models are computer programs that act like the real thing.

Name _____

# Word Play

**1** Use the words in the box to complete the puzzle.

| computer model* | real-time |
|---|---|
| mental model | model* |
| scale model | satellite |
| two-dimensional model* | weather |
| three-dimensional model* | |

*Key Lesson Vocabulary

**Across**

2. A type of model that is in your head
4. Something that represents the real thing
6. These kinds of models can save lives
7. A type of model that has length and width
9. A device that sends weather images back to Earth

**Down**

1. A type of model made with a computer program
3. A type of model that has length, width, and height
5. In this type of model, a measurement on the model stands for a measurement on the real thing
8. Data that scientists can see as soon as it is collected

# Apply Concepts

Tell how making or using each model below could help people.

**2** A model to show where lightning is likely to strike

_____

_____

_____

_____

**3** A model to show where water flows during a storm

_____

_____

_____

**4** A model to show how traffic moves in a city

_____

_____

**5** A model to show equipment for a new playground

_____

_____

Take It Home!

Many kids' toys are models of real things. Challenge your family to find such toys at home, in ads, or where you shop. Ask yourself: How is this toy like the real thing? How is it different?

Name _____

**Essential Question**

# How Can You Model a School?

## Set a Purpose
What inquiry skills will you practice in this investigation?

_____

_____

_____

## Think About the Procedure
How will you decide what part of your school to model?

_____

_____

_____

_____

How will you choose the two types of models?

_____

_____

_____

_____

## Record Your Observations
Identify the part of your school you modeled.

_____

_____

_____

_____

Identify the two types of models you made and describe them.

_____

_____

_____

_____

_____

_____

## Draw Conclusions

What was something you learned about your school from making the models?

_____

_____

_____

## Analyze and Extend

1. Why is it helpful to compare results with others?

_____

_____

_____

2. What was the hardest part of making the models? Explain.

_____

_____

_____

_____

3. Why is it important to be accurate when making your measurements?

_____

_____

_____

4. Why is it important for engineers to make and try out models before making a real building or bridge?

_____

_____

_____

_____

_____

_____

5. What other things or places would you like to learn about by making a model? Explain why.

_____

_____

_____

_____

_____

6. What other questions would you like to ask about making models?

_____

_____

_____

_____

_____

# Unit 1 Review

## Vocabulary Review

Use the terms in the box to complete the sentences.

> inference
> investigation
> observation
> pan balance
> spring scale

1. When people collect information by using their five senses,

   they make a(n) _____.

2. A tool used to measure the mass of an object

   is a(n) _____.

3. When people ask questions, make observations, and use other methods to gather data about an event or

   object, they are doing a(n) _____.

4. Someone who makes a statement that explains an

   observation is making a(n) _____.

5. If you want to measure the pull of a force, such as the force of gravity, you would use a tool called

   a(n) _____.

## Science Concepts

Fill in the letter of the choice that best answers the question.

6. Amira wants to compare close-up views of different bird feathers. Which tool should she use?

   (A) measuring cup

   (B) meterstick

   (C) microscope

   (D) pan balance

7. Camilla is studying minerals in different types of rocks. Which of the following would **not** help Camilla obtain data about a rock?

   (A) measuring the volume of the rock

   (B) inferring that the rock is millions of years old

   (C) testing the effect of dripping vinegar onto the rock

   (D) making observations of the rock's minerals

**8.** Junichi looks at this 2-D model of a classroom on a computer screen that uses perspective so it appears as a 3-D model.

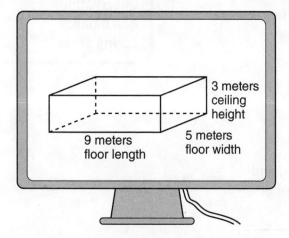

3 meters
ceiling
height

9 meters
floor length

5 meters
floor width

Junichi wants to know if the classroom is longer than it is tall. How can he use evidence from this model to answer the question?

Ⓐ He can look at the length of the floor.

Ⓑ He can look at the height of the ceiling.

Ⓒ He can compare the length and the width.

Ⓓ He can compare the length and the ceiling height.

**9.** During gym class, Julia had an ice pack on one arm. You think she must have hurt her arm. What scientific skill did you use?

Ⓐ communicating

Ⓑ comparing

Ⓒ inferring

Ⓓ measuring

**10.** Diego has been observing how well one type of plant grows in different locations. He concludes that a location with bright sunlight is best for the plant. Which of the following could be a reason for his conclusion?

Ⓐ His friend told him that all plants need bright sunlight to grow.

Ⓑ Plants that he kept in shade grew better than plants that he kept in sunlight.

Ⓒ Plants that he kept in shade did not grow as well as plants that he kept in sunlight.

Ⓓ He thinks that the plants he kept in sunlight would have grown better with more water.

**11.** A scientist is using a scientific method. She studies a table of data she has collected and recorded. What does the scientist do next?

Ⓐ She draws a conclusion.

Ⓑ She makes a hypothesis.

Ⓒ She conducts an experiment.

Ⓓ She studies the results one more time.

**12.** Scientists state a hypothesis for each experiment. What is one way that scientists can test a hypothesis?

Ⓐ asking questions

Ⓑ conducting an experiment

Ⓒ drawing conclusions

Ⓓ gathering materials

**13.** A scientist has spent a year conducting an experiment. He concludes that evidence from his experiment does not support his hypothesis. What should the scientist do next?

(A) Forget this experiment and choose a new problem.

(B) Try to make up evidence that supports his hypothesis.

(C) Look at the evidence and see if he can make a new hypothesis.

(D) Look at the information and find a different way to organize his results.

**14.** Gia hypothesizes that hot water will cause a sugar cube to dissolve faster than cold water will. She investigates by filling three cups: one with hot water, one with cold water, and one with ice water. She drops a sugar cube in each cup. Which observation will help Gia decide whether her hypothesis is correct?

(A) which cup the sugar cube dissolves in first

(B) the time it takes for two sugar cubes to dissolve

(C) changes in water temperature from start to finish

(D) changes in the size of the sugar cube in cold water

**15.** The local news station asks viewers to measure the amount of rain that falls in their neighborhoods. Four measurements are shown below.

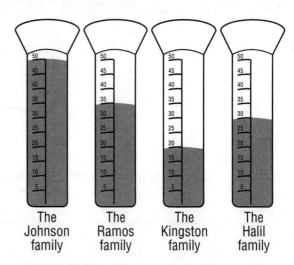

The Johnson family   The Ramos family   The Kingston family   The Halil family

Which family measures the most rain?

(A) Halil family

(B) Johnson family

(C) Kingston family

(D) Ramos family

**16.** Seiji wonders why flowers will not grow in his garden. What part of the inquiry process does this represent?

(A) asking a question

(B) conducting an investigation

(C) drawing a conclusion

(D) making a prediction

# Apply Inquiry and Review the Big Idea

**Write the answers to these questions.**

**17.** Luis fed his cat in the kitchen. These pictures show what Luis saw
as he left the kitchen and then what he saw when he returned.

Luis figured out that the cat jumped on the table and knocked the mitt
onto the floor. What inquiry skill did Luis use? Give a reason for your answer.

_____

_____

**18.** Write three observations about this leaf.

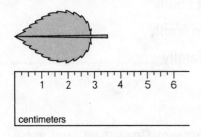

**My Observations**

a. _____

b. _____

c. _____

**19.** Rachel wonders if a heavy ball rolls down a ramp faster than a light ball.
Describe an investigation she could do to find out.

_____

_____

_____

# The Engineering Process

Houghton Mifflin Harcourt Publishing Company (bg) ©Steve Cole/Getty Images; (inset) ©Warren Morgan/Corbis; (border) ©ND/a-Age Fotostock

## Big Idea

**Engineers use a process to design products and processes that solve human problems.**

## I Wonder Why

Ancient people used stone tools. Today, scientists study these tools to learn how ancient people lived. I wonder how scientists know why ancient people made these tools? *Turn the page to find out.*

**Here's Why** Throughout history, people have designed and built tools to help meet their needs. Whether a tool is a simple stone or a high-tech electronic device, it can help solve a problem. By figuring out how an ancient tool was used, scientists can draw conclusions about the needs of the person who made it.

In this unit, you will explore the Big Idea, the Essential Questions, and the Investigations on the Inquiry Flipchart.

**Levels of Inquiry Key** ■ DIRECTED ■ GUIDED ■ INDEPENDENT

Track Your Progress

**Big Idea** Engineers use a process to design products and processes that solve human problems.

## Essential Questions

**Now I Get the Big Idea!**

**Science Notebook**

Before you begin each lesson, be sure your thoughts about the Essential Que

**Essential Question**

# What Is an Engineering Design Process?

## Engage Your Brain!

Find the answer to the following question in this lesson and record it here.

Why would a car company want a wooden car?

_____

_____

_____

_____

## Active Reading

### Lesson Vocabulary

List the terms. As you learn about each one, make notes in the Interactive Glossary.

_____

_____

_____

### Signal Words: Sequence

Signal words show connections between ideas. Words that signal sequence include *now, before, after, first,* and *next.* Active readers remember what they read because they are alert to signal words that identify sequence.

# What Is ENGINEERING?

From the food we eat and the clothes we wear, to the cars we drive and the phones we talk on, science is at work in our lives every day.

Electrical engineers use their knowledge of physics to build things like this robot.

© Houghton Mifflin Harcourt Publishing Company ©Peter Menzel/Photo Researchers, Inc.

Knowledge of math and geology allows surveyors to make maps of Earth.

This biomedical engineer uses his knowledge of biology to make glass eyes.

Look around. Many of the things you see are products of engineering. **Engineering** is the use of scientific and mathematical principles to develop something practical. Some engineers use biology. Others use geology, chemistry, or physics.

Engineers use this knowledge to create something new. It might be a product, a system, or a process for doing things. Whatever it is, it's practical. People use it. Engineers develop things that people use.

▶ In the space below, draw a picture of something you can see around you that was probably designed by an engineer.

# What Is the DESIGN PROCESS?

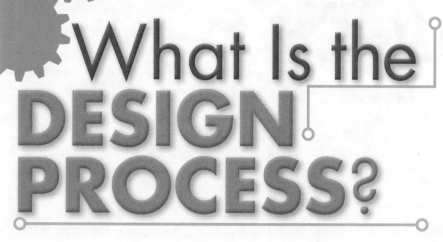

It has been said that necessity is the mother of invention. But once you find a need, how do you build your invention? That's the design process!

**Active Reading** As you read these two pages, draw boxes around clue words or phrases that signal a sequence or order.

**W**hat is design? **Design** means to conceive something and prepare the plans and drawings for it to be built. Engineers use the design process to develop new technology, but anyone can follow the design process.

From basic to complex, skateboards have changed over time.

The design process starts with identifying a need or a problem. Next, you brainstorm and write down ideas on how to plan and build a potential solution. Once you have some options, select a solution to try. Usually, engineers test possible solutions using a prototype.

A **prototype** is an original or test model on which a real product is based. If the prototype works, then the real product is made. Usually, after testing a prototype, improvements have to be made. The prototype is then tested again. Finally, a finished product is made.

## Design Process Steps

- Find a problem
- Plan and build
- Test and improve
- Redesign
- Communicate

Even something seemingly simple takes a lot of thought, planning, testing, and improvement.

## How was it improved?

Look at the skateboards. Describe two design features that have been improved over time.

_____

_____

_____

_____

# Design YOU CAN USE

Look around you at all the things you use every day. Do you have ideas about improving them?

## Who Needs It?

The first step in any design process is identifying a need or problem. Is there a chore that could be easier, a tool that could work much better, a car that could go faster or be safer? Often, the design process begins with the phrase "What if?"

## Prototype!

A prototype is a test version of a design. To build a prototype, a person has to have plans. Early sketches give a rough idea. More detailed drawings provide exact measurements for every piece. Keeping good records and drawings helps to make sure that the prototype can be replicated.

This skateboard turns fairly well. But what if it could go around curves even better?

© Houghton Mifflin Harcourt Publishing Company   HMH Credits

# Details

Draw a blueprint of a school supply, favorite toy, or tool. Label its parts and include exact measurements.

Sketches and detailed drawings are an important step in planning a product.

Every part of a product can become an opportunity for a design change.

**wheel**

**trucks**

**deck**

# Are We DONE YET?

Now that the prototype has been built, can the final product be far behind? Yes, it can. But it might not be. It all depends.

**Active Reading** As you read these two pages, draw a box around the clue word or phrase that signals one thing is being contrasted with another.

## Test It and Improve It!

Prototypes are carefully tested. This testing helps answer questions such as, *Does it work the way it should? Is it easy to use? How does it hold up under normal working conditions?*

The first prototype you build may pass all its tests. If so, the prototype can go into production. However, it is more likely that testing shows that the design needs to change. Once the test results are analyzed, it's back to the drawing board. The product may need only a few minor improvements, or it may need to be completely redesigned.

If a prototype works as expected, it will become a finished product.

# Redesign and Share

When a prototype fails to meet a design goal, it may be redesigned. Redesign takes advantage of all work done before. Good design features are kept, and those that fail are discarded.

When the final working prototype is done, team members communicate the design. Sketches, blueprints, and test data and analysis are shared. Often, the product details are recorded in a legal document called a *patent*.

Sometimes, one prototype leads to ideas for others.

## Spin Off!

Imagine a normal bicycle. Now think of three ways it could be modified to work better in different environments.

_____

_____

_____

_____

_____

New ideas keep the engineering design process constantly moving forward.

When you're done, use the answer key to check and revise your work.

**Use information in the summary to complete the graphic organizer.**

## Summarize

The first step in the design process is to identify a need or a problem to be solved. The next step is to plan and build a prototype. Brainstorming ideas and drawing detailed sketches of potential solutions are important parts of this step. The third step is to test and improve a prototype. After testing, a prototype might need to be redesigned and tested again. A prototype that meets all its design goals is ready for production. The final step in the design process is to communicate to others the details of a working prototype.

**1** The design process starts with identifying a need or _____ _____.

**3** _____ _____ _____

**5** The final step in the design process is to _____ _____.

**2** _____ _____ _____ _____

**4** _____ _____ _____ _____

**Answer Key: 1.** problem to be solved **2.** The second step in the design process is to plan and build a prototype. **3.** The third step is to test and improve the prototype. **4.** After testing, a prototype might need to be redesigned and tested again. **5.** communicate

Name _____

# Word Play

**1** Use the clues to help you write the correct word in each row. Some boxes have been filled in for you.

A. To conceive something and prepare plans to build it

B. The use of scientific and mathematical principles to develop something practical

C. A prototype may undergo many rounds of this.

D. Engineers have to be familiar with these principles.

E. The answer to a problem

F. A test version of something

G. Is identified during the first step in the design process

H. What comes after sketches, plans, and the prototype?

I. Something that people will use is described as this.

J. Engineers have to be familiar with these principles.

| | | | | | E | | I | | |
|---|---|---|---|---|---|---|---|---|---|
| | | | | | E | | I | | G |
| | | | | | | | I | | G |
| | | | | | | | I | | I | C |
| | | | | | | | I | | |
| P | | | | | | | | P | E |
| P | | | | | | | | | |
| P | | | | | | | | | |
| P | | | | | | C | | L |
| | | | | | | | C | | L |

# Apply Concepts

**2** Write numbers in the circles to put the pictures in the correct order.

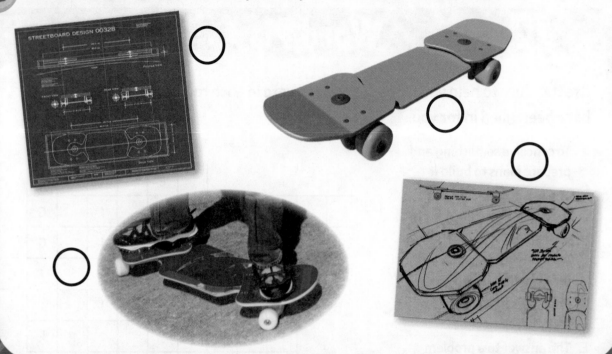

**3** How is a prototype different from the finished product?

_____

_____

_____

_____

_____

**4** Why is it better to build and test a prototype of a product than to produce tens of thousands of the product and then test it?

_____

_____

_____

**5** The owner of a safety apparel company asks an engineer to "design a better helmet for skateboarders." How would you improve this instruction?

_____

_____

_____

_____

_____

_____

_____

_____

**6** Which job is more likely to be done by an engineer? Why?

| Developing a new material that will be used to make the outer covering of vitamin capsules | Determining how vitamins are absorbed into the bloodstream |
|---|---|

_____

_____

_____

_____

_____

_____

**7** The engineers at an appliance company have developed a new dishwasher. It looks very different from previous models. The controls look different and work differently. The part of the machine that heats the water has been completely redesigned. Now that the plans are completed, should the company start producing thousands of these dishwashers? Why or why not?

_____

_____

_____

_____

_____

_____

_____

_____

_____

_____

_____

_____

_____

**Take It Home!**

With your family, find a product in your home that needs improving. Suppose you work for the company that makes this product and brainstorm a new prototype to test.

**Name** _____

**Essential Question**

# How Can You Design a Solution to a Problem?

## Set a Purpose
**What do you think you will learn from this experiment?**

_____

_____

_____

_____

## Think About the Procedure
**How will the equipment you design be similar to safety belts and airbags in a car?**

_____

_____

_____

_____

_____

_____

**Why is it a good idea to make sure the plastic bag is tightly sealed before you test your prototype?**

_____

_____

_____

## Record Your Data
**In the space below, draw a table to record the materials you used in your prototype and your observations from each test.**

## Draw Conclusions

What conclusions can you draw as a result of your test observations?

_____

_____

_____

## Analyze and Extend

1. Was your design successful? Why or why not?

_____

_____

_____

2. Based on your results, how could you improve your design? Describe and draw the changes you would make to your prototype.

_____

_____

_____

3. Were there any aspects of someone else's design you might incorporate into your design?

_____

_____

_____

4. What is the difference between a successful design and a successful prototype?

_____

_____

_____

_____

5. Think of other questions you would like to ask about forces and transportation.

_____

_____

_____

# What Is Technology?

## Engage Your Brain!

Find the answer to the following question in the lesson and record it here.

This robot is riding a bicycle, just like a human, and not falling over. How is this possible?

_____

_____

_____

_____

## Active Reading

### Lesson Vocabulary

List the terms. As you learn about each one, make notes in the Interactive Glossary.

_____

_____

_____

### Main Ideas

The main idea of a paragraph is the most important idea. The main idea may be stated in the first sentence, or it may be stated elsewhere. Active readers look for main ideas by asking themselves, What is this paragraph mostly about?

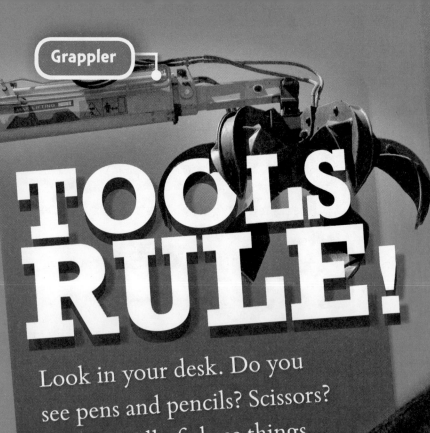

# TOOLS RULE!

A bulldozer and a shovel serve the same purpose. However, because of a bulldozer's size, it can move huge amounts of material much more quickly than a shovel can.

Look in your desk. Do you see pens and pencils? Scissors? A ruler? All of these things are tools.

**Active Reading** As you read these two pages, put brackets [ ] around the sentences that describe a problem. Underline the sentences that describe the solution.

Planting a vegetable garden? You'll need a shovel, a rake, and a spade. All these items are tools. A **tool** is anything that helps people shape, build, or produce things to meet their needs.

Your family's toolbox probably contains a hammer and screwdrivers. Construction workers have similar tools that do the same jobs, only on a larger scale. Instead of hammering nails by hand, construction workers use tools that quickly drive nails into wood with the push of a button. Their tools are sized and powered differently to meet different needs.

Some tools are designed to do one task. You use a pen to write a note to a friend. You keep your science notes organized in a notebook. You talk to your grandmother on the phone. What if you had one tool that could do all these tasks? A smartphone is a tool that can help you send a message, organize information, *and* talk to people.

A smartphone, like all tools, is an example of technology. **Technology** is any designed system, product, or process that people use to solve problems. Technology doesn't have to be complex. The pencil you write with and the cell phone you text with are both technology. Technology changes as the needs of people change.

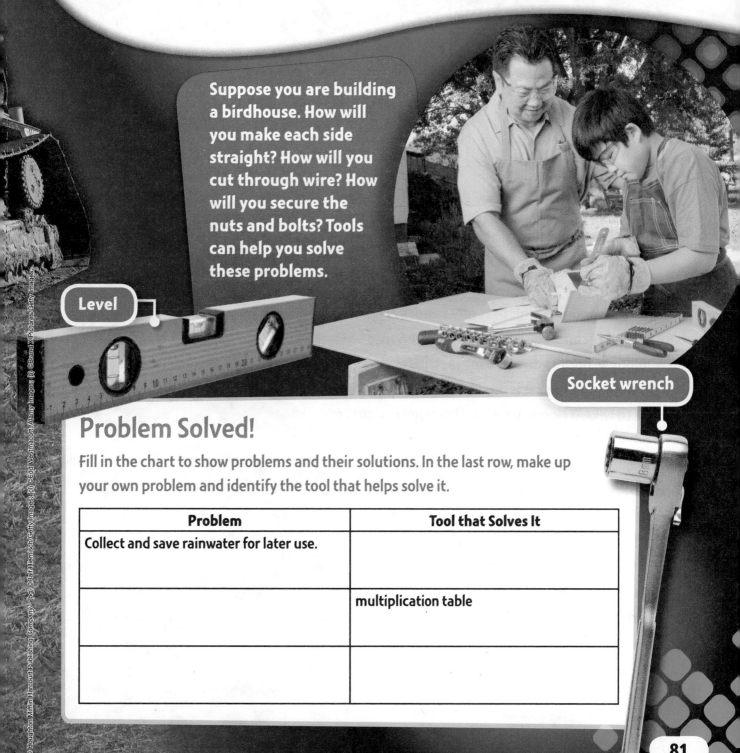

Suppose you are building a birdhouse. How will you make each side straight? How will you cut through wire? How will you secure the nuts and bolts? Tools can help you solve these problems.

Level

Socket wrench

## Problem Solved!

Fill in the chart to show problems and their solutions. In the last row, make up your own problem and identify the tool that helps solve it.

| Problem | Tool that Solves It |
|---|---|
| Collect and save rainwater for later use. | |
| | multiplication table |
| | |

# WHAT IS TECHNOLOGY?

Vending machines, televisions, and video games are examples of technology products you know—but there are more. Technology is all around you.

**Active Reading** As you read this page, underline technology products. On the next page, circle the paragraph that describes examples of a technology process.

A video game is the end product of a technology process. Programming a video game involves technology you can't hold in the palm of your hand.

You've learned that technology is any designed system, product, or process. A *technology product* is anything designed to meet a need or desire. Some people think that electronics are the only type of technology product. However, most technology products do not use electricity!

This book, the desk it is on, and the backpack you use to take it home are all technology products. Your bike and the sidewalk you ride it on are technology products, too. Technology products can be very large or very small. They can be a single thing like a stone brick or made of many things put together. Some technology products, such as medicine, are made to keep us healthy. Others, such as construction tools, are made to shape the world around us. We also invent technology products just to have fun.

▶ Circle three examples of technology in this photo.

The way a product is made is also a form of technology. A *technology process* is a series of steps used to achieve a goal or make a product. The steps in a technology process are like the steps in a scientific investigation. They are carefully designed for doing something a certain way.

Many things you do are a technology process. You follow a series of steps to make gelatin dessert, tie your shoelaces, and add music to your MP3 player. If you have ever played baseball, you are familiar with its rules. The rules of a game are a technology process.

Safety gear and clothing are types of technology that help baseball players perform. The bleachers and the backstop are types of technology that let spectators watch safely.

## Play Ball

The ballpark, scoreboard, rules, and baseball equipment are all examples of technology. How can technology help deliver the game's events to people who aren't at the ballpark?

_____

_____

_____

# TECHNOLOGICAL SYSTEMS

The next time you ride in a car, look at how many parts it has. It took many tools and hundreds of steps to produce this technology.

**Active Reading** As you read this page, underline the sentence that describes what makes a designed system.

Groups of things that work together to achieve a goal make up a *system*. Tools, parts, and processes that work together form a *designed system*. Designed systems help us travel and ship goods. They help us communicate and grow our foods.

You are a part of many designed systems. Whether you ride the bus or walk to school, you are a part of a transportation system. This system is made up of the sidewalks, roads, and traffic signs. It also includes the cars, buses, planes, and trains that move people and materials from place to place.

Designed systems help us shape the world around us. When you ride around your town, you might see cars, roadways, buildings, or farm fields. All these things make up the *designed world*. The designed world is the part of your community that is designed and built by people.

Many designed systems work together in the designed world. For example, the agricultural system produces the food that we need. Ships, trains, and trucks in the transportation system carry food where it is needed.

A water irrigation system is a tool that helps farmers grow crops. It includes water, hoses, and pipes. It also includes the people who run the system and fix it when it breaks down.

## PARTS OF A DESIGNED SYSTEM

| Part | Example: Rail Transportation System |
|------|-------------------------------------|
| Goal—what the system aims to do | Goal—to move cargo and passengers safely from place to place |
| Input—what is put into the system to meet the goal | Inputs—fuel for the train, cargo, and people to ride the train |
| Processes—describe how the goal is to be achieved | Processes—train tracks and departure and arrival schedules |
| Output—the end product | Output—safe and timely delivery of people and cargo |
| Feedback—information that tells whether or not the output is successful | Feedback—records of whether trains left and arrived on time |

A railroad system includes trains, rails, and safety signals at road crossings. The system also has parts you can't see. Radio signals keep track of where trains are. The signals raise and lower crossing arms, too.

## Tech Systems

What do you think would be the goal of a farming system?

_____

_____

_____

# THE GOOD AND THE BAD OF IT

A light bulb that can save you $100 a year? What's the catch?

Compact fluorescent lights (CFLs) and light emitting diodes (LEDs) use less energy than incandescent bulbs. However, CFLs contain mercury, which can be hazardous if the bulbs break open, and LEDs are more expensive than regular light bulbs.

Technology is constantly changing. Anyone can invent or improve a technology product or process. It takes new ideas and knowledge for technology to change. The goal of any new technology is to better meet people's needs. However, new technology can also bring new risks.

Changes in technology often involve making things safer, quicker, easier, or cheaper. For example, people once used candles and lanterns to light their homes. These things helped people see at night, but they could also cause fires. Electricity and incandescent light bulbs helped solve this problem, but this technology also has its risks.

We burn coal to generate electricity. When coal burns, harmful ash and gases are produced. The potential harm these substances can cause leads to negative feedback. Such feedback helps people think of ways to improve technology.

Sometimes the problems with a technology are caused by the way people use technology. For instance, pesticides are helpful technology products. They are used to protect people, crops, and farm animals from harmful organisms. However, when used incorrectly, they can contaminate the soil, the water, and the air. Living things exposed to pesticides by accident can get sick and die.

## Do the Math!
### Interpret a Table

Use the data in the table to answer the questions below.

| Light Bulb Cost Comparisons | | |
|---|---|---|
| | 25-Watt CFL | 100-Watt incandescent |
| Cost of bulb | $3.40 | $0.60 |
| Bulb life | 1,667 days (4.5 years) | 167 days (about half a year) |
| Energy cost per year | $6.00 | $25.00 |
| Total cost over 4.5 years | $27.00 | $118.50 |

1. How much more is the total cost of an incandescent bulb than a CFL?

_____

2. How much would your yearly energy cost be if you had 20 CFL bulbs in your home?

_____

3. Which bulb lasts longer?

_____

Airplanes can transport a lot of people at one time. However, they burn a lot of fuel and release pollution into the atmosphere. Engineers redesign airplanes to improve their performance.

# OUT WITH THE OLD

Computers, cell phones, and flat-screen TVs are fun and useful. But like all technology, electronic gadgets have drawbacks.

Electronic technology seems to change at the blink of an eye. New electronic devices rapidly replace old ones. People benefit from new or improved electronic devices, but they also bring new problems.

Not long ago, most televisions and computer monitors were large, bulky things. New technology has made these large devices a thing of the past. They have been replaced by thin, lightweight flat screens.

But what do we do with old electronics? Some are taken apart and recycled; however, like the devices shown on this page, most end up in landfills. At landfills, electronics may release harmful chemicals into the environment.

Many electronic devices contain lead. Lead can be harmful to people and other organisms in the environment.

Electronics are helpful communication, work, and entertainment tools. They can also be a distraction. Some people spend a lot of time playing video games or on the Internet. They send text messages or listen to MP3 players while they are with other people. Some might even operate electronics while driving and cause a safety hazard for themselves and others.

People can solve these problems. They can set limits on computer and game time. They can put the phone away and pay attention to people and driving. These are ways to be responsible with technology.

▶ On the chart below, fill in the pros and cons of each electronic technology. Some examples have been provided for you.

| | Pros | Cons |
|---|---|---|
| Television | can be educational; can provide breaking news quickly | |
| Smartphones | | can take time away from doing other activities or being social; can cause drivers to be a hazard |
| Video games | fun; can be social when played with others | |

When you're done, use the answer key to check and revise your work.

**Complete the graphic organizer below.**

**1** _____ changes with new ideas and knowledge of science and engineering.

is made up of any

**2** _____ is tools, parts, and processes that work together.

**4** _____ is a series of steps used to achieve a goal or make a product.

**3** _____ includes electronic and nonelectronic devices that meet a need or a desire.

## Summarize

**Fill in the missing words that help summarize ideas about technology.**

A shovel is a tool that can help move dirt. A [5] _____ can do the same job in a bigger way. Tools are technology that help people shape, build, or produce things.

[6] _____ changes to meet the growing needs and desires of people.

A computer is an electronic product of technology. A [7] _____

is a nonelectronic product of technology. [8] _____ and

[9] _____ often work in teams to develop new technology.

With technology, there is often risk to people and to the [10] _____.

Name _____

# Word Play

**1** Use the clues below to fill in the words of the puzzle.

1. Any designed system, product, or process

2. Anything that helps people shape, build, or produce things to meet their needs

3. Tools, parts, and processes that work together

4. Things that are made to meet a need

5. The end product or service of a system

6. Anything that is put into a system to meet a goal

7. Information that tells whether or not the output is successful

8. This is made up of all products of technology

9. A series of steps that result in a product

designed world

feedback        input

process        products

output        system

technology*    tool*

*\* Key Lesson Vocabulary*

Read down the squares with red borders. The word will answer the question below.

Murata Boy is a bicycling robot. He can ride forward, backward, and stop without falling over. Where does he get the ability to do it?

— — — — — — — — — —

# Apply Concepts

Passenger jets can transport people quickly from one place to another. Modern computer electronics help pilots fly these planes.

**2** Describe two technological systems that are related to airplanes.

_____

_____

_____

**3** What are some of the risks of global airline travel? What are some of the benefits?

_____

_____

_____

**4** Write a problem associated with each example of electronic technology.

1. Compact fluorescent light bulbs

2. Video games

3. Cell phones

_____    _____    _____

_____    _____    _____

_____    _____    _____

Work with a family member to make a list of tools found in your kitchen. Sort the items in your list into simple and complex tools. Share your work with your class. Explain how you categorized the items in your list.

Name _____

Essential Question

# How Do We Use Technology?

## Set a Purpose
What do you think you will learn from this activity?

_____

_____

## Think About the Procedure
What does the spring scale measure?

_____

Why is it a good idea to repeat each trial in Steps 1 and 2 three times?

_____

_____

_____

_____

What is being modeled when some of the marbles are replaced with cubes?

_____

_____

_____

## Record Your Data
Record your observations for Trials 1–3 in the space below.

| | Measured Force (N) | | |
|---|---|---|---|
| Trial | Bare table | Marbles | Marbles and cubes |
| 1 | | | |
| 2 | | | |
| 3 | | | |
| Average | | | |

## Draw Conclusions

Calculate the average force needed to move the book stack in each setup. Show your work and record your answers in the table above.

## Draw Conclusions (continued)

**Which problem did the tool you built help solve?**

_____

_____

_____

**Which setup required the greatest amount of force to move the book stack? Why?**

_____

_____

_____

_____

_____

## Analyze and Extend

1. **Which products of technology did you use to build your tool?**

_____

_____

2. **What other objects could you have used in place of marbles?**

_____

_____

_____

3. **In the space below, draw a bar graph to show the average force needed to move the book stack in each setup.**

4. **What could cause the marbles to become more like cubes?**

_____

_____

_____

_____

_____

5. **How could you redesign this tool to move larger things?**

_____

_____

_____

_____

# 8 Things YOU SHOULD KNOW ABOUT Ayanna Howard

**1**
Dr. Ayanna Howard is a roboticist. She designs and builds robots.

**2**
Dr. Howard is making robots that will make decisions without the help of people.

**3**
To get a robot to make decisions on its own, Dr. Howard must teach the robot how to think.

**4**
Dr. Howard uses computer programs to teach robots. She observes the robots. Then she changes her computer programs to get better results.

**5**
Dr. Howard studies how robots can help explore outer space and unsafe places on Earth.

**6**
Dr. Howard taught a robot called SmartNav to move around things in its path. This robot could explore the surface of Mars.

**7**
Scientists want to understand why the ice in Antarctica is melting. Dr. Howard's SnoMote robots can safely gather data on the cracking ice sheets.

**8**
In 2003, Dr. Howard was named a top young inventor.

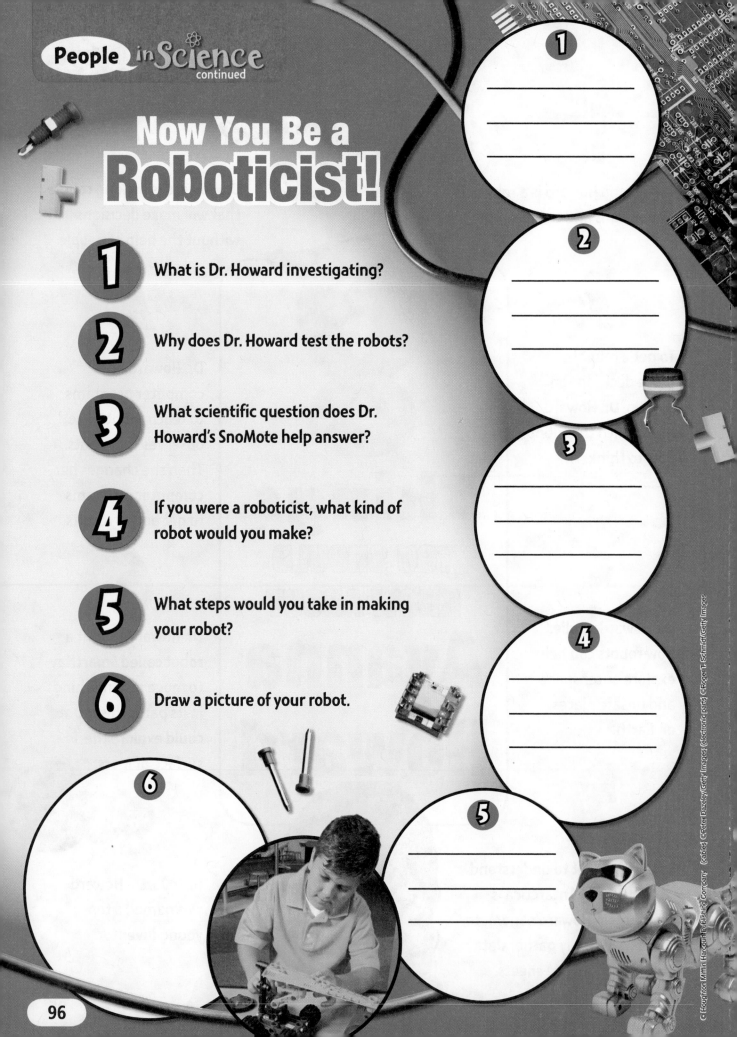

# Now You Be a Roboticist!

**1** What is Dr. Howard investigating?

**2** Why does Dr. Howard test the robots?

**3** What scientific question does Dr. Howard's SnoMote help answer?

**4** If you were a roboticist, what kind of robot would you make?

**5** What steps would you take in making your robot?

**6** Draw a picture of your robot.

1

2

3

4

5

6

Name _____

## Vocabulary Review

Use the terms in the box to complete the sentences.

> design
> designed system
> engineering
> process
> prototype
> technology
> technology product
> tool

1. Anything that is made to meet a need or desire is

   a(n) _____.

2. To conceive of something and prepare the plans and drawings

   for it to be built is _____.

3. A designed system, product, or process that people use to solve

   problems is called _____.

4. A series of steps used to achieve a goal or make a product is

   called a(n) _____.

5. The use of scientific and mathematical principles to develop

   something practical is called _____.

6. An original or test model on which a real product is based is

   called a _____.

7. Tools, parts, and processes that work together form

   a(n) _____.

8. Anything that helps people shape, build, or produce things

   to meet their needs is called a _____.

# Science Concepts

Fill in the letter of the choice that best answers the question.

9. A group of researchers is working on a way to make winter coats warmer. The first coat the researchers design is not very warm. What should they do?

 (A) They should try again without using tools.

 (B) They should find a different designed system.

 (C) They should continue their work without using technology.

 (D) They should examine their test data for ways to improve the coat's design.

10. Sylvia works for a car company. She uses her knowledge of math and science to design dashboards that make it easier to operate cars. What is Sylvia's profession?

 (A) analyst

 (B) biologist

 (C) engineer

 (D) geologist

11. Marco is using this object to help him find information for a report.

 Which statement best describes this object?

 (A) It is a technology process.

 (B) It is an engineer.

 (C) It is a prototype.

 (D) It is a tool.

12. Researchers want to build a new type of spaceship for transporting astronauts to the moon. What should they do **first**?

 (A) They should test the prototype.

 (B) They should plan a prototype.

 (C) They should build a model.

 (D) They should evaluate how the prototype worked.

13. Bulldozers, measuring cups, pencils, and hammers are all examples of tools. What else can be said about all of them?

 (A) They are all technology products.

 (B) They are all in the prototype stage.

 (C) They all release harmful gases into the atmosphere.

 (D) They all require power sources other than their users.

14. New solutions to problems often begin with a "What if?" question. Which "What if?" question might an engineer ask after seeing the electrical energy station shown below?

 (A) What if we burned trees instead of coal?

 (B) What if we could find even more coal to burn?

 (C) What if we all threw away all of our electrical appliances?

 (D) What if we could burn coal to make electricity without polluting the air?

**15.** Angie tested a reflector that she hopes will make bicycles safer. Although her first test went well, she repeated the test three more times. Which of these statements is **true**?

Ⓐ She skipped the step of asking "What if?"

Ⓑ She wasted her time by repeating the same test.

Ⓒ She obtained unreliable data, because there were more chances for mistakes.

Ⓓ She obtained more accurate data than if she had only tested the reflector once.

**16.** You probably use the tools shown below every day.

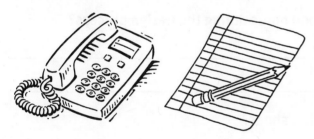

Which statement about these tools is **true**?

Ⓐ They cost about the same to produce.

Ⓑ They are both examples of technology.

Ⓒ They are examples of identical technology.

Ⓓ They are each designed for many different tasks.

**17.** Sometimes, a prototype tests poorly or fails completely. What should be done when that happens?

Ⓐ The prototype should be abandoned.

Ⓑ A second prototype should be built.

Ⓒ The prototype should be modified, with the good parts of it kept.

Ⓓ The prototype should be examined to see if it has other uses.

**18.** A fuel-efficient automobile is an example of a designed system. What is an example of feedback for such an automobile?

Ⓐ safe arrival at the destination

Ⓑ fuel for the car and the roads on which it will travel

Ⓒ data on how much fuel the car used to travel 100 km

Ⓓ to move a family of four 100 km using only 2 liters of gasoline

**19.** Long ago, there were few roads. Now there are many roads. How has a system of roads changed most communities?

Ⓐ People can easily get from one place to another.

Ⓑ People live closer to where they work and drive less.

Ⓒ People travel less and rarely see family members that live far away.

Ⓓ Use of fossil fuels has decreased with the increase in roads and highways.

# Apply Inquiry and Review the Big Idea

Write the answers to these questions.

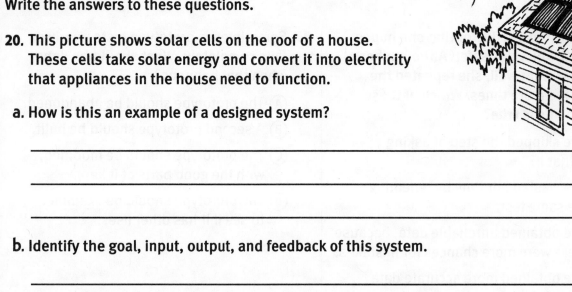

**20.** This picture shows solar cells on the roof of a house. These cells take solar energy and convert it into electricity that appliances in the house need to function.

**a.** How is this an example of a designed system?

_____

_____

_____

**b.** Identify the goal, input, output, and feedback of this system.

_____

_____

_____

**21.** An engineer follows the design process to improve soccer shoes. First, he studies shoes on the market and reads about what people have to say about them. Then, he starts to design his prototype.

**a.** Why is it important for the engineer to keep good notes during the design process?

_____

_____

**b.** Why should the engineer build a prototype of the shoes?

_____

_____

**c.** Describe a part of the design process the engineer should do **after** testing the prototype.

_____

_____

_____

_____

_____

# Plants and Animals

## Big Idea

Living things are adapted for survival in their environment.

## I Wonder Why

This insect looks like a leaf. When it walks, it rocks back and forth. Why? *Turn the page to find out.*

**Here's Why** This bug is a walking leaf. It mimics leaves to hide from predators. It rocks back and forth when it walks, which makes it look like a leaf blowing in the wind—a bird won't think this bug is food!

In this unit, you will explore the Big Idea, the Essential Questions, and the Investigations on the Inquiry Flipchart.

Levels of Inquiry Key ■ DIRECTED ■ GUIDED ■ INDEPENDENT

Track Your Progress

**Big Idea** Living things are adapted for survival in their environment.

## Essential Questions

**Now I Get the Big Idea!**

**Science Notebook**

Before you begin each lesson, be sure to write your thoughts about the Essential Question.

© Houghton Mifflin Harcourt Publishing Company  (b) ©Cris Mattison/Alamy Images; (inset) ©blickwinkel/Alamy Images; (border) ©DLILLC/Age Fotostock

**Essential Question**

# What Are Some Plant Structures?

## Engage Your Brain!

Find the answer to the following question in this lesson and record it here.

How does the stem of this tree differ from the stems of other plants?

_____

_____

_____

## Active Reading

### Lesson Vocabulary

List the terms. As you learn about each one, make notes in the Interactive Glossary.

_____ _____

_____ _____

_____

### Main Idea and Details

Detail sentences give more information about a main idea. The information may be examples, features, characteristics, or facts. Active readers stay focused when they ask, What fact or information does this sentence add to the main idea?

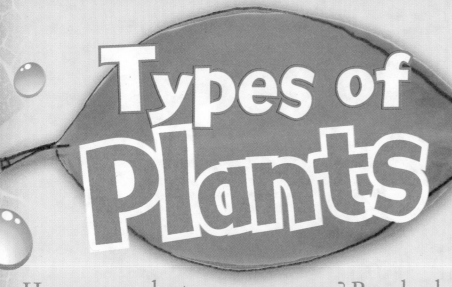

# Types of Plants

How many plants can you name? Rosebushes, maple trees, cacti, ferns, and mosses are just a few examples. Scientists have identified more than 310,000 types of plants on Earth! How do scientists group all of them?

As you read these two pages, circle the two types of plants that are being compared each time they appear.

Scientists classify plants into two groups: *nonvascular plants* and *vascular plants.*

Nonvascular plants are the simplest types of plants that grow on land. These small plants grow close to the ground and soak up water and minerals like a sponge. Some parts of nonvascular plants look like structures on vascular plants, but the functions are different. For example, nonvascular plants have parts that look like roots, but the parts don't take in water. Instead they help anchor the nonvascular plant in the ground. Nonvascular plants don't have stems or leaves, either. Instead they have a stalk on which leaflike structures grow.

Mosses are nonvascular plants. Most types of moss grow to a height of less than 10 cm.

Vascular plants, such as this rosebush, have roots, stems, and leaves. Water and nutrients taken in by the roots move through the stem to the leaves in tubes. The tube system also moves food from the leaves to other parts of the plant.

Most plants that you see every day are vascular plants. Vascular plants have a system of tubes that carry water and nutrients through the plant. These tubes run through the plant's roots, stems, and leaves. Roots take in water and minerals and also anchor the plant in the ground. Stems hold up the plant's leaves, which make food for the plant.

All plants that produce flowers, such as rosebushes and magnolia trees, are vascular plants. *Flowers* are reproductive structures, but not all vascular plants have flowers. Some vascular plants, such as pine trees, produce reproductive structures called cones.

# Do the Math!
## Work with Fractions

About $\frac{1}{10}$ of the 310,000 known types of plants are nonvascular. The remaining $\frac{9}{10}$ are vascular plants. Use this information, and two different colors, to color in and label the circle below.

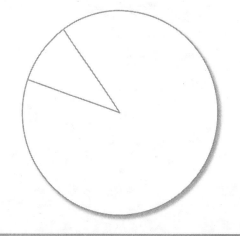

# Using the Tubes

What type of tool do you use to drink juice in a pouch? A straw, of course! Vascular plants have tubes that work like straws to move water, minerals, and sugars through the plant.

**Active Reading** As you read this page, draw two lines under the main idea.

Vascular plants have structures called roots. **Roots** are usually underground and absorb water and minerals from soil. If you have ever helped weed a garden, you know that roots also help anchor a plant in the soil. There are two main types of roots—fibrous roots and taproots.

*Taproots* are thick, strong roots that grow deep in the soil. Some plants use taproots to store food. When you eat a carrot or a beet, you are eating a taproot!

*Fibrous roots* are thin, branching roots that grow close to the surface. Grasses and most trees have fibrous roots.

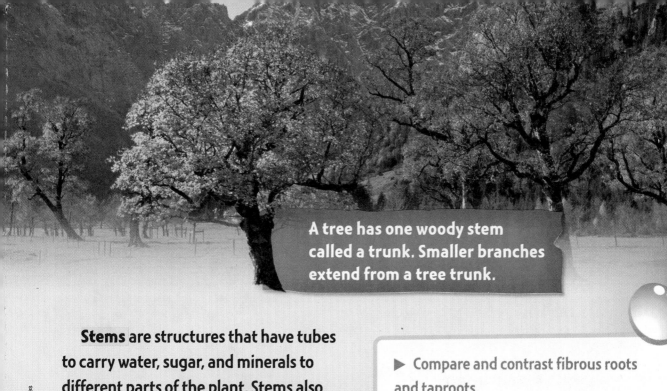

A tree has one woody stem called a trunk. Smaller branches extend from a tree trunk.

**Stems** are structures that have tubes to carry water, sugar, and minerals to different parts of the plant. Stems also support the plant. Stems may look very different. Most plant stems grow above the ground, but some plants have stems that remain underground.

There are many types of stems. Some plants, such as trees, have a single hard woody stem called a trunk. Shrubs have many smaller, woody stems. Soft green stems support other plants, such as daisies. Trees and shrubs live for more than one growing season. Many plants with soft stems sprout, grow, and die all in one season.

▶ Compare and contrast fibrous roots and taproots.

_____

_____

_____

_____

_____

_____

This goldenrod plant has a soft green stem. The plant will die at the end of its growing season.

A shrub has many woody stems that begin at ground level. Most shrubs, such as this daphne plant, are less than 6 m high.

# Lots of Leaves

Leaves can be long, short, wide, narrow, smooth, rough, shiny, or dull. Some leaves even have fuzzy surfaces!

**Active Reading** As you read the paragraph on this page, underline two facts about leaves.

Leaves are another part of vascular plants. **Leaves** are plant parts that use sunlight to produce sugar for the plant's food. While leaves may have the same function, leaves come in many shapes and sizes. Some plants, such as water lilies, have round leaves. On other plants, such as redbud trees, the leaves are heart-shaped. Grasses have leaves that are long and narrow. Leaves can even be triangular, as they are on a gentian sage plant.

► Scientists often use leaf shape to identify plants. Label each leaf shape.

Vascular plants, such as maple trees, have leaves with veins.

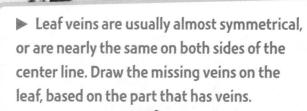

Leaves also have different textures. Tomato plant leaves have tiny hairs on their surfaces that make them look and feel fuzzy. These hairs may keep the tomato plant from drying out and protect its leaves from animals. Other leaves, such as an aloe leaf, feel smooth and waxy. The waxy coating keeps the plant from drying out. Can you think of a plant with shiny leaves?

If you look at a leaf, you may see veins running across it. These veins are small tubes that carry food made by the leaves to the plant's flowers, stems, and roots. Veins also carry water and minerals through the leaves. When the veins are filled with water, they even help support the leaves!

▶ Leaf veins are usually almost symmetrical, or are nearly the same on both sides of the center line. Draw the missing veins on the leaf, based on the part that has veins.

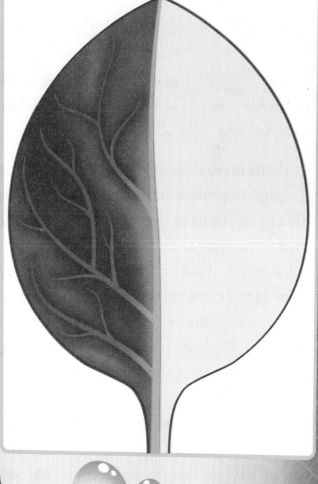

# Plants Make Food

How would your day be different if you didn't need to stop to eat? Plants don't need to eat. They work to make their own food all day long.

**Active Reading** As you read this page, underline the sentence you think is most important and be ready to explain why.

Plants make their food through a process called photosynthesis. During **photosynthesis**, plants use energy from the sun to change carbon dioxide and water into sugar and oxygen. Photosynthesis takes place in the leaves of plants. A substance in the leaves called **chlorophyll** captures energy from the sun during the day. Chlorophyll is what makes leaves appear green in color. It also helps plants make sugars, which the plants store in their stems, roots, and in some plants, in their leaves.

*Carbon dioxide* is a gas that plants get from the air. Plants take in carbon dioxide for photosynthesis and give off oxygen. This oxygen becomes part of the air that you breathe. These two gases move through small openings in a plant's leaves.

sunlight

water

food

oxygen

carbon dioxide

## The Ins and Outs of Photosynthesis

Fill in the blanks to show what happens during photosynthesis.
Some of the words are filled in for you.

Sunlight + _____ + _____ yields _____ + Oxygen

# Sum It Up!

When you're done, use the answer key to check and revise your work.

**Draw a line to match each description of a plant part with its picture.**

**1** Part that supports the plant and has tubes

**2** Part where photosynthesis takes place

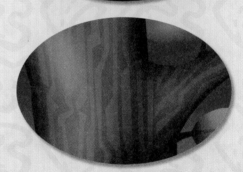

**3** Part that anchors the plant in the soil and absorbs water and minerals

## Summarize

**Fill in the missing words to describe leaves.**

Leaves have [4]_____ shapes. Some plants, like water lilies, have

[5]_____ leaves. Leaves can also be [6]_____,

triangular, or shaped like needles. Some leaves look fuzzy. These leaves have tiny

[7]_____ on their surface that help keep a plant from

[8]_____. Some leaves are [9]_____,

while others are dull.

Answer Key:1. stem 2. leaf 3. root 4. many 5. round 6. heart-shaped 7. hairs 8. drying out 9. shiny

Name _____

# Word Play

**1** Use the words in the box to complete each sentence. Then use the circled letters to answer the question below.

| photosynthesis* | chlorophyll* | flowers | root* |
|---|---|---|---|
| veins | vascular | leaf* | stems* |

*Key Lesson Vocabulary

The process of changing carbon dioxide and water into sugar and oxygen using energy from sunlight is __ __ __ __ __ __ Ⓞ __ __ __ __ __ __.

Plants may have hard woody or soft green Ⓞ__ __ __ __.

Plants with tubes that move water, minerals, and sugar are called __ __ __ __Ⓞ__Ⓞ__ plants.

The part of the plant that absorbs water and minerals is the Ⓞ__ __ __.

All plants that produce __Ⓞ__ __ __ __ are examples of vascular plants.

The part of the plant where food is made is the __ __Ⓞ__.

The lines in a leaf that contain tubes are called Ⓞ__ __Ⓞ__.

The substance in leaves that captures sunlight is called Ⓞ__ __ __ __Ⓞ__ __ __ __ __.

Mosses are examples of which type of plant?

__ __ __ __ __ __ __ __ __ __

# Apply Concepts

**2** Contrast vascular plants and nonvascular plants.

_____

_____

_____

_____

**3** Draw and label arrows to show how water and food move around in the vascular plant below. Then explain your diagram.

_____

_____

_____

_____

_____

_____

_____

_____

_____

_____

**Take It Home!**

With an adult family member, take a walk in your neighborhood or visit a local park or nursery. Identify plants you see as vascular or nonvascular. Explain the function of each visible plant part to your family member.

# How It Works:
## Water Irrigation System

A water irrigation system moves water to where it is needed. This water may come from rivers, lakes, or wells. Pumps and valves control the movement of water into and through the system. Farmers use a control panel to determine how much and how quickly water moves through a field.

- pipe and drip pipes
- center pivot gear
- system control panel
- "A" frame
- pump and check valve
- wheel

## Troubleshooting

Find and circle the pump on the diagram. What would happen to the irrigation system if the pump stopped working?

_____

_____

_____

# Show How It Works

People use irrigation systems to water their vegetable gardens at home.
Look at the picture of a backyard irrigation system. Label its parts.
Then answer the questions.

Name some parts of the irrigation system not shown in the diagram.

_____

_____

_____

Identify some problems with this irrigation system. Then, describe how you would solve them.

_____

_____

_____

_____

## Build On It!

Rise to the engineering design challenge—complete **Make a Process:
Planting and Caring for a Garden** on the Inquiry Flipchart.

Essential Question

# How Do Plants Reproduce?

**Engage Your Brain!**

Find the answer to the following question in this lesson and record it here.

Bees need flowers for food. How do flowers need bees?

_____

_____

_____

_____

## Active Reading

### Lesson Vocabulary

List the terms. As you learn about each one, make notes in the Interactive Glossary.

_____  _____

_____  _____

_____

### Signal Words

In this lesson, you will read about the sequence of stages in a plant's life cycle. Words that signal sequence include *now, before, after, first, next, start,* and *then.* Active readers look for signal words that identify sequence to help them remember what they read.

# How Does a
# Garden Grow?

Think of some of the plants you saw on your way to school today. You might have seen trees, grasses, flowers, or even weeds. Where did all of these plants come from?

**Active Reading** As you read the next page, circle the signal words that show the sequence in which a plant grows.

## Radish Life Cycle

A seed, such as this radish seed, contains the embryo of a plant.

When a seed sprouts during a process known as **germination**, the embryo in the seed begins to grow.

When a plant grows to its full size, it reaches **maturity**. Mature plants make seeds that can grow into new plants.

As the plant continues to grow, it gets larger. It also gets more roots.

When a plant grows, it goes through a series of set stages. The series of stages that a living thing goes through as it develops is called a *life cycle*. It is important for people to understand plant life cycles, because most of the food we eat comes from plants.

Most plants grow from seeds. First, a seed is placed in soil, so it can sprout. Next, the plant grows until it reaches maturity. A mature plant may grow flowers or cones. Then these structures make more seeds. You will learn about flowers and cones on the next pages.

## Lima Bean Life Cycle

Place the pictures in the correct sequence to show the life cycle of a lima bean plant. Write a number next to each picture. Start with the seed.

# Flowers and Cones

There are about 310,000 types of plants. Almost 90% of them produce seeds. How do plants produce seeds?

Flowers and cones are reproductive structures that make seeds. They produce sex cells. Sex cells are used during *sexual reproduction*. Male sex cells are called sperm, and female sex cells are called eggs. **Fertilization** is the process of a sperm and an egg cell joining together. A fertilized egg grows into an embryo inside a seed.

About 1,000 types of plants produce seeds in cones. In plants with cones, sperm are made in male cones and eggs are made in female cones.

Most plants produce seeds in structures called flowers. In plants with flowers, grains of pollen, produced in parts called anthers, contain the sperm. Eggs are made in a structure called a pistil. Many flowers have both anthers and a pistil. As you can see in the picture, flowers have many other parts as well.

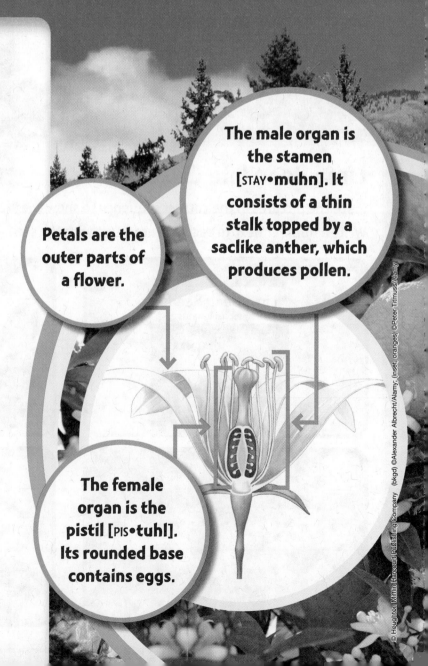

Petals are the outer parts of a flower.

The male organ is the stamen [STAY•muhn]. It consists of a thin stalk topped by a saclike anther, which produces pollen.

The female organ is the pistil [PIS•tuhl]. Its rounded base contains eggs.

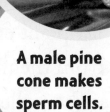

Most cone-bearing plants are trees. Pines, spruces, and cycads [SY•kadz] are all cone-bearing plants.

A female pine cone makes egg cells.

A male pine cone makes sperm cells.

## Plant Parts

Add labels to the flower.

# The Power of Pollen

In order for plant eggs to be fertilized, pollen has to move from the male parts to the female parts. How does the pollen get there?

**Active Reading** Underline ways plants can be pollinated.

Plants reproduce through pollination. **Pollination** is the process of pollen moving from a male plant part to a female plant part. There are several ways this can happen. Sometimes wind can blow the pollen from one plant to another, which is how many grasses and trees are pollinated.

Other plants are pollinated by *pollinators*. Some bees, birds, butterflies, and other animals are pollinators. For example, a butterfly goes from flower to flower drinking nectar. At each flower, the pollen on the stamens rubs off on the butterfly. When the butterfly visits the next flower, the pollen may drop off and fall on the pistil. As a result, the flower will be pollinated.

Brightly colored flower petals attract pollinators.

Some water plants are pollinated by water. Flowing water carries the pollen from plant to plant.

Pollen Cloud

## Do the Math!
### Work with Fractions

Animals pollinate $\frac{3}{4}$ of seed-making plants. Wind and water pollinate the other $\frac{1}{4}$ of plants. Use this information to label the parts of the circle.

Wind blows pollen from male cones. The wind may carry the pollen to a female cone.

# Seeds on the Move

Unlike most animals, plants cannot move around in their environment. So how can a plant's seeds be spread from place to place?

**Active Reading** As you read, underline three things that help seeds move from place to place.

Animals play a big role in moving plant seeds. The base of the pistil of flowers grows into a fruit that contains the flower's seeds. Think of the seeds in an apple or in a blackberry. When an animal eats these fruits, the seeds pass through the animal's body before being deposited elsewhere.

Other animals will find and bury seeds. Think of squirrels. Squirrels bury acorns so that they will have food in the winter. The squirrels will dig up and eat most of the acorns, but they may forget a few. These acorns will grow into new oak trees.

Seeds, such as burs, can also travel on an animal's body. Other kinds of seeds are very light. They can be carried by the wind. Still other seeds, including coconuts, float in water.

**Some seeds are very light. They can be blown around by the wind.**

Some seeds are covered in little hooks. These seeds are called burs. They can easily attach to fur or even to your socks!

▶ How are each of these seeds most likely spread from place to place?

_____

_____

_____

_____

Many animals eat fruit. This helps spread the seeds contained in fruit.

# Other Ways Plants Grow

Pine trees, beans, and sunflowers all grow from seeds. Other plants do not grow from seeds. These plants grow from structures called spores.

Have you ever looked at the underside of a fern leaf? You may have seen black or brown spots, like the ones in this picture. These spots are made up of pockets filled with spores.

A **spore** is a cell that can grow into a new plant when the conditions are right. Some plants, such as mosses and ferns, grow from spores instead of seeds. Plants that grow from spores have two distinct forms in their life cycles.

Spores are released when the structures that hold them break open. Wind carries the spores to new places. If a spore lands in a good spot, it will grow into a plant.

Spores are very tiny. They can be carried long distances by the wind.

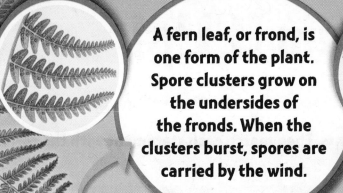

A fern leaf, or frond, is one form of the plant. Spore clusters grow on the undersides of the fronds. When the clusters burst, spores are carried by the wind.

The new plant reaches maturity when it can reproduce.

If a spore lands in a place with good light and water, it begins to grow into a tiny, flat, heart-shaped structure.

The heart-shaped structure is the other form of the plant. It produces eggs and sperm. If a sperm cell fertilizes an egg cell, a curled frond will begin to develop and push out of the ground.

▶ Fill in the chart to compare and contrast characteristics of seeds and spores.

| Seeds | Both | Spores |
|-------|------|--------|
|       |      |        |
|       |      |        |
|       |      |        |
|       |      |        |
|       |      |        |

When you're done, use the answer key to check and revise your work.

**Read the summary statements. Then match each statement with the correct image.**

## Summarize

____ 1. When a seed germinates, the embryo in the seed grows.

**A**

____ 2. The female organ of the flower is the pistil. The male organ of the flower is the stamen.

**B**

____ 3. In order to make new seeds, flowers or cones need to be pollinated by animals, wind, or water.

**C**

____ 4. Seeds can travel by water or wind, on an animal's body, or inside an animal's body.

**D**

____ 5. Spores are stored in clusters on the underside of fern leaves.

**E**

Answer Key: 1. D  2. B  3. E  4. A  5. C

# Brain Check

Name _____

## Word Play

**1** Use the terms in the box to complete the puzzle.

**cone**

**cycle**

fertilization*

**flower**

germination*

maturity*

**pollen**

pollination*

**seed**

spore*

*Key Lesson Vocabulary

### Across

3. Which process happens when a sperm joins with an egg?

4. When a plant has grown enough to reproduce, it has reached which stage in its life cycle?

5. What forms when an egg within a pistil is fertilized?

6. All of the stages a plant goes through as it develops is called its life _____ .

8. Which process happens when pollen falls on a flower's pistil?

9. Which cell grows into a new plant, such as a fern or moss, if it lands in a spot with the right conditions?

### Down

1. Which process happens when a small root and stem begin to grow out of a seed?

2. Which structures in seed-forming plants contain male sex cells?

6. Which structure do pine trees and spruce trees use to reproduce?

7. Which structure do rose bushes and apple trees use to reproduce?

# Apply Concepts

**2** Draw the life cycle of a flowering plant.

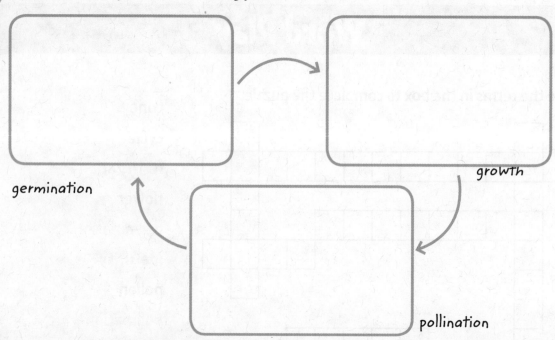

germination

growth

pollination

**3** Circle the structure(s) that plants use to reproduce.

**4** List three ways a seed-forming plant can be pollinated.

1. _____
_____

2. _____
_____

3. _____
_____

**5** Look at the seed shown here. How do you think this seed is spread? Explain your answer.

_____

_____

_____

_____

**6** Draw a picture of a flower and label its parts.

**7** Explain how pollination is different from fertilization in flowers. (Hint: Which needs to happen first—pollination or fertilization?)

_____

_____

_____

_____

_____

**8** Circle the pollinator(s) below.

With your family, go on a walk through your neighborhood or a local park. Locate plants that have flowers or cones. Examine the flowers or cones, and describe their structures to your family members.

Name _____

# How Can We Observe a Plant's Life Cycle?

## Set a Purpose
What will you learn from this experiment?

_____

_____

## Think About the Procedure
What are the conditions that you will control, or try to make the same, for each seed?

_____

_____

Why is it important that each seed is exposed to the same conditions?

_____

_____

_____

_____

_____

## Record Your Data
In the space below, draw a table to record your observations.

## Draw Conclusions

Which seed germinated the fastest? Which germinated the slowest?

_____

_____

_____

What would you expect to happen if you planted the germinated seeds in soil?

_____

_____

_____

## Analyze and Extend

1. Which factors do you think determine how fast a seed germinates?

_____

_____

_____

2. Explain how you could test the effect of one of the factors you listed in Question 1 on the germination rate of seeds.

_____

_____

_____

_____

_____

3. How do you think the plant would look if it was kept in the dark? How do you think the plant would look if it was kept in low light?

_____

_____

_____

_____

_____

4. Compare with a classmate the number of days it took for your seeds to germinate. Account for any differences and explain what you think happened.

_____

_____

_____

_____

_____

5. What other questions do you have about how seeds germinate?

_____

_____

_____

_____

# How Do Animals Reproduce?

## Engage Your Brain!

Find the answer to the following question in this lesson and record it here.

How do you think these young egrets will change as they grow up?

_____

_____

_____

_____

## Active Reading

### Lesson Vocabulary

List the terms. As you learn about each one, make notes in the Interactive Glossary.

_____

_____

_____

_____

### Sequence

Many ideas in this lesson are in a sequence, or order, that describes the steps in a process. Active readers stay focused on sequence when they go from one stage or step in a process to another.

# Life in Full Circle

Like plants, animals have life cycles. Animals are born and then begin to grow up. When animals become adults, they may have young of their own. In this way, life continues to renew itself.

**Active Reading** As you read the next page, underline the description of each stage of an animal's life, and number the stages in the correct order.

When a bird reaches adulthood, it mates with another bird.

Over time, the bird grows. Soon it can live on its own.

After the eggs hatch, the parents feed the young birds.

After mating, a female bird lays eggs. Birds hatch from eggs.

# Matching Game

Use the terms on the right to identify the correct life stages in each series of pictures.

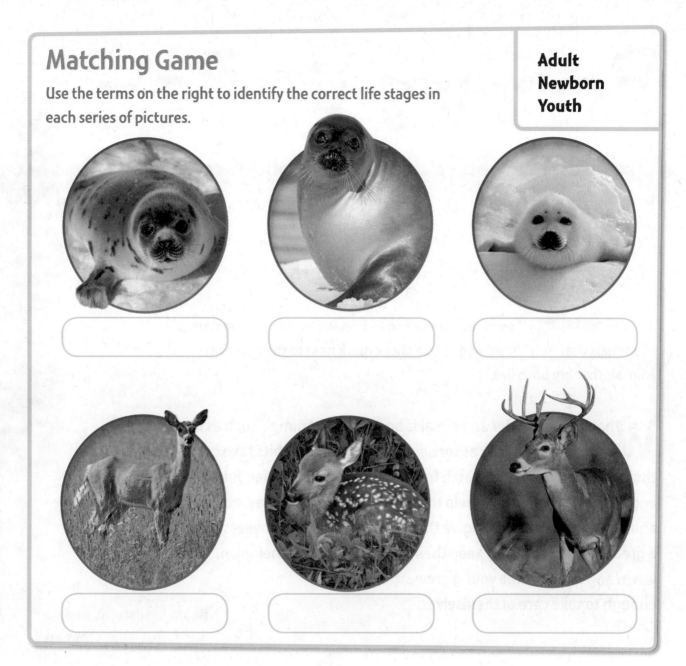

M ost animals reproduce sexually. During sexual reproduction, sperm from a male joins an egg from a female. The fertilized egg can then develop into a new animal.

In some animals, such as many kinds of fish, eggs are fertilized outside of the female's body. In other animals, such as birds, eggs are fertilized inside the female's body. After the eggs are fertilized, birds lay the eggs. Bird parents then protect the eggs until they have hatched.

After the young are born, they begin to grow and change. Over time, newborns develop into youths. Youths continue to develop until they grow into adults. Adult animals mate with one another to produce offspring. An animal's life cycle ends when the animal dies. However, the animal's offspring will likely have offspring of their own. In this way, the life cycle repeats again and again.

# Bringing Up Baby

Like birds, many other animals hatch out of eggs. For example, most fish, reptiles, and spiders hatch from eggs. Other animals give birth to live young. Dogs, horses, and mice are all born this way.

**Active Reading** As you read these pages, draw a star next to the names of animals that hatch from eggs and a check mark next to the names of animals that are born live.

What happens after an animal is born? Some animals, such as turtles, are on their own as soon as they hatch from their eggs. Their parents do not help them. Other animals, such as penguins, give their young a great deal of care. They keep their young warm and fed until the young grow strong enough to take care of themselves.

Animals such as deer, bears, and rabbits take care of their young by feeding them milk. These animals may stay with their parents for months or years until they are able to live on their own.

Birds' eggshells are hard, but alligators and other reptiles have soft, leathery shells.

▶ What are young kangaroos called?

_____

Cats give birth to live young.
Young cats drink their mother's milk.

## Do the Math!
### Solve a Problem

Raccoons usually give birth to 3 to 5 young at one time. Raccoons give birth only once a year. Suppose a female raccoon lives 10 years. She is able to give birth for 9 of those years. How many offspring will she have?

_____

_____

When kangaroos are born, they are about the size of a dime. They then develop in their mother's pouch.

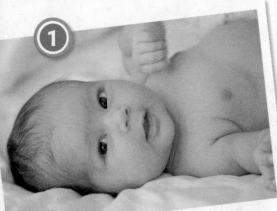

When babies are born, they drink their mother's milk. They have no teeth, and they are not able to walk on their own.

**2** Babies grow into toddlers. Toddlers learn how to walk. They also start learning how to speak. Humans get their first set of teeth when they are toddlers.

# Growing Up

Just like other animals, humans go through stages of development. After a human egg is fertilized, it grows inside the mother. After nine months, the baby is born. It takes many years for a human baby to grow into an adult. Study these pages to see all of the growth stages humans go through.

**Active Reading** Put a star next to the life stage that you are currently in.

**3** As a child develops, the first set of teeth is replaced by permanent teeth. The child grows and develops many physical and mental skills.

# Growth Chart

At age 2, children are about 2 ft 10 in. tall.
By age 5, children are about 3 ft 6 in. tall.
Place these measurements into the chart.
Then, measure yourself and an adult.
Place those measurements in the chart.

How do you change as you get older?

_____

| Age | Height |
|-----|--------|
| 2 | |
| 5 | |
| You | |
| Adult | |

**During the teenage years, boys and girls start looking more like adults. For example, boys start growing facial hair.**

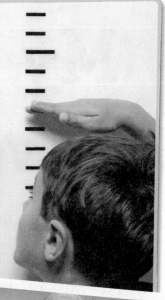

6 **As an adult ages, they lose some of their physical abilities. The body changes in other ways, as well. For example, the hair turns gray.**

5 During adulthood, people reach maturity. Often, adults marry and have children of their own.

# My, How You've Changed!

A young frog, or tadpole, has a long tail and no legs. As it grows, its tail becomes shorter, and it begins to grow legs. An adult frog has no tail, but has legs. The young go through a series of changes known as *metamorphosis*.

**Active Reading** As you read the next page, underline the sentences that contain vocabulary terms.

▶ Write a caption for this photo of a butterfly breaking out of its chrysalis.

_____

_____

_____

_____

## Complete Metamorphosis

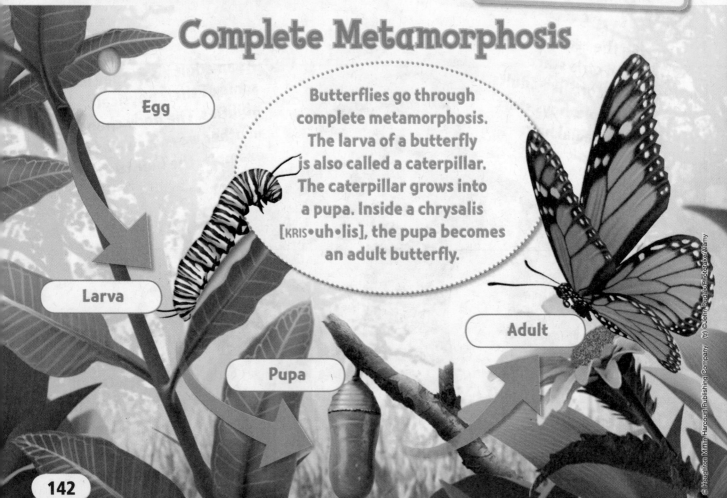

Egg

Butterflies go through complete metamorphosis. The larva of a butterfly is also called a caterpillar. The caterpillar grows into a pupa. Inside a chrysalis [KRIS•uh•lis], the pupa becomes an adult butterfly.

Larva

Pupa

Adult

# Incomplete Metamorphosis

**Adult**

Grasshoppers will molt five times before they reach the adult stage.

Grasshoppers go through incomplete metamorphosis. Young grasshoppers hatch as nymphs. A nymph grows and molts.

**Nymph**

The female grasshopper lays eggs in the soil.

**Eggs**

In many animals, the young look similar to the adults. But in other animals, the young look very different. In **complete metamorphosis** [met•uh•MAWR•fuh•sis], an animal goes through four different stages in its life cycle. The egg hatches into a *larva*. The larvae [LAR•vee] of many insects look like worms. A larva develops into a *pupa* [PYOO•puh]. The pupa of a moth is enclosed in a cocoon. While in the cocoon, the pupa develops into an adult moth. The adult splits its cocoon and flies out.

Some insects, such as dragonflies and termites, go through a different series of changes. In **incomplete metamorphosis**, an animal goes through three different stages in its life cycle. First, the animal hatches from the egg as a **nymph** [NIMF]. Nymphs look like tiny adults, but they don't have wings. As the nymph grows larger, it molts. Molting happens when an insect sheds its hard outer skeleton. After several moltings, the insect, which now has wings, reaches its adult stage.

# Saving (the) Sea Turtles

Some kinds of animals are endangered. That means there are not many of them left. Scientists study the life cycles of endangered animals to try to save them and help them increase their numbers.

Sea turtles are one example of an endangered animal. Hunting, pollution, and beach erosion have caused the number of sea turtles to go down. To help sea turtles, people have learned about the sea turtle's life cycle. They have used what they learned to rear sea turtles. The turtles are then released into the wild. Over time, scientists hope this will help increase the number of sea turtles.

To rear sea turtles, eggs are collected.

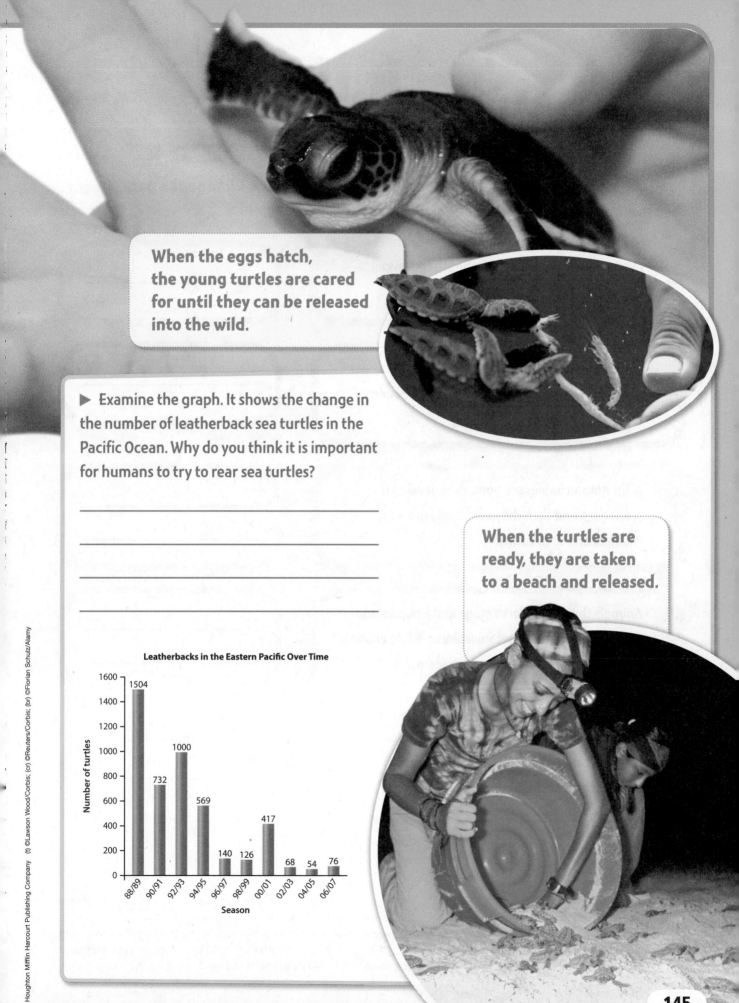

When the eggs hatch, the young turtles are cared for until they can be released into the wild.

▶ Examine the graph. It shows the change in the number of leatherback sea turtles in the Pacific Ocean. Why do you think it is important for humans to try to rear sea turtles?

_____

_____

_____

_____

When the turtles are ready, they are taken to a beach and released.

**Leatherbacks in the Eastern Pacific Over Time**

Number of turtles

1504, 732, 1000, 569, 140, 126, 417, 68, 54, 76

Season: 88/89, 90/91, 92/93, 94/95, 96/97, 98/99, 00/01, 02/03, 04/05, 06/07

When you're done, use the answer key to check and revise your work.

**Read the summary statements below. Each one is incorrect. Change the part of the summary in blue to make it correct.**

**1** Most animals grow from a fertilized sperm cell.

_____

**2** Some animals, such as cows, cats, and rabbits, give birth to live young and care for the young by feeding them worms.

_____

**3** After human babies are born, they develop into teenagers, and then they eventually grow into toddlers and then adults.

_____

**4** Animals that have a larva stage and a pupa stage undergo incomplete metamorphosis, while animals that have a nymph stage undergo complete metamorphosis.

_____

**5** Humans can try to help endangered animals by rearing them and releasing them into cities.

_____

Name _____

# Word Play

**1** Match the words to the correct picture.

_____ 1. metamorphosis

_____ 2. incomplete metamorphosis

_____ 3. larva

_____ 4. nymph

_____ 5. molt

_____ 6. pupa

A

B

C

D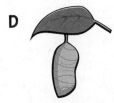

E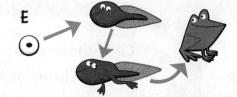

F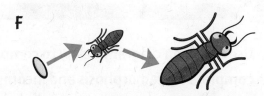

# Apply Concepts

**2** Circle the animals that hatch from eggs.

# Apply Concepts

**3** Draw the life cycle of an eagle.

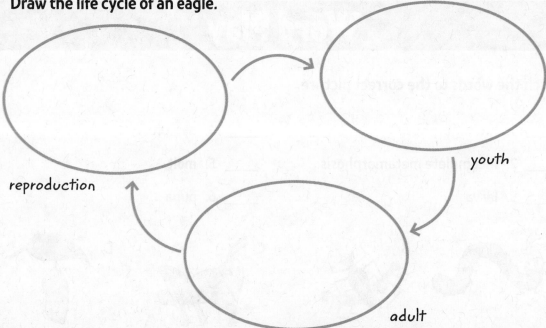

reproduction

youth

adult

**4** Use the Venn diagram below to compare complete metamorphosis and incomplete metamorphosis.

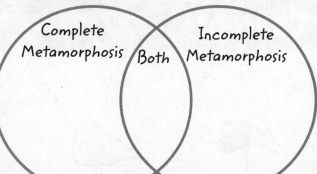

Complete Metamorphosis        Both        Incomplete Metamorphosis

**5** Circle the one that undergoes incomplete metamorphosis.

**Take It Home!**

Ask to see childhood photographs of adult family members. How did your family members change as they grew and developed?

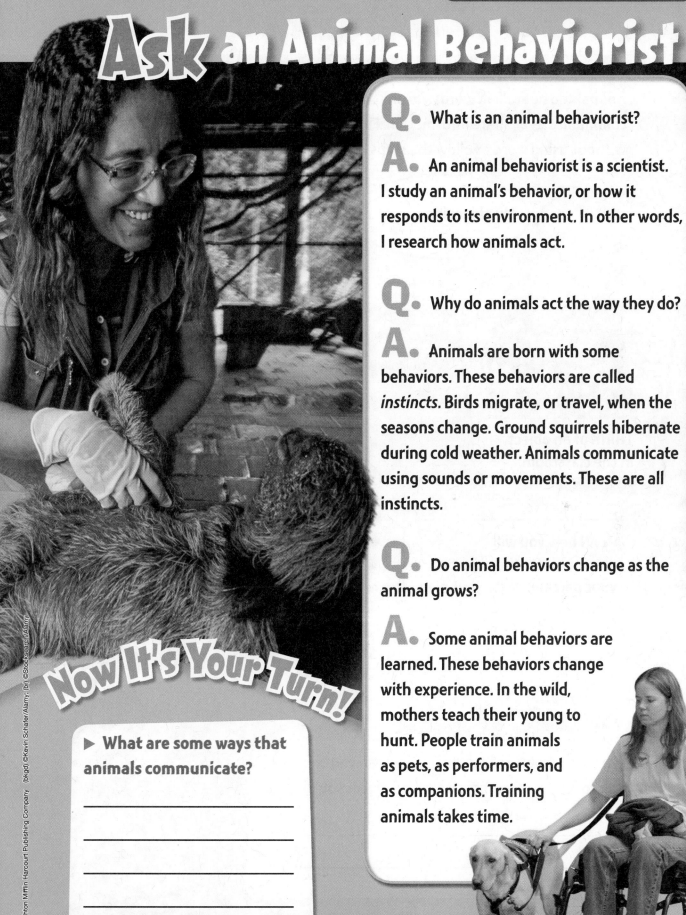

# Ask an Animal Behaviorist

**Q.** What is an animal behaviorist?

**A.** An animal behaviorist is a scientist. I study an animal's behavior, or how it responds to its environment. In other words, I research how animals act.

**Q.** Why do animals act the way they do?

**A.** Animals are born with some behaviors. These behaviors are called *instincts*. Birds migrate, or travel, when the seasons change. Ground squirrels hibernate during cold weather. Animals communicate using sounds or movements. These are all instincts.

**Q.** Do animal behaviors change as the animal grows?

**A.** Some animal behaviors are learned. These behaviors change with experience. In the wild, mothers teach their young to hunt. People train animals as pets, as performers, and as companions. Training animals takes time.

## Now It's Your Turn!

▶ What are some ways that animals communicate?

_____

_____

_____

_____

149

# Be an Animal Behaviorist

Animals do not talk in words. An animal behaviorist finds other ways to *communicate,* or share information. Find a partner and communicate without using words. Follow the steps below.

My object is a _____.

**1** THINK of an object in the classroom.

**2** PLAN how you will communicate the object to your partner. Write your plan.

**3** Taking turns, COMMUNICATE the object to your partner.

**4** DRAW what your partner communicated.

## Think About It!

After seeing your partner's drawing, how can you change your plan to better communicate which object you picked?

_____

_____

**Essential Question**

# How Are Living Things Adapted to Their Environment?

## Engage Your Brain!

Find the answer to the following question in this lesson and record it here.

How do the characteristics of this fox help it survive in its environment?

_____

_____

_____

_____

## Active Reading

### Lesson Vocabulary

List the terms. As you learn about each one, make notes in the Interactive Glossary.

_____ _____

_____ _____

_____ _____

_____ _____

### Signal Words: Details

This lesson gives details about the types of adaptations that help plants and animals survive in different environments. Signal words, such as *for example, for instance,* and *like,* link main topics to added details. Active readers look for signal words that link a main topic to its details.

# Life on the Blue Planet

Because most of Earth is covered by water, it is often called the Blue Planet. Life is found in water, on land, and everywhere in between!

**Active Reading** As you read this page, circle signal words that indicate details about the environment.

The **environment** consists of all the living and nonliving things in an area. Look at the picture on these pages. The environment shown here includes the animals, plants, water, soil, air, and everything else in the picture. Animals and plants depend on their environment to meet their needs. For example, the zebras in the picture get food, water, and shelter from their environment.

Earth has many types of environments. For instance, Arctic environments are very cold; tropical rainforests are very hot. Some types of environments are deep in the ocean. Others are on dry land with very little rainfall. Because there are so many types of environments on Earth, there are also many types of living things. Each living thing, or organism, is able to survive in its own environment.

> All living things need food, water, air, and shelter. Organisms in the same environment share resources.

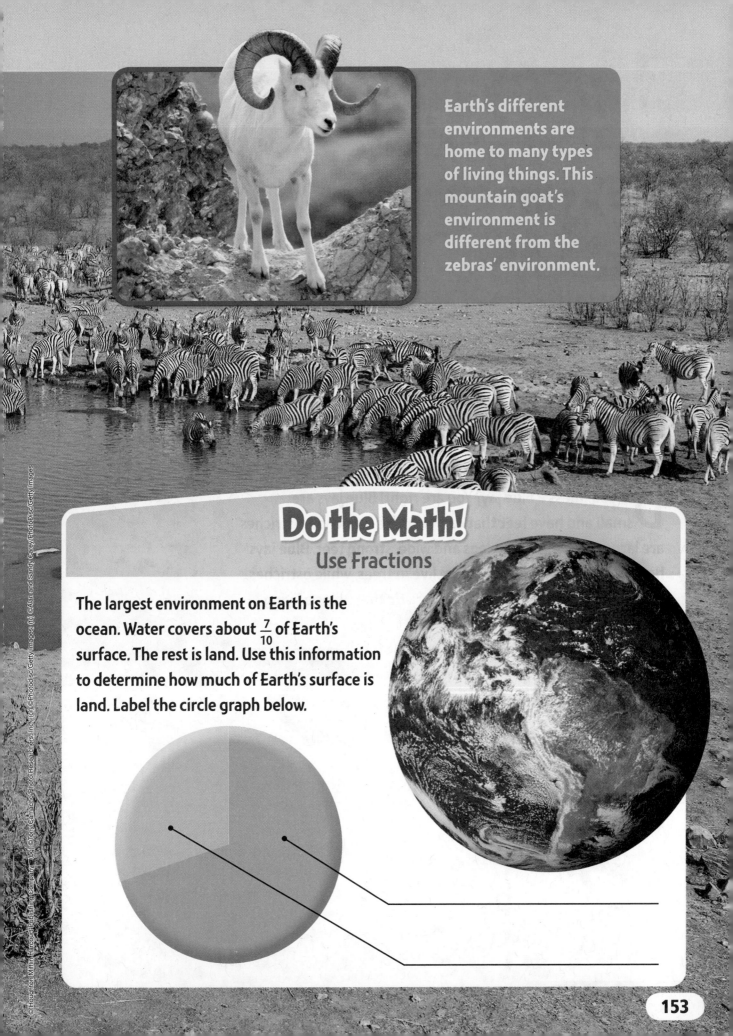

Earth's different environments are home to many types of living things. This mountain goat's environment is different from the zebras' environment.

# Do the Math!
## Use Fractions

The largest environment on Earth is the ocean. Water covers about $\frac{7}{10}$ of Earth's surface. The rest is land. Use this information to determine how much of Earth's surface is land. Label the circle graph below.

# Who Is out on a Limb?

If you were in a forest, which bird would you expect to see up in the trees—a blue jay or an ostrich?

**Active Reading** As you read this page, underline the definition of *adaptation*.

Did you guess a blue jay? You are right! Blue jays are small and have feet that can grip tree branches. Ostriches are large. They have long legs and wide, strong feet. Blue jays have adaptations that help them live in trees, while ostriches do not. An **adaptation** is a characteristic that helps a living thing survive.

Ostriches live on grasslands. They have long, strong legs that enable them to run quickly in open spaces. Their brown color helps them blend in.

Prairie dogs have strong paws for digging burrows. Their brown color enables them to blend in with their environment.

A **physical adaptation** is an adaptation to a body part. Living things have different physical adaptations based on their specific environments. For example, plants and animals in open spaces have different physical adaptations than living things in forests.

In open spaces, grasses can bend in strong winds. Grassland animals have coverings to blend in with the grass. These animals may be able to run fast or have shovel-like paws for burrowing.

Living things in forests have physical adaptations to live in and around trees. Vines can climb up trees to reach sunlight they need. Many forest animals can grip branches.

This blue jay's curved feet help it grip small branches. Its wings enable it to fly from branch to branch.

This sloth's long claws help it to hang from tree branches for most of its life. A sloth can even sleep without letting go of the branch.

▶ Compare the prairie dog's grassland adaptations with the sloth's forest adaptations.

_____

_____

_____

_____

_____

_____

_____

_____

# Who Can Go with the Flow?

Some living things swim upstream while others go with the flow. Which adaptations do living things need in different water environments?

**Active Reading** As you read the paragraph below, circle examples of fish physical adaptations.

Imagine you live in a constantly flowing stream of water. How could you stay in the same part of the stream without being carried away? Many fish that live in streams have smooth bodies and strong tails. These characteristics help fish swim against the current. Water plants have flexible stems that allow them to bend with the flow. Many water insects are able to hold on tightly to water plants. Other insects burrow into the soil at the bottom of the stream.

This fish has a smooth, streamlined body. Its body shape allows it to swim quickly in fast-moving water.

*Elodea* are very flexible plants, so flowing water is less likely to break them. If a piece of elodea is pulled off, though, the piece can sprout roots and start to grow in a new part of the stream.

Plants in still water, such as ponds and lakes, have different adaptations. Some plants are tall and have strong stems, so they can grow above the water. Others, such as water lilies, float on the surface.

Animals that live in lakes and ponds are excellent swimmers. Many are adapted to living in deep water with little light. Catfish have whiskers that sense chemicals in the water to help them find food in the dark. Some birds wade at the shore and hunt. Their long, thin legs look like the cattails, so fish do not see them until it's too late.

Cattails grow in relatively still, shallow water, such as the water of a pond. Their stems are strong and stiff. Cattails can grow to more than 3 m tall.

Pond turtles are strong swimmers. They are also able to hold their breath for long periods of time. Their dark color allows them to stay hidden in dark, muddy water.

▶ Compare the elodea's adaptations with the cattail's adaptations.

_____

_____

_____

_____

_____

_____

# Who Can Take the Heat?

Deserts are places that get very little rain. Some deserts are very hot. How do plants and animals live in such hot, dry places?

**Active Reading** As you read these two pages, circle the words or phrases that describe desert environments.

Desert plants and animals have physical adaptations that help them stay cool and conserve water. Many desert plants have waxy coatings on their stems to minimize water loss. Many of these plants have very long roots to reach water that is deep underground. Some desert plants have wide root systems that can absorb lots of water when it rains. Desert animals have physical adaptations to keep cool. Some have short, thin fur, or no fur at all.

Jackrabbits have large ears. Their ears release body heat and help the rabbits stay cool.

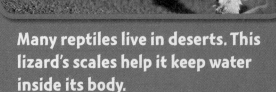

Many reptiles live in deserts. This lizard's scales help it keep water inside its body.

A **behavioral adaptation** is something an organism does to help it survive. For example, most desert animals are active at night to avoid the heat of the day. An instinct is a type of behavioral adaptation.

An **instinct** is an inherited behavior an animal knows how to do without having to learn it. For instance, jackrabbits stay crouched in one position whenever they sense danger. This instinct helps them hide from predators.

Other behaviors help organisms survive in the desert. For example, some seeds of desert plants stay dormant, or inactive, until it rains. When it rains enough, the seeds grow quickly into plants that flower and make more seeds.

Saguaro cactus flowers open and release their fragrance at night and close the next day. It is cooler at night in the desert. As a result, the flowers do not wilt as quickly as they would during the day.

▶ Describe a living thing with adaptations that help it survive in the desert. Explain how each adaptation helps.

_____

_____

_____

_____

_____

_____

# Who Can Take the Cold?

Polar environments are very cold places. How do plants and animals survive in cold places such as Antarctica and the Arctic?

**Active Reading** As you read these pages, circle the words or phrases that describe polar environments.

Temperatures in Antarctica rarely get above freezing—even in summer! Plants and animals that live there have adaptations to live in extreme cold. Emperor penguins have a thick layer of fat—a physical adaptation that keeps them warm on land and in the water. To protect themselves from very cold winds, male penguins huddle together in large groups. The behavior is an instinct that helps male penguins and their newly hatched baby penguins keep warm.

The Antarctic pearlwort grows close to the ground in the warmer, wetter parts of Antarctica.

Black feathers on the backs of emperor penguins absorb heat from the sun, which helps them keep warm.

The Arctic has extremely cold winters and very short summers. Arctic animals have thick fur and a layer of fat to keep in body heat. Some Arctic animals are often white in the winter, which helps them blend in with the snow. These characteristics are physical adaptations. Arctic animals also have behavioral adaptations. For example, many Arctic animals live in dens dug into the ground or snow during very cold months.

Most Arctic plants have short roots because the ground there is frozen the majority of the year. These plants produce seeds during the short summer when the ground isn't frozen. Most Arctic plants grow close to the ground, which helps protect them from strong, cold Arctic winds.

This prairie crocus has fuzzy hairs that cover its flowers and seeds. The hairs protect the plant from wind and trap heat from the sun.

► Compare the adaptations that help the desert jackrabbit and the Arctic hare survive in their environments.

_____
_____
_____
_____
_____
_____
_____
_____

Arctic hares grow white fur in winter to blend in with the snow. They sit with their paws, tails, and ears tucked in to keep from losing body heat.

# Sum It Up!

When you're done, use the answer key to check and revise your work.

**The outline below is a summary of the lesson. Complete the outline.**

## Summarize

I. Match each description to the living thing that has that adaptation.

A. flexible stem that bends in flowing water          Arctic hare

B. grows white fur in the winter                       sloth

C. long claws to hang from tree branches       saguaro

D. flowers open at night when it's cooler        prairie dog

E. long claws for digging burrows               *Elodea*

II. Identify each adaptation described below as a physical adaptation or a behavioral adaptation.

A. An ostrich has long, strong legs. _____

B. An Arctic hare sits for hours to conserve heat. _____

C. A catfish has whiskers that sense chemicals in the water. _____

D. Male penguins huddle together to stay warm. _____

E. A fish has a smooth, streamlined body. _____

Name _____

# Word Play

**1** Complete the crossword puzzle.

## Across

4. Desert animals are active at night to avoid the heat. Which type of adaptation is this?

5. Which type of behavior does an animal know how to do without having to learn it?

## Down

1. What are all of the living and nonliving things in an area called?

2. A blue jay's small, curved feet help it grip branches. Which type of adaptation is this?

3. What is a body part or behavior that helps a living thing survive called?

# Apply Concepts

**2** Draw a circle around the plant that would most likely live in a forest environment. On the line below, write an adaptation the plant has that helps it live in a forest.

_____

**3** Snakes and lizards are rarely found living near polar environments.
Explain why.

_____

_____

_____

**4**

This spider monkey lives in the forest. What physical adaptations does it
have that help it survive in this type of environment?

_____

**5** Why is it better for an animal to know how to hide from predators because
of an instinct than to have to learn how to hide from them?

_____

_____

_____

_____

**Take It Home!**

Take a walk with your family through your neighborhood or a
local park. Look at different plants and animals, and point out the
adaptations these plants or animals have to help them survive.

Name _____

**Essential Question**

# Why Do Bird Beaks Differ?

## Set a Purpose

**Why do you think different birds have beaks with different shapes?**

_____

_____

_____

_____

**Write a statement summarizing what you plan to investigate.**

_____

_____

_____

_____

**What will you be modeling in this investigation?**

_____

_____

_____

_____

## Record Your Data

**In the space below, make a table in which you record your observations.**

## Draw Conclusions

Did some beaks work for more than one kind of food? What might this suggest about the bird's ability to survive?

_____

_____

_____

_____

Did one kind of beak work for eating all of the different foods?

_____

_____

_____

_____

## Analyze and Extend

1. Which bird's beak would be best for eating flower nectar? Which beaks would be best for picking insects out of wood and worms out of sand?

_____

_____

_____

_____

_____

2. A toucan is a bird that eats very large, tough tropical fruit. What would you expect a toucan's beak to look like?

_____

_____

_____

3. Look at the bird beaks below. Tell which tool in the investigation was most similar to each of the beaks.

hummingbird

finch

_____     _____

macaw

shorebird

_____     _____

woodpecker

duck

_____     _____

4. Think of other questions you would like to ask about how adaptations relate to the food an animal eats.

_____

_____

_____

# Unit 3 Review

Name _____

## Vocabulary Review

Use the terms in the box to complete the sentences.

1. The process by which plants use energy from the sun to change carbon dioxide and water into sugar and oxygen

   is called _____.

2. Animals that have three stages in their life cycles go

   through _____.

3. A characteristic that helps an organism survive is

   a(n) _____.

4. The substance in leaves that makes them appear green

   in color is _____.

5. The process by which a sperm cell joins with an egg cell

   is called _____.

6. A cell from a fern plant that can produce a new plant is

   called a _____.

7. All of the living and nonliving things in an area make up

   an _____.

8. The movement of sperm cells from the male part of a flower to the female part occurs through the process

   of _____.

# Science Concepts

Fill in the letter of the choice that best answers the question.

9. Plants get the energy they need to live by changing substances into the sugars they use for food. Which two substances do plants change during photosynthesis to make food?

   (A) sugar and water

   (B) sugar and oxygen

   (C) carbon dioxide and water

   (D) carbon dioxide and oxygen

10. Which stage below is part of incomplete metamorphosis—but not of complete metamorphosis?

    (A) adult

    (B) egg

    (C) nymph

    (D) pupa

11. The bristlecone pine tree produces cones that are either male or female. In contrast, the fishpoison tree has flowers that contain both male and female parts. What can you infer about these two trees?

    (A) Both trees carry out sexual reproduction.

    (B) Both trees have incredibly long life cycles.

    (C) Both trees can disperse their seeds very far.

    (D) Both trees need insects to carry out pollination.

12. Examine the beak on the bird below.

   For which type of feeding is the shape of this beak best suited?

   (A) tearing food

   (B) eating small seeds

   (C) getting flower nectar

   (D) digging insects from bark

13. The bald cypress tree produces seeds protected within cones. This type of tree is found in swampy areas where heavy rains produce floods. The flood waters help spread the cones throughout the swampy areas. What role do the flood waters play in the life cycle of the bald cypress tree?

    (A) pollination

    (B) fertilization

    (C) seed dispersal

    (D) removal of dead leaves

**14.** This picture shows a butterfly and bees visiting a flower to obtain nectar.

Which process are these insects helping the plant carry out?

(A) pollination

(B) germination

(C) seed dispersal

(D) photosynthesis

**15.** The caddis fly is an insect that can live in streams for months. When its body is more wormlike, this fly builds an underwater house from pebbles to protect it from predators. Which stage of metamorphosis is the fly in at this point?

(A) egg

(B) adult

(C) larva

(D) pupa

**16.** Sharks can smell very small amounts of substances in ocean water. What does this physical adaptation most likely help sharks do?

(A) sense water temperature

(B) find a place to lay eggs

(C) find a safe place to hide

(D) find food that is far away

**17.** Monarch butterflies migrate to warm places every winter. What is their migration an example of?

(A) a trait    (C) a characteristic

(B) an instinct    (D) a learned behavior

**18.** Sarai visits the local nature center. She sees a number of young animals. Which of the animals hatches from an egg?

(A) a turtle    (C) a dolphin

(B) a cheetah    (D) a bear

**19.** A mahogany tree produces seeds that look like the picture below.

Fan-like blades

Notice the blades on the surface of this seed. What role do these blades play in the life cycle of a mahogany tree?

(A) protect the seed

(B) end the plant's life cycle

(C) store food for the seedling

(D) help disperse the tree's seeds

**20.** Which of the following lists stages in the life cycle of a seed plant?

(A) spore, reproduction, maturity

(B) germination, maturity, reproduction

(C) egg, larva, pupa, adult

(D) germination, nymph, spore, death

# Apply Inquiry and Review the Big Idea

Write the answers to these questions.

21. The illustration shows common structures of a flowering plant. Identify each plant part, and describe its function.

Structure A:_____

_____

_____

Structure B:_____

_____

_____

Structure C:_____

_____

_____

Structure D:_____

_____

22. Sayana is testing where bean seeds germinate more quickly. She places several bean seeds into two plastic bags—one containing moist soil and the other moist paper towels. What does she need to do to make this a fair experiment?

_____

_____

23. This picture shows organisms that live in a desert environment. Choose one of the organisms. Identify one of its physical adaptations, and describe how the adaptation helps the organism live in a desert environment.

_____

_____

_____

_____

# Energy and Ecosystems

## Big Idea

Ecosystems are made up of both living and nonliving parts that impact one another.

## I Wonder Why

Why are these living things able to move and grow? How do they get their energy? *Turn the page to find out.*

**Here's Why** Living things get the energy they need to move and grow from food. Plants make their own food. Animals eat plants or other animals.

In this unit, you will explore the Big Idea, the Essential Questions, and the Investigations on the Inquiry Flipchart.

Levels of Inquiry Key ■ DIRECTED ■ GUIDED ■ INDEPENDENT

**Big Idea** Ecosystems are made up of both living and nonliving parts that impact one another.

# Essential Questions

Now I Get the Big Idea!

**Science Notebook**

Before you begin each lesson, be sure to write your thoughts about the Essential Question.

**Essential Question**

# What Are Populations, Habitats, and Niches?

## Engage Your Brain!

Find the answer to the following question in this lesson and record it here.

Bears are rarely found in groups. Why are so many bears in this stream at the same time?

_____

_____

_____

_____

## Active Reading

### Lesson Vocabulary

List the terms. As you learn about each one, make notes in the Interactive Glossary.

_____  _____

_____  _____

_____  _____

_____  _____

### Main Idea and Details

Details give information about a topic. The information may be examples, features, or characteristics. Active readers stay focused on the topic when they ask, What facts or information do these details add to the topic?

# Who Lives Where?

Rain forests have rainy weather. Deserts have dry weather. Each place meets the needs of the organisms that live in it.

**Active Reading** As you read this page, underline the main idea.

All of the living and nonliving things in an area make up an environment. The living things in an environment include people, plants, and animals. The nonliving things include water, air, soil, and weather. All of the living and nonliving things in an area and their interactions make up an **ecosystem** [EE•koh•sis•tuhm].

An ecosystem may be as large as a lake or as small as the area under a rock. Ecosystems are found everywhere organisms live and interact—in water or on land. Some ecosystems include coral reefs, savannas, swamps, rain forests, and the polar ecosystems.

All parts of an ecosystem are connected. For example, the soil and the temperature of a place determine the types of plants that can grow there. In turn, the types of animals in an ecosystem depend on the plants it contains.

A great variety of plants and animals thrive in rain forests, where the weather is always warm and wet.

Coral reefs are made up of the outer skeletons of coral animals. These reefs are home to many types of organisms.

Polar ecosystems are very cold and dry. Organisms that live there have adaptations to survive the cold weather. Organisms that live in wetlands such as swamps, where pools of water cover the land, have adaptations, too. Cypress trees, for example, have strong trunks and thick roots that hold the tree in place.

Organisms are not evenly distributed among the different ecosystems. The greatest diversity of plants are found in tropical rain forests. By comparison, few plants live in polar ecosystems.

Within a large ecosystem, there are smaller ecosystems. Some frogs in tropical rain forests, for example, live their entire lives perched on a few trees.

Similarly, in the ocean, certain fish, sponges, seaweeds, sharks, and sea turtles make their homes in or around coral reefs. Many of these organisms could not live elsewhere in the ocean. Coral reefs make up less than one-tenth of ocean ecosystems. But about one-fourth of all kinds of sea organisms live in or around coral reefs.

▶ Match each animal with the ecosystem where it lives. Then describe one way each animal interacts with its ecosystem.

**Walrus**

**Giraffe**

**African savanna**

**Polar ecosystem**

_____
_____
_____
_____
_____
_____
_____
_____
_____
_____
_____
_____

# Nearby Neighbors

You and your neighbors are part of a community.
Plants and animals form communities, too.

**Active Reading** As you read these two pages, put brackets [ ] around each paragraph's main idea.

Look at this picture. The zebras, the elephants, the grasses, and the shrubs—in fact, all the living things shown—form a community. A **community** is made up of all the organisms that live in the same place.

Natural and human activities change communities over time. On the savannas of Africa, for example, water is scarce during the dry season. As a result, many organisms die. Fires are also common. Lightning causes most of these fires; however, people start some, too.

Fires kill some organisms, but many more survive. Grasses have deep roots that are not harmed by fire. Some trees have thick, fire-resistant bark. Moles, gophers, and other small animals stay away from fire by hiding underground. Larger animals, such as zebras, antelopes, lions, and hyenas, run fast to escape fire.

Spring thunderstorms bring the rainy season to the savanna. Grasses, shrubs, and trees grow back quickly. Animals that survived the fire give birth to their young. With so much grass to eat, the mothers are able to make enough milk to feed the calves, and the animal populations grow.

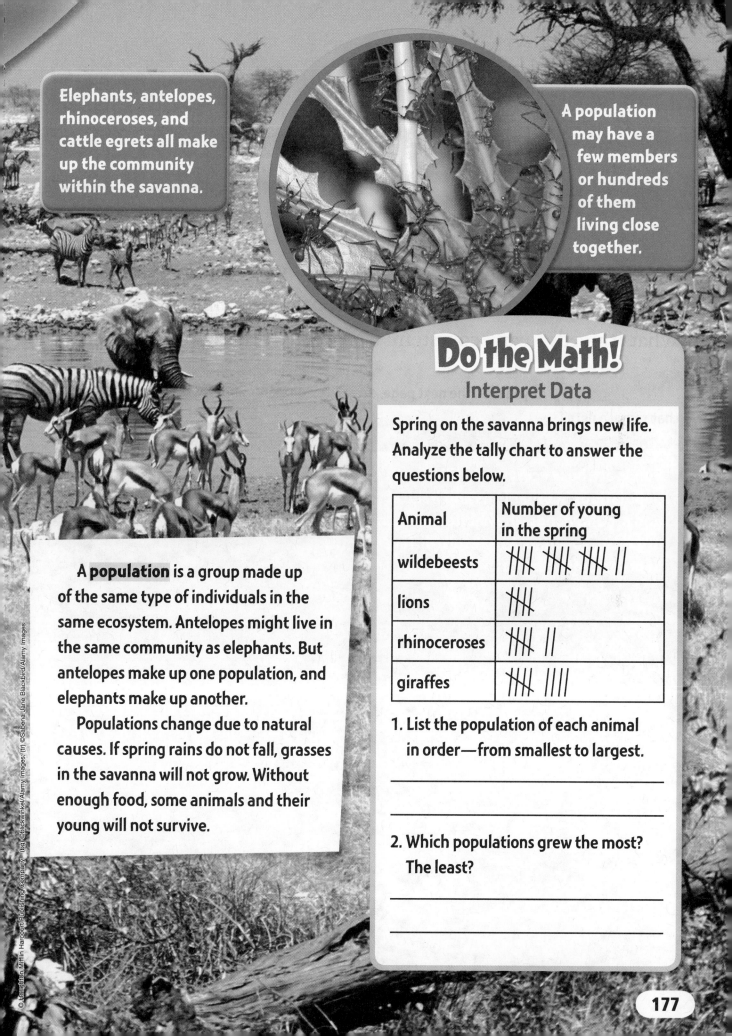

Elephants, antelopes, rhinoceroses, and cattle egrets all make up the community within the savanna.

A population may have a few members or hundreds of them living close together.

A **population** is a group made up of the same type of individuals in the same ecosystem. Antelopes might live in the same community as elephants. But antelopes make up one population, and elephants make up another.

Populations change due to natural causes. If spring rains do not fall, grasses in the savanna will not grow. Without enough food, some animals and their young will not survive.

## Do the Math!
### Interpret Data

Spring on the savanna brings new life. Analyze the tally chart to answer the questions below.

| Animal | Number of young in the spring |
|--------|-------------------------------|
| wildebeests | ⅷ ⅷ ⅷ || |
| lions | ⅷ |
| rhinoceroses | ⅷ || |
| giraffes | ⅷ |||| |

1. List the population of each animal in order—from smallest to largest.

_____

_____

2. Which populations grew the most? The least?

_____

_____

# A Place of One's Own

All organisms have the same basic needs. Different organisms meet their needs in a number of ways. Read on to find out about where an organism finds what it needs in an ecosystem.

**Active Reading** As you read the next page, circle the clue words or phrases that signal a detail.

Ponds are busy ecosystems filled with different populations of organisms and habitats. In and around ponds, the habitats of many organisms overlap. As a result, different kinds of organisms often have to interact.

Tadpoles

Mosquito larvae and tadpoles often share the same habitat. They use the same resources for food and shelter

Mosquito larvae

Organisms find the resources they need in their habitat. A **habitat** is the physical part of the ecosystem that meets the needs of an organism. Organisms find food and shelter in their habitats.

Every organism in a habitat has a role, or **niche**. The way an organism interacts with the habitat and gets food and shelter are part of its niche. Every organism has body parts that help it fit its niche. A duck, for example, has webbed feet and oily feathers to help it swim and stay warm.

Some animals, such as frogs, change niches during their life cycle. At first, tadpoles live in water, breathe through gills, and eat algae. As adults, frogs breathe through lungs, live at the water's edge, and eat insects.

Organisms compete for resources when their habitats and niches overlap. Tadpoles and mosquito larvae, for instance, compete for algae in a pond. Crowded plants at a pond's edge may compete for a place to grow and for sunlight.

Tree swallow

As tadpoles grow into adult frogs, their niche changes. Adult frogs compete with tree swallows for food. They both eat insects.

Adult frog

▶ Identify two organisms that share food or other resources in an ecosystem.

_____

_____

_____

# Dinner Time!

Water, air, sunlight, and presto, dinner is served! Plants are able to use water, air, and solar energy to make their own food. Read these pages to learn how other living things get their food.

**Active Reading** As you read these pages, circle the words that signal details.

A strawberry plant uses water, carbon dioxide, and energy from the sun to make its own food. The boy and the squirrel eat the strawberries for energy.

Any living thing that makes its own food is called a **producer**. Trees and algae are types of producers. Animals can't make their own food, but they need energy, too. An animal that eats plants or other animals to get energy is called a **consumer**.

A field of strawberry plants may provide energy for many organisms. For example, consumers, such as birds, opossums, mice, squirrels, and people may eat the plant's fruit. Deer, rabbits, and insects may prefer to eat the plant's leaves.

Consumers often compete for food in their habitats. When there is too much competition, some organisms die. For example, if there are too many rabbits in a habitat, they all won't have enough food to eat. Some will die, and the rabbit population will decrease. In time, when the plants they eat grow back, the rabbit population may grow larger again.

An overripe fruit, a falling leaf, or a dying strawberry plant provides energy for another group of organisms called decomposers. A **decomposer** is a living thing that breaks down wastes and the remains of plants and animals for energy. Fungi and bacteria are two types of decomposers.

Gray mold covers these strawberries. As the mold breaks down the fruit, it returns nutrients back to the soil for the plant to use.

▶ What could happen if too many consumers were competing for the same food source in a habitat?

_____

_____

_____

_____

# Doing the Dirty Work

You open a bag of bread and right away your nose detects a musty scent. You see greenish-blue dots in the bread and think, *"Yuck, mold!"*

Usually, finding mold growing in our foods in not a pleasant experience. Yet mold and other decomposers play important roles. Molds, mushrooms, and yeasts are types of fungi. Fungi and bacteria are the main types of decomposers.

Decomposers help recycle materials in ecosystems. When an organism dies, decomposers go to work. Fungi and bacteria produce chemicals that help them break down and absorb nutrients from dead organisms and wastes. As decomposers feed, they release useful materials back into the environment. Plants use these materials to grow. When these plants die, the decomposers go to work again.

These fungi grow on dead tree trunks, which helps the trunks decay.

Bacteria in some foods, such as cheese and yogurt, help you absorb nutrients.

In a compost bin, moldy bread can be turned into soil nutrients.

Sometimes having decomposers in our food is exactly what we want. For example, yeast is used in baking to make bread rise, and bacteria add taste and texture to milk products, such as sour cream and cheese.

Decomposers can even help with human-made pollution. Scientists and engineers use bacteria and fungi to break down oil spills. Often, they simply add nutrients or oxygen to help decomposers already in the environment do their work.

Corn rust is a fungus that infects and kills sweet corn plants.

▶ Identify harmful and beneficial effects of decomposers.

_____

_____

_____

_____

_____

When you're done, use the answer key to check and revise your work.

## Use the information in the summary to complete the idea web by writing a definition or a description for each term.

### Summarize

All the living and nonliving things found in an area make up an ecosystem. Within an ecosystem, all the organisms that live in the same place make up a community. A group of elephants that live on a savanna is a population. A habitat is the phyiscal part of an ecosystem that meets the needs of an organism. Each living thing in a habitat has a role, or niche. Plants are producers because they make their own food. Animals are consumers because they get energy by eating other living things. Organisms that feed on the waste and remains of plants and animals are called decomposers.

**Habitat**

2 _____
_____
_____

**Niche**

3 _____
_____
_____

**Ecosystem**

1 _____
_____
_____

**Population**

4 _____
_____
_____

**Community**

5 _____
_____
_____

Name _____

# Word Play

**1** **Use the examples to help unscramble the words.**

1. S C R O D E P O M E  _ _ _ _ _ _ _ _ _ _
   a bacteria found in yogurt

2. B A I T A T H  _ _ _ _ _ _ _
   where an organism finds food and shelter

3. R E C R O P U D  _ _ _ _ _ _ _ _
   grass

4. N A T I L O P U P O  _ _ _ _ _ _ _ _ _ _
   a group of elephants living on the savanna

5. N E C I H  _ _ _ _ _
   an adult frog in a pond eating dragonflies

6. M E S S Y O C T E  _ _ _ _ _ _ _ _ _
   a rain forest

7. U S E R M O N C  _ _ _ _ _ _ _ _ _
   a lion

8. M I N T M U C O Y  _ _ _ _ _ _ _ _ _
   frogs, birds, and plants at a pond

# Apply Concepts

**2** Draw a picture of the different producers and consumers in a pond ecosystem. Identify the different populations that make up your pond's community.

_____

_____

_____

_____

_____

_____

_____

_____

_____

**3** Label each picture as a *consumer*, *producer*, or *decomposer*.

_____     _____     _____

_____     _____     _____

**4** Use the picture to answer the questions below.

a. Which organisms make up this ecosystem's community?

_____

_____

_____

_____

b. Which organism has the smallest population? The largest?

_____

_____

_____

_____

**5** Complete the Venn diagram to compare and contrast decomposers and consumers.

Decomposer            Both            Consumer

**6** Is mold that grows on bread a consumer, a producer, or a decomposer? How do you know?

_____

_____

_____

**7** Identify the parts of the ecosystem shown.

_____

_____

_____

_____

_____

_____

_____

_____

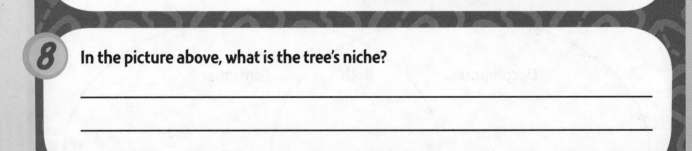

**8** In the picture above, what is the tree's niche?

_____

_____

_____

**Take It Home!**

Share with a family member what you learned about decomposers. Together, use the Internet and other resources to find how people use decomposers to solve problems. Share your findings with the class.

## Essential Question

# What Are Food Chains?

### Engage Your Brain!

Find the answer to the following question in this lesson and record it here.

Is this frog a predator, or is it prey?

_____

_____

_____

## Active Reading

### Lesson Vocabulary
List the terms. As you learn about each one, make notes in the Interactive Glossary.

_____   _____

_____   _____

_____

### Main Ideas
The main idea is the most important idea of a paragraph or section. The main idea may be stated at the beginning, or it may be stated elsewhere. Active readers look for main ideas by asking themselves, What is this paragraph or section mostly about?

# Food Chains

Did you know that you are fed by the sun? Find out how!

**Active Reading** As you read these two pages, circle common, everyday words that have a different meaning in science.

Lettuce is a plant that uses energy from the sun to make its own food. When you eat lettuce, some energy passes from the lettuce to you. You can show this relationship in a food chain. A **food chain** is the transfer of food energy in a sequence of living things. In a diagram of a food chain, arrows show how energy moves. Here is a food chain that shows how energy moves from lettuce to you.

lettuce ⟶ you

The food chain above has only two steps, or links. Food chains can have more than two links. Look at the pictures to see a food chain with five links.

Producers make up the first link. In this pond, tiny algae [AL•jee] are the producers. Mosquito larvae eat the algae. They make up the second link in this food chain.

# Make a Food Chain

Choose a food that you ate for breakfast or lunch today. Make a food chain showing how energy from the sun flowed from the food to you.

**Minnows are small fish. They eat the mosquito larvae. They make up the third link in this food chain.**

**Bass are bigger fish. They eat the minnows. They make up the fourth link in this food chain.**

**People eat the bass. People make up the last link in this food chain.**

# You Are What You Eat

A zebra and a lion are both consumers. But they eat very different foods. How can you group consumers by what they eat?

**Active Reading** As you read this page, underline the sentence that identifies one characteristic that is used to classify consumers.

Consumers eat other living things. They can be placed into groups according to the kind of food they eat.

- A consumer that eats only plants is a **herbivore**. A zebra is a herbivore. It eats grasses and other plants.

- A consumer that eats other animals is a **carnivore**. A lion is a carnivore. It eats zebras and other animals.

- A consumer that eats both plants and animals is an **omnivore**. People are omnivores. They eat plants such as tomatoes and animals such as fish.

- A consumer that eats dead plants and animals is a scavenger.

A crocodile is a carnivore. It eats mainly fish. But it will eat big animals, such as hippos, when it can catch them.

A rabbit is a herbivore. It eats leafy plants during spring and summer, and woody plants during fall and winter.

Raccoons are omnivores. They eat fruit, acorns, fish, and mice. They'll eat sweet corn right from your garden!

Vultures are scavengers. They eat dead animals.

## What Does It Eat?

Look at the pictures below. The top row shows different kinds of consumers. The bottom row shows the kinds of food they eat. Draw lines to match the consumers to the foods they eat. Some consumers might eat more than one kind of food.

# Hunt or Be Hunted

A lion crouches in the tall grass. Nearby, a zebra nibbles on the grass. Who is the hunter? Who will be hunted?

A hawk can see the movement of small animals, like this mouse, from high in the sky.

Consumers are grouped by what they eat. But you can also group consumers by whether they hunt or are hunted.

A *predator* is an animal that hunts other animals. Lions are predators. They often hunt in packs. This helps them catch big animals, like hippos and rhinos. They hunt smaller animals, too.

An animal that is eaten is called *prey*. Deer, elk, and moose are all prey for wolves in the Rocky Mountains.

Some animals can be both predator and prey. A frog might eat insects in a forest. But the frog might be eaten by a snake.

Lions can run fast for short bursts. Zebras may not run as fast, but they can run for a much longer time.

Sharks feed on many kinds of prey. Fish stay in large groups to make it difficult for predators to hunt individuals.

## Who's the Hunter? Who's Hunted?

Fill in the table below. Classify the animals shown on these pages as predators or prey.

| Animals | |
| --- | --- |
| Predators | Prey |
|  |  |
|  |  |
|  |  |

# Food Webs

A food chain shows how energy moves from one living thing to another. But living things often eat more than one kind of food. How can you show these different feeding relationships?

**Active Reading** As you read these two pages, draw a line under the main idea.

Lobsters eat clams. But they also eat crabs, sea stars, and mussels. Other animals, like the shark and the octopus, eat the lobster. You can use a model to show all these feeding relationships. A **food web** shows the relationships among different food chains. Food web models use arrows to show who eats what.

These green plankton are producers. They are eaten by clams, small fish, whales, and other organisms.

## Desert Food Chain

Use arrows to show how energy moves from one living thing to another in this desert food chain.

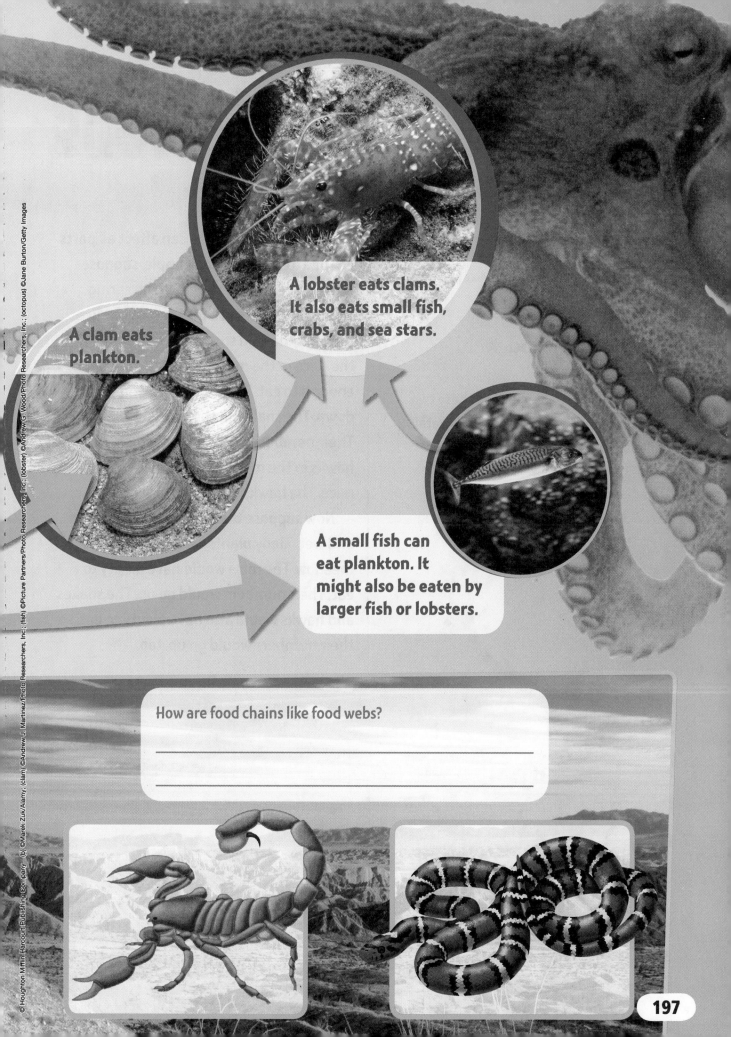

A clam eats plankton.

A lobster eats clams. It also eats small fish, crabs, and sea stars.

A small fish can eat plankton. It might also be eaten by larger fish or lobsters.

How are food chains like food webs?

_____

_____

# Changes in Food Webs

Imagine that one animal disappeared. What would happen to the other living things in the food web?

**Active Reading** As you read these two pages, circle clue words that signal a detail such as an example or an added fact.

Changes in food webs can affect all parts of a food web. For example, suppose the weather was very cold in the spring. Only a few plants in a meadow might live through the cold spring. This means that the mice in the meadow would not have enough to eat. Their numbers would go down. The snakes in the meadow eat mice. Their numbers would also go down. The hawks in the meadow hunt snakes and mice. The hawks would be hungry, too.

Now suppose that the spring was warm and wet. Many plants would grow in the meadow. The mice would have plenty to eat. Their numbers would go up. The snakes and hawks would also have plenty to eat, so their numbers would go up, too.

Food webs can be disrupted when one member of a food web goes away. This happened in Yellowstone National Park. During the early 1900s, the gray wolf was hunted in the park. Eventually, no gray wolves were left.

The gray wolf preyed mostly on elk. The number of elk in the park increased after the wolves disappeared. In 1995, scientists returned 14 gray wolves to the park. The number of wolves has since increased. As a result, the number of elk in the park has decreased.

Other changes happened, too. Elk eat trees. Before the wolves were reintroduced, the elk overgrazed the trees in the park.

This harmed the trees. Since beavers had fewer trees to build dams with, the beaver population decreased. After the wolves were reintroduced to the park, both the trees and beavers began to thrive.

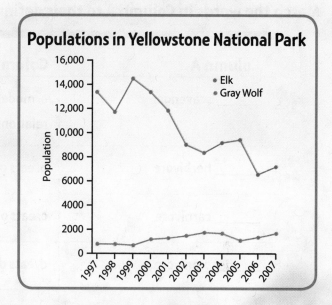

Populations in Yellowstone National Park

# Do the Math!
## Interpret Tables

The table shows the height of trees in Yellowstone National Park before and after the gray wolves returned. Study the table, and then answer the questions.

| Kind of tree | Average height before 1995 | Average height after 2002 |
|---|---|---|
| Cottonwood | less than 1m | 2 to 3 m |
| Willow | less than 1m | 3 to 4 m |

1. Describe the heights of the trees before the gray wolves were brought back to Yellowstone National Park.

_____

2. Describe the heights of the trees after the gray wolves were brought back to Yellowstone National Park.

_____

3. Why do you think the heights of the trees changed?

_____

_____

_____

# Sum It Up!

When you're done, use the answer key to check and revise your work.

**Match the words in Column A to their definitions in Column B.**

| | Column A | Column B |
|---|---|---|
| 1 | _____ scavenger | a. model that shows all the feeding relationships in an ecosystem |
| 2 | _____ herbivore | b. eats other animals |
| 3 | _____ carnivore | c. eats only plants |
| 4 | _____ omnivore | d. eats dead animals and plants |
| 5 | _____ food web | e. eats both plants and animals |

## Summarize

**The idea web below summarizes the lesson. Complete the web.**

Food chains show how energy moves from one living thing to another. The first link in a food chain is always a(n) 6. ____________________.

Herbivores are consumers that 7. ____________________.

Omnivores are consumers that 8. ____________________.

Carnivores are consumers that 9. ____________________.

Scavengers are consumers that 10. ____________________.

Answer Key: 1. d 2. c 3. b 4. e 5. a 6. producer 7. eat only plants 8. eat plants and animals 9. eat other animals 10. eat dead animals and plants

© Houghton Mifflin Harcourt Publishing Company

# Word Play

**1** Use the clues to complete the crossword puzzle.

## Across

1. The transfer of energy from one living thing to another
3. Consumer that eats both plants and animals
5. Consumer that eats other animals
7. Animal that is hunted

## Down

2. Consumer that eats only plants
4. Shows the relationship among all the food chains in an ecosystem
6. Animal that hunts
8. Consumer that breaks down the remains of plants and animals

# Apply Concepts

**2** The food chain below is in scrambled order. Put the links of the food chain in the correct order.

| wolf | → | rabbit | → | grass |

_____ → _____ → _____

**3** Fill in this graphic organizer about different kinds of consumers.

KINDS OF CONSUMERS

a. _____

scavenger

herbivore

b. _____

eats other animals

e. _____

c. _____

d. _____

**4** The pictures below show a lion and a zebra. Label the animals as *predator* or *prey*.

_____    _____

Name _____

**5** The picture shows different animals in a pond food web. Use arrows to show who eats what. Remember that arrows should point from the living thing that is being eaten to the living thing that is eating.

**6** In the space below, draw an ocean food chain and a forest food chain.

**7** The pictures show different kinds of consumers. Label each consumer as a herbivore, carnivore, omnivore, or scavenger.

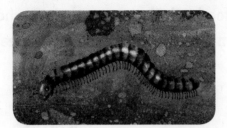

_____

_____

**8** The population of a predator in an area has gone up. What do you think will happen to the population of prey in the area? Explain your answer.

_____

_____

_____

_____

_____

_____

**Take It Home!**

Share what you have learned about food chains with your family. With a family member, tell which of the foods you ate for dinner came from plants and which came from animals.

**Name** _____

**Essential Question**

# How Can We Model a Food Web?

## Set a Purpose
**What will you learn from this investigation?**

_____

_____

## Think About the Procedure
**Which parts of an ecosystem will you model?**

_____

_____

_____

**Why is it important to have plants, animals, and decomposers in your food web?**

_____

_____

_____

_____

_____

_____

## Record Your Data
Make a chart to classify the organisms in your ecosystem as producers, consumers, or decomposers. Describe how each organism gets its energy.

## Draw Conclusions

How are ecosystems different from one another?

_____

_____

_____

What roles do plants have in a food web?

_____

_____

_____

## Analyze and Extend

1. Suppose an animal with no natural predator in an ecosystem comes to live there. How would this animal affect the food web?

_____

_____

_____

2. Suppose a fungus grows on some of the plants. How might this fungus affect the food web?

_____

_____

_____

3. What other events might affect the food web?

_____

_____

_____

4. In the space below, draw two food chains that overlap in your food web. Then, write a caption that describes your picture.

_____

_____

5. Think about other questions you would like to ask about food webs. Write your questions below.

_____

_____

_____

_____

**206**

Essential Question

# What Are Natural Resources?

## Engage Your Brain!

Find the answer to the following question in this lesson and record it here.

What types of natural resources can be found in this setting?

_____

_____

_____

_____

## Active Reading

### Lesson Vocabulary
List the terms. As you learn about each one, make notes in the Interactive Glossary.

_____

_____

_____

### Signal Words: Contrasts
Words that signal contrasts, or differences, include *unlike*, *but*, *different from*, and *on the other hand*. Active readers remember what they read because they are alert to signal words that identify contrasts.

# Resources You Can Rely On

Soap, water, clothes, wood, bricks, pencils, paper. What do all these things have in common? They are all natural resources or things made from these resources.

**Active Reading** As you read the next page, circle examples of renewable resources.

These pictures show natural resources. **Natural resources** are materials found in nature that are used by living things. Can you identify the natural resources in the pictures?

▶ Look at the picture. What renewable resources are found in this setting?

_____

_____

_____

_____

Some natural resources, such as water and air, are used again and again. Other resources form quickly in nature and are easy to replace. If a tree is cut to make paper, a new tree can be grown in a short time. The new tree will replace the old tree. Natural resources that can be replaced quickly are called **renewable resources**. Scientists also consider sunlight and wind renewable resources.

People need to use renewable resources wisely. The wise use of resources is called *conservation* [kahn•ser•VAY•shuhn]. Why is conservation important? People can use up renewable resources. Think about this: What would happen to fish if people ate more fish than could be replaced? Soon there would be no fish left!

**209**

# nonrenewable Resources

Not all natural resources can be replaced quickly. Some natural resources take thousands or millions of years to form.

**Active Reading** On these two pages, circle phrases that show how nonrenewable resources are different from renewable resources.

**N**atural resources that aren't replaced easily are called **nonrenewable resources**. It can take thousands or millions of years to replace a nonrenewable resource. Fossil fuels are an example of a nonrenewable resource. Coal, oil, and natural gas are all types of fossil fuels. Some are used to produce electricity. Some are used to run planes, cars, and other vehicles.

Because they form so slowly, there are limited amounts of fossil fuels and other nonrenewable resources. Once nonrenewable resources are used up, they cannot be replaced in our lifetimes. If people keep using fossil fuels at the same rate they use them today, these fuels will be gone very soon.

Oil is found deep underground. It is pumped to the surface and then refined before it can be used.

Soil takes hundreds of years to form. It is made of weathered rock and once-living plants and animals.

Limestone and aluminum are mined. Limestone is used to make cement, and aluminum is used to make cans.

Soil is a nonrenewable resource that people use to grow crops. It can be washed away if it is left uncovered or used improperly. As a result, it is important for people to conserve soil.

Minerals and rocks are other types of nonrenewable resources. A *mineral* is a nonliving solid with a crystal form. A *rock* is a solid substance made of one or more minerals. A rock that contains a valuable mineral is called an *ore*. Many minerals and rocks, such as limestone and aluminum ore, are mined. Once they have been removed from a mine, there are none left. It takes a long time for more minerals or rocks to form.

## Do the Math!
### Interpret a Graph

The graph shows the percentage of different natural resources used to produce electricity in the United States. How much comes from nonrenewable resources? _____

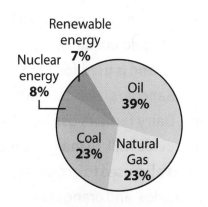

Renewable energy **7%**

Nuclear energy **8%**

Oil **39%**

Coal **23%**

Natural Gas **23%**

# From Coast to Coast

You use natural resources every day. Some natural resources provide shelter. Others help you learn in school. On these pages, you will learn where some natural resources come from.

**Active Reading** As you read these pages, circle examples of land used as a natural resource in order to produce food.

Every state has natural resources. Many natural resources are found in greater quantities in some parts of the United States than in others. Trees, silver, wind, coal, and fish are just a few examples of natural resources found in the United States.

People mine land to get many natural resources. Some mining is done to get valuable minerals, such as silver, iron, and copper. Mining also takes place to get fossil fuels. Other mining gets rocks used to construct roads and buildings.

Sometimes land is used for food production. Ranchers raise cattle that graze on the land. Dairy farmers use land to raise cows that provide milk to make cream and cheese. Soil is also used to grow crops, such as corn, avocados, and oranges.

Some land is used to produce *green energy*, or energy generated using renewable resources. Wind farms, solar cells, and hydroelectric dams use wind, sunlight, and water to produce electrical energy.

*Forests*, or areas with large numbers of trees, provide lumber. People use lumber to make paper and furniture and to build houses.

▶ Look at the Natural Resources map, and locate the region where you live. Circle the renewable resources, and draw an *X* over the nonrenewable resources found there.

**People use land to raise livestock and grow crops.**

People use trees for lumber.

People use hydroelectric dams, wind turbines, and solar panels to produce green energy.

People mine land to get minerals, rocks, and fossil fuels.

## Natural Resources

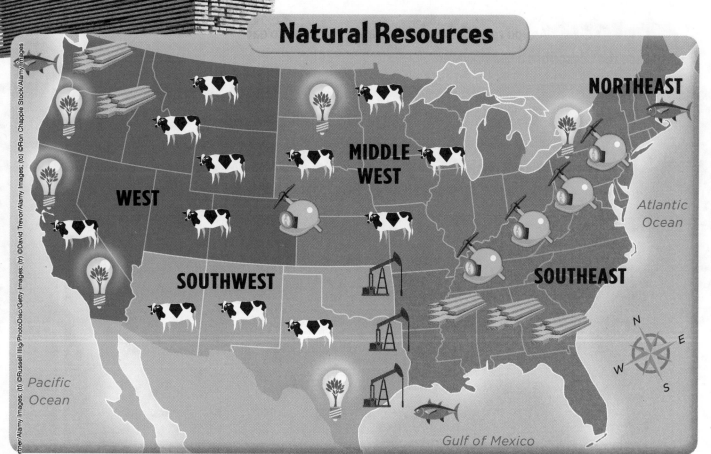

NORTHEAST

WEST

MIDDLE WEST

Atlantic Ocean

SOUTHWEST

SOUTHEAST

Pacific Ocean

Gulf of Mexico

### Legend

| | | |
|---|---|---|
| Fisheries | Timber | Mining |
| Oil | Green Energy | Farming |

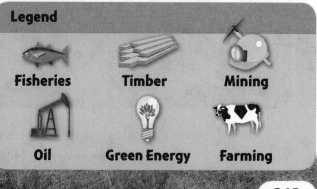

# Flowing Down Slope

Every second, millions of gallons of water flow from the Mississippi River into the Gulf of Mexico. Where does all this water come from?

**Active Reading** As you read these pages, draw a star next to each sentence that describes a use of water.

The Mississippi River watershed is an important natural resource. It is home to many living things.

From its source as a tiny stream in northern Minnesota to where it empties into the Gulf of Mexico, the Mississippi River spans 3,782 km (2350 mi). Along the way, it connects with hundreds of rivers and streams, including the Missouri and the Ohio Rivers.

Water from 31 states drains into the Mississippi River. All of this water makes the Mississippi River system one of the world's largest watersheds. A *watershed* is all of the land and water that drain into a river system.

A watershed is an important natural resource. States often share the water in a watershed. Virginia, for example, shares the water in the Chesapeake Bay watershed with five other states as well as the District of Columbia.

The rivers and streams in a watershed are used in many ways. For example, the Mississippi River supplies drinking water to more than 50 cities. People also use water from the Mississippi River to grow crops, for recreation, and for transportation.

## A Day Without Water

How many ways do you use water each day? Make a list. Then describe what a day without water would be like.

_____

_____

_____

_____

_____

People use water for recreational activities such as fishing, canoeing, and swimming.

Farmers use water to grow food.

Cargo ships and barges use the Mississippi to move goods.

# Keeping It Clean

Using up natural resources too quickly is a problem. Another problem is pollution, or harmful materials in the environment. Pollution is harmful to natural resources. How can you help to conserve natural resources and prevent pollution?

Pollution can harm air, water, and soil. It can also harm plants and animals.

Many communities have cleanup projects to make the environment healthier for everyone.

## Reasons to Recycle

**What happens to trash? It ends up in a landfill, which is wasteful. Many things we throw away can be reused. For example, some things, such as paper, glass, plastic, and metal, can be recycled and made into new products. By reducing, reusing, and recycling we help conserve natural resources.**

## How Can You Help?

What can you do to help cut down on air pollution caused by cars and trucks? Draw a picture of your solution in the space above.

When you're done, use the answer key to check and revise your work.

**Read the summary statements below. Each one is incorrect. Change the part of the summary in blue to make it correct.**

## Summarize

**1** Nonrenewable resources can be quickly replaced or renewed after they are used.

_____
_____
_____

**2** Examples of renewable resources are rocks and coal.

_____
_____
_____

**3** Oil, minerals, and soil are all renewable resources that will be gone forever once they are used up.

_____
_____
_____

**4** Nonrenewable resources can take 10 or 20 years to be replaced.

_____
_____
_____

**5** You conserve natural resources so that they disappear faster.

_____
_____
_____

Answer Key: 1. Renewable resources 2. Sample answers: plants, animals, sunlight, water, air, wind 3. nonrenewable resources 4. thousands or millions of years 5. Sample answer: will be around for people in the future

218

© Houghton Mifflin Harcourt Publishing Company

Name _____

## Word Play

**1** Use the words in the box to complete each sentence.

| | | | |
|---|---|---|---|
| watershed | fossil fuels | nonrenewable resources* | pollution |
| recycling | natural resources* | renewable resources* | |

*Key Lesson Vocabulary

Materials found in nature and used by living things are _____ .

All of the land and water that drain into a river system forms a _____ .

When _____ are burned, they cause pollution.

Resources that are limited and cannot be replaced quickly are called

_____ .

Fish, trees, and other similar resources should be protected

because if they are used too quickly, they will no longer be

_____ .

Resources such as plastic, metal, glass, and paper can be

conserved by _____ them.

Harmful materials in the environment are forms of

_____ .

## Apply Concepts

**2** Circle the renewable resource.

**3** List four different resources and products made from those resources.

_____

_____

_____

_____

**4** Name three ways you use water.

_____

_____

_____

**5** Draw a natural resource found in your state or region and describe how it is used.

_____

_____

_____

_____

_____

_____

_____

_____

Take It Home!

With your family, make a list of all of the natural resources you use in one day. Research to find out where each one comes from. For example, where does the cotton used to make a T-shirt come from?

**Essential Question**

# How Do People Impact Ecosystems?

## Engage Your Brain!

Find the answer to the following question in this lesson and record it here.

What has caused millions of ash trees to die?

_____

_____

_____

_____

## Active Reading

### Lesson Vocabulary
List the terms. As you learn about each one, make notes in the Interactive Glossary.

_____

_____

_____

### Cause and Effect
Some ideas in this lesson are connected by a cause-and-effect relationship. Why something happens is a cause. What happens as a result of something else is an effect. Active readers look for effects by asking themselves, What happened? They look for causes by asking, Why did it happen?

# The Natural Environment

Look around you. What do you see? You may see trees, land, water, and sky. All of these things make up the natural environment.

**Active Reading** As you read these pages, circle words that identify nonliving parts of the environment.

Our environment is made up of living and nonliving things. Things that make up the natural environment include the air we breathe and the water we drink. They also include the living and nonliving things that people and animals use for shelter. The natural environment is the source for all the natural resources that organisms need to stay alive.

Bald eagle

_____

_____

Rainbow trout

_____

_____

Mountains, valleys, rivers, and oceans make up the nonliving part of the natural environment. Different parts of the environment support different types of organisms. Some trees can only grow near the top of a mountain. Others can only grow near the valley floor.

Environmental factors, such as temperature, moisture, and availability of food, may affect where an organism can live. Some organisms can only live in the water. Others can live both in the water and on land.

## My Place

▶ Describe the place in the environment where each animal on these pages finds food and shelter.

**Deer**

_____

_____

_____

Animals and plants make up the living part of the environment. Organisms get what they need from the environment.

223

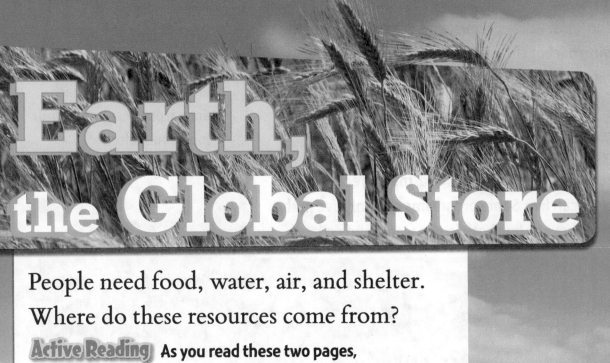

# Earth, the Global Store

People need food, water, air, and shelter. Where do these resources come from?

**Active Reading** As you read these two pages, underline the main idea.

Natural resources found in the environment help us meet most of our needs. These resources were used to build the road, the farm buildings, and the fence shown in this picture.

Farmers use water to help crops grow. Food such as milk, yogurt, and cheese comes from dairy farms.

Many of our natural resources come from plants. We use wood from trees to build homes, tools, and furniture. Plants are also used to make health products. Aspirin, for example, is a medicine used to relieve pain. It comes from the bark of a tree.

Land and soil are useful natural resources, too. Farmers use land to plant and grow crops, such as spinach, cotton, and pineapples. They also use land to raise animals, such as cattle and sheep, that graze on grass-covered land.

We can use a natural resource that is unchanged in its raw form or we can change it into something new. Rocks, for example, are used in their natural form to pave roads, decorate buildings, and to make floor tiles. Sand might be combined with cement to make concrete. Sand may also be heated and changed to glass that is used to make windows. We burn fossil fuels, such as oil and coal, to produce energy.

Some natural resources are required to sustain life. Plants, animals, and people would die without air and water. People drink water and use it to keep clean. On farms, we use water in irrigation systems to water fields where crops grow.

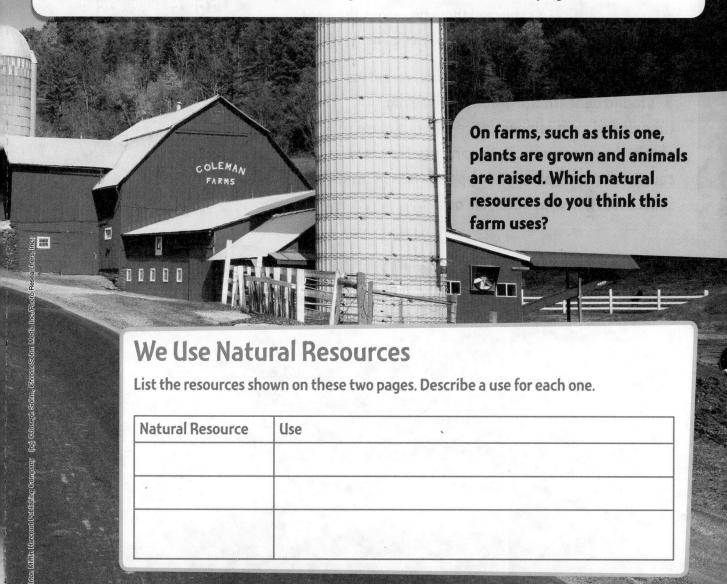

On farms, such as this one, plants are grown and animals are raised. Which natural resources do you think this farm uses?

## We Use Natural Resources

List the resources shown on these two pages. Describe a use for each one.

| Natural Resource | Use |
|---|---|
|  |  |
|  |  |
|  |  |

# People Change the Environment

Sometimes people do things that can change the environment. Some of these changes can be very harmful.

**Active Reading** As you read these two pages, draw one line under each cause. Then draw two lines under its effect.

Rocks, ores, oil, and coal are natural resources found beneath the ground. People dig tunnels and even remove entire mountaintops to obtain these resources. In the process, they may cause pollution. **Pollution** happens when harmful substances mix with water, air, or soil.

The emerald ash borer beetle is not from North America. It came here on shipping crates from Asia. The emerald ash borer larvae feed on the inner bark of ash trees, killing them.

Mining for resources can damage the land.

Farming can also harm the environment. Large herds of grazing animals can eat all the grass in a place, which loosens the soil. As a result, running water and wind can carry the soil away. Plowing fields for crops also loosens the soil. Once soil is gone, it takes a very long time to form again.

A forest also takes many years to form. People clear forests to make lumber and to make space for new roads, buildings, or homes. Plants die when a forest is cleared. The animals that live in the forest must move to find new homes. If they don't find another habitat that meets their needs, they might die.

Sometimes people introduce nonnative plants and animals to the environment. These *invasive species* have no natural enemies to control their population and can be very destructive. The kudzu plant and the emerald ash borer beetle are two nonnative organisms. They have invaded ecosystems in various regions of the United States, killing millions of trees.

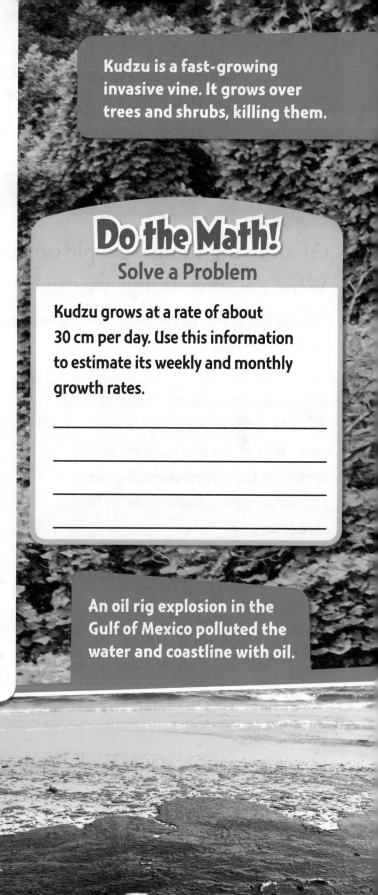

Kudzu is a fast-growing invasive vine. It grows over trees and shrubs, killing them.

# Do the Math!
## Solve a Problem

Kudzu grows at a rate of about 30 cm per day. Use this information to estimate its weekly and monthly growth rates.

_____

_____

_____

_____

An oil rig explosion in the Gulf of Mexico polluted the water and coastline with oil.

# Caring for Our Ecosystems

Of all living things, people can affect ecosystems the most. What are some things we can do to care for ecosystems?

**Active Reading** As you read these pages, circle cause-and-effect signal words or phrases.

People share natural resources with other living things in the environment. We also have the ability to change the environment the most. Therefore, we are responsible for taking care of it.

We can practice conservation to care for the environment. **Conservation** is the use of less of something to make its supply last longer. Conservation also means preserving the natural condition of the environment.

People, communities, businesses, and governments all help care for the environment. People, for example, volunteer to locate and remove invasive species from ecosystems. Communities operate water treatment facilities, where polluted water is cleaned up before it is released to the environment.

Many businesses have adopted more efficient technology. As a result, they have found ways to make products using less energy. They have also designed *biodegradable* materials that break down quickly in the environment.

Governments have passed laws to protect the environment. As a result, many rivers and streams are cleaner than they used to be. Governments have also set aside millions of acres of land to use as national parks and animal refuges. As a result, some **endangered species**, organisms whose whole population was at risk of dying out, have thrived.

Millions of American bison lived in the United States before people reduced their population to less than 1,000 animals. Today, because of government laws, there are about 450,000 American bison in the United States.

Water treatment facilities capture and remove pollutants in wastewater before the water is released into the environment.

A federal law passed in 1977 requires that land be reclaimed or restored once mining activities end.

## What Can You Do?

List two ways you can practice conservation.

_____

_____

_____

# Sum It Up!

When you're done, use the answer key to check and revise your work.

**Use the information from the lesson and the summary below to complete the graphic organizer.**

## Summarize

People can change the environment in both positive and negative ways. We change the environment to meet our needs. People need shelter, food, air, and water to live. Some of the changes people make can be harmful to the environment. For example, plants and animals lose their homes when people clear forests. People can also cause pollution. However, people can have a positive impact on the environment. We all can practice conservation. We can use natural resources wisely and use less of some things to make their supplies last longer.

[1] Main Idea: _____
_____.

[2] Detail: Why do people change the environment?
_____
_____
_____

[3] Example: What do living things need to live?
_____
_____

[4] Detail: How can people harm the environment?
_____
_____
_____

[5] Example: What is pollution?
_____
_____

[6] Detail: Who is responsible for caring for the environment?
_____
_____

[7] Example: How can we care for the environment?
_____
_____
_____

© Houghton Mifflin Harcourt Publishing Company   HMH Credits

# Brain Check

Lesson **5**

Name _____

## Word Play

**1** Use the words in the box to complete the puzzle.

### Across

5. When harmful substances mix with air, water, or soil
6. Interaction between organisms and their surroundings
7. To save natural resources
8. _____ species are organisms whose whole population are at risk of dying out.

### Down

1. Oil or coal used to produce energy
2. An organism with no natural enemy in an area
3. A material that breaks down over time
4. The living and nonliving things in an area

| biodegradable | fossil fuel |
|---|---|
| conservation* | nonnative |
| ecosystem | pollution* |
| environment | endangered species* |

\* Key Lesson Vocabulary

# Apply Concepts

**2** Match each natural resource with a product made from it.

sand

trees

coal

electricity generating station

glass cup

rocking chair

**3** Identify each statement as helpful or harmful to the environment.

Cut down trees.

_____

Ride a bike.

_____

Clean up water pollution.

_____

**4** Think of a product you buy, such as your favorite juice. Then describe how you could redesign its packaging to conserve resources.

_____

_____

_____

**Take It Home!** Take a walk in your neighborhood with an adult family member. Describe ways that people have changed the environment.

Name _____

Essential Question

# How Do People Affect Their Environment?

## Set a Purpose
How does this activity show how people affect the environment?

_____

_____

_____

_____

## Think About the Procedure
Why did you need to observe the trash for three weeks?

_____

_____

_____

_____

Why did you wear gloves?

_____

_____

_____

_____

## Record Your Data
In the space below, write or draw your results.

## Draw Conclusions

What did the plastic container and soil represent?

_____

_____

_____

What did you observe about the different materials after observing them for three weeks?

_____

_____

_____

## Analyze and Extend

1. Compare your results with those of other groups. Did everyone have the same results? If not, what might have made the results differ?

_____

_____

_____

_____

2. What did you learn about materials that go into landfills?

_____

_____

_____

3. Look at the table. How could you display this data in another way? Show your work below.

| Object | Time it takes to decompose |
|--------|----------------------------|
| Diaper | 75 yr |
| Paper | 2–3 months |
| Milk carton | 5 yr |
| Aluminum can | 200–500 yr |
| Plastic bag | 10–20 yr |

4. Think of other questions you would like to ask about trash disposal.

_____

_____

_____

234

# Meet the Tree-Planting Scientists

## Wangari Maathai

Wangari Maathai was born in Kenya. Maathai started an organization that conserves Kenya's forests by planting trees. She recruited Kenyan women to plant native trees throughout the country. In 1977, this organization became known as the Green Belt Movement. The Green Belt Movement has planted more than 40 million trees. Maathai's work inspires other African countries to start community tree plantings.

Seeds from nearby forests are used to grow native trees.

## Willie Smits

Willie Smits works to save orangutans in Indonesia. By clearing the forests, people are destroying the orangutan's habitat. The orangutan is endangered. Smits's plan helps both orangutans and people. Smits is growing a rain forest. The new forest gives people food and rainwater for drinking, so they protect it. The sugar palm is one of the trees planted. In 2007, Smits started using sugar palms to make sugar and a biofuel called ethanol. The sugar palms provide income for the community.

Sugar palms are fire-resistant. This protects the forest from fires.

Smits has rescued almost 1,000 orangutan babies. However, his goal is to save them in the wild.

# Scientist saves the Day!

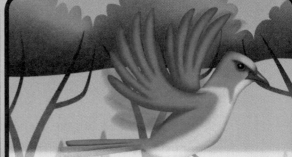

Read the story about the Florida scrub jay. Draw the missing pictures to complete the story.

**The Problem:** Florida scrub jays are endangered. They are found only in parts of Florida with shrubs and other short plants.

Fires kill tall trees that grow in the scrub jay's habitat. But people put out the fires, so the trees survive.

Trees are now growing, so there are fewer shrubs. The scrub jays can't live there.

**The Solution:** Scientists and firefighters start fires that can be kept under control. These fires kill the tall trees.

Shrubs grow and the scrub jays return.

# Underwater Exploration

When you think of underwater exploration, you may think of scuba. The word *scuba* comes from the first letters of the phrase "self-contained underwater breathing apparatus." Scuba divers take everything they need with them; they are not connected to anything on the surface. Follow the timeline to learn how underwater diving equipment has changed over time.

### 1530s
**Guglielmo de Lorena—Diving Bell**
Diving bells are airtight containers opened at one end. De Lorena's diving bell rested over a diver's shoulders, allowing the diver to breathe the trapped air and to walk on the ocean floor. Ropes connected the diver to the surface.

### 1830s
**Augustus Siebe—Diving Dress**
A metal diving helmet is sealed onto a watertight canvas suit. An air hose and a cable connect the diver to the surface. In this closed-circuit system, used-up air is released into the suit. The diver controls when air is released.

### 1940s
**Jacques Cousteau and Emile Gagnan—Aqua-Lung**
This breathing system passes air to a diver from a tank carried on the diver's back. This is an open-circuit system that releases used-up air into the water. Divers can swim without any cables or hoses connecting them to the surface.

## Critical Thinking

How are the first two types of diving equipment similar?

_____

_____

_____

# S.T.E.M.
## continued

# Make Some History

Research another type of diving equipment. Describe how it works and where it should be placed on the timeline.

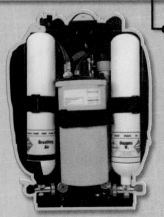

**1960s**
**Rebreather**

Rebreathers are closed-circuit systems. A diver breathes through a mouthpiece and used-up air is not released into the water. Instead, it is filtered to remove carbon dioxide and used again. This design feature extends the amount of time a diver can spend underwater.

**1980s**
**ADS**

Atmospheric Diving Suits (ADS) were developed for deep diving activities. They use rebreather technology and a hard suit that enable divers to safely dive to great depths. Modern ADS can work in water up to 610 m deep!

# Design Your Future

What features do you think the next diving suit should have? What needs would those features meet?

# Build On It!

Rise to the engineering design challenge—complete **Solve It: Getting Around a Dam** on the Inquiry Flipchart.

# Unit 4 Review

## Vocabulary Review

Use the terms in the box to complete the sentences.

> conservation
> consumer
> ecosystem
> endangered
>   species
> habitat
> niche
> population
> producer

1.  All of the leopard frogs that live in a pond make up

    a(n) _____.

2.  A community of organisms and the physical environment in

    which they live is called a(n) _____.

3.  The use of less of something to make its supply last longer is

    called _____.

4.  A place in the environment that meets the need of an organism

    is called a(n) _____.

5.  An organism that makes its own food is called

    a(n) _____.

6.  Organisms whose whole kind is at risk of dying out are

    called _____.

7.  An organism's role in its habitat is known as

    its _____.

8.  An animal that eats plants or other animals to get energy is

    called a(n) _____.

# Science Concepts

Fill in the letter of the choice that best answers the question.

9. Many household items are made from renewable resources. Which of these objects is made from a renewable resource?

   (A)
   plastic bag

   (C)
   computer keyboard

   (B)
   wooden spoon

   (D)
   motor oil

10. Tony is studying the natural resources that supply water to his home. He traces the water from a mountain, through several small rivers, and to the large river that supplies his town with water. What is Tony studying?

    (A) an ecosystem

    (B) a habitat

    (C) a niche

    (D) a watershed

11. Carla wants to show how living things get energy. Which sequence is correct?

    (A) Decomposer → Consumer → Sunlight → Producer

    (B) Consumer → Sunlight → Producer → Decomposer

    (C) Producer → Decomposer → Producer → Consumer

    (D) Sunlight → Producer → Consumer → Decomposer

12. The picture below shows some animals you can find in grassland food chains.

    Which animal is the carnivore?

    (A) animal 1

    (B) animal 2

    (C) animal 3

    (D) animal 4

13. Mica is identifying natural resources used to produce many of the items he uses every day. He has identified the source of paper and wood furniture. Which natural resource has he identified?

    (A) water

    (B) forest

    (C) animals

    (D) energy resources

**14.** The table below shows how long it takes for some biodegradable items to decompose in salt water.

| Item | Decomposition time |
|------|-------------------|
| Cardboard box | 2 months |
| Newspaper | 6 weeks |
| Paper towel | 2–4 weeks |
| Waxed milk carton | 3 months |

Which item will decompose the fastest?

Ⓐ newspaper

Ⓑ paper towel

Ⓒ cardboard box

Ⓓ waxed milk carton

**15.** It takes a long time for rocks to form. Limestone is a type of rock used in buildings and in road construction. Which type of resource is limestone?

Ⓐ green

Ⓑ energy

Ⓒ renewable

Ⓓ nonrenewable

**16.** A new highway is planned to replace a pond habitat where a frog population lives. How will this change **most likely** affect the frog population?

Ⓐ The frog population will double.

Ⓑ The frog population will increase.

Ⓒ The frog population will decrease.

Ⓓ The frog population will not change.

**17.** Emily is studying animals that live in marshes. She makes the following graphs to show how the number of fish and marsh birds changed in a certain area over time.

Fish

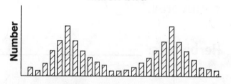

Marsh bird

What **most likely** happened when the number of fish was highest?

Ⓐ The bird population began to decrease.

Ⓑ The birds moved away for lack of food.

Ⓒ The fish population continued to increase.

Ⓓ The bird population increased because there was more food.

**18.** People use land resources to help them meet their needs. Coal is a fossil fuel that people mine from the land. They burn coal to make electricity. Which type of resource is coal?

Ⓐ a green living resource

Ⓑ a green energy resource

Ⓒ a renewable energy resource

Ⓓ a nonrenewable energy resource

# Apply Inquiry and Review the Big Idea

Write the answers to these questions.

19. This illustration shows a food web.

   a. Identify the organisms shown in the food web as producers, consumers, or decomposers.

   Producers:_____

   Consumers:_____

   Decomposers:_____

   b. Classify the consumers as herbivores, omnivores, or carnivores.

   Herbivores:_____

   Omnivores:_____

   Carnivores:_____

   c. Explain why all animals depend on producers such as plants. Use an example from the food web in your explanation.

   _____

   _____

   _____

   _____

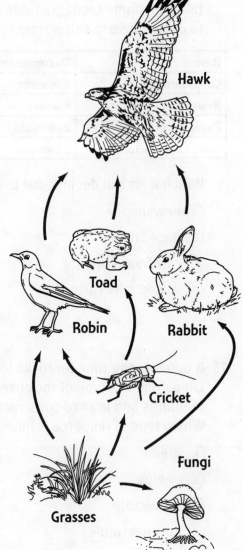

Hawk

Toad

Robin

Rabbit

Cricket

Fungi

Grasses

20. Juan studied this food web and said that hawks were the last link in every food chain shown. Vicky pointed to a different organism and said that it was the last link. Which organism did Vicky identify? What was her reasoning?

_____

_____

_____

_____

# Weather

## Big Idea

Water moves in a regular cycle that influences the weather.

## I Wonder Why

As the sun rises, the clouds glow red. Late morning brings sunny skies. Then puffy white clouds appear. A thunderstorm rages by late afternoon! Why? *Turn the page to find out.*

**Here's Why** The color of the early morning or evening sky is a clue people can use to predict changes in weather. In places where weather systems move from west to east, red skies in the morning signal an approaching storm.

In this unit, you will explore the Big Idea, the Essential Questions, and the Investigations on the Inquiry Flipchart.

**Levels of Inquiry Key** ■ DIRECTED ■ GUIDED ■ INDEPENDENT

**Track Your Progress**

**Big Idea** Water moves in a regular cycle that influences the weather.

## Essential Questions

**Now I Get the Big Idea!**

**Science Notebook**
Before you begin each lesson, be sure to write your thoughts about the Essential Question.

**Essential Question**

# What Is the Water Cycle?

## 🧠 Engage Your Brain!

Find the answer to the following question in this lesson and record it here.

Where is all this water going?

_____

_____

_____

_____

## Active Reading

### Lesson Vocabulary

List the terms. As you learn about each one, make notes in the Interactive Glossary.

_____  _____

_____  _____

_____  _____

_____

### Sequence

In this lesson, you'll read about a process of change called the *water cycle*. As you read about the water cycle, focus on the sequence, or order, of events in the process. Active readers stay focused on a sequence when they mark the transition from one step in a process to another.

# Water on the Move

The water that you drink may have once been under ground or high in the sky. How does water get from Earth's surface to the air and back again?

▶ On the diagram, draw an X on three places where evaporation may take place.

**Active Reading** As you read the next page, underline the main idea and circle details that provide information about it.

Earth's water is always being recycled. It evaporates from bodies of water, the soil, and even from your skin. Water exits plants' leaves through a process called transpiration. In the air, winds and clouds can help move water from one place to another.

Condensation    Transpiration

Evaporation

After it rains, this birdbath is filled with water. When the sun comes out, its energy heats the water. The birdbath becomes empty as water changes to water vapor and returns to the atmosphere.

About three-fourths of Earth's surface is covered by water. Most of the water is stored in oceans. Water moves between Earth's surface and the atmosphere through a process called the **water cycle**.

The sun provides the energy for water to move through the water cycle. Sunlight heats up water particles near the ocean's surface. It causes water to evaporate.

**Evaporation** is the change from a liquid to a gas. When water evaporates, it forms an invisible gas called *water vapor*.

Water vapor rises into the atmosphere. The **atmosphere** is the mixture of gases that surrounds Earth. In the atmosphere, water vapor cools to form clouds. At any time, about three-fifths of Earth's surface is covered by clouds.

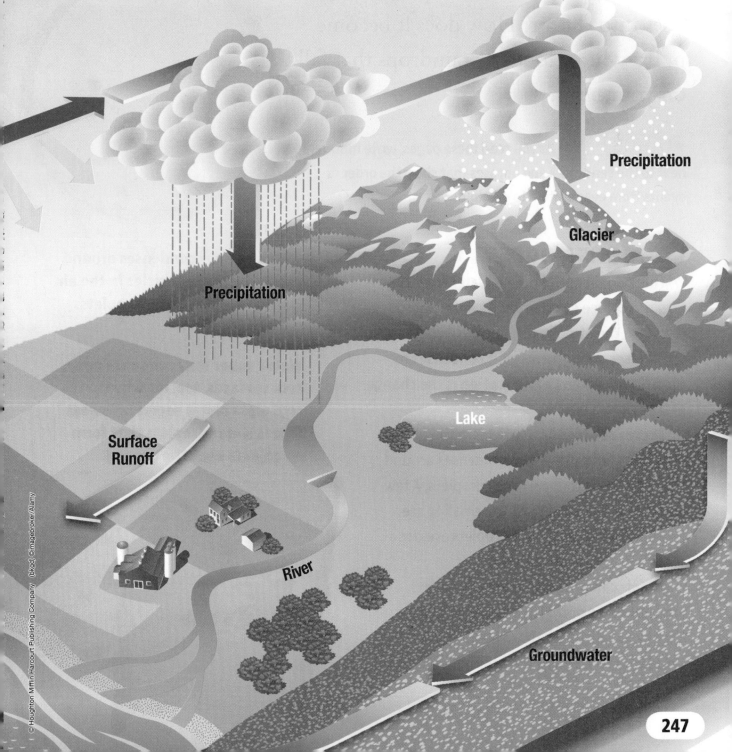

Precipitation

Precipitation

Glacier

Lake

Surface Runoff

River

Groundwater

# What Goes Up
## Comes Down

What happens to water vapor after it rises into the air? How does it become puffy white clouds or raindrops that fall on your head?

**Active Reading** As you read these pages, write numbers next to the sentences and phrases that show the order of events from evaporation to precipitation.

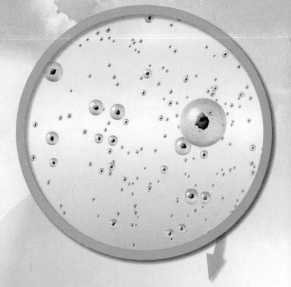

## Condensation

Think again of the ocean. Water from the ocean's surface evaporates. As water vapor rises into the atmosphere, it cools. When water vapor loses enough energy, it condenses to form liquid water. **Condensation** is the change of a gas into a liquid.

There are tiny solid particles in the atmosphere. Water vapor condenses around these particles to form water droplets. A few water droplets are almost too small to see. However, when billions of droplets are close together, they form clouds.

Clouds can be made of water droplets, ice crystals, or both. They can form high in the sky or just above the ground. *Fog* is a cloud that forms near the ground.

Water vapor condenses around salt and dust particles in the air to form these water droplets.

Water vapor may condense on cool surfaces, too. It's why the cool glass below seems to "sweat." *Dew* is water droplets that form on objects near the ground.

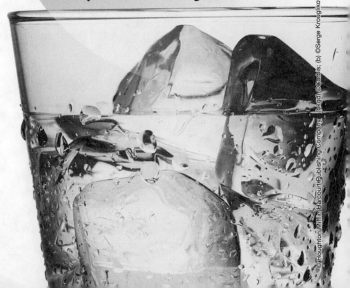

**Water droplets in a cloud collide and join together. It takes many droplets to form a single raindrop.**

# Precipitation

Air currents keep water droplets in the air. But as droplets and snow crystals grow inside clouds, they become too heavy and fall to Earth as precipitation. **Precipitation** is water that falls from clouds to Earth's surface. Rain, snow, and hail are all forms of precipitation.

Precipitation that falls into the oceans may quickly evaporate back into the atmosphere. Precipitation that falls on land may be stored, it may flow across the land, or it may be used by living things. Depending on where it falls, water from precipitation may move quickly or slowly through the water cycle.

# Do the Math!
## Order Fractions

A raindrop is many times bigger than a water droplet and a dust particle. The table shows the size of droplets and dust particles in relation to the size of raindrops. Order the fractions from least to greatest.

| Fractions | Ordered fractions |
|-----------|-------------------|
| $\frac{1}{100}$ | |
| $\frac{1}{1}$ | |
| $\frac{1}{5000}$ | |
| $\frac{1}{20}$ | |

Use the ordered fractions to correctly label the items on the diagram.

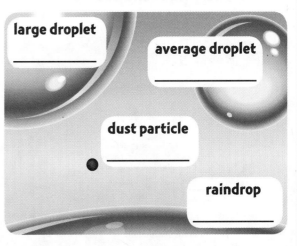

large droplet
_____

average droplet
_____

dust particle
_____

raindrop
_____

# Where Does Water Go?

Most precipitation falls into oceans and evaporates back into the air. But some water takes a more roundabout path on its way through the water cycle.

Imagine a rainstorm. Heavy rain falls on the ground. Some of this water will evaporate from shallow puddles quickly. It goes from Earth's surface directly back into the atmosphere.

Much of the rainfall will not reenter the atmosphere right away. Some will seep into the ground. Water that is stored underground is called **groundwater**. Groundwater can be found near the surface or very deep underground. Some groundwater may eventually return to the surface at places such as natural springs. Then it moves on through the water cycle.

As rainwater soaks into the ground, it fills up spaces between soil particles and cracks in rocks. Water that seeps deep underground becomes groundwater. Groundwater moves very slowly—if at all!

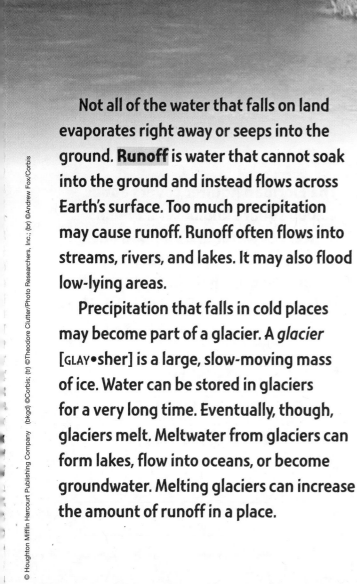

When glaciers melt, they quickly release stored water. Some of it may evaporate, some may seep into the ground, and some may move across the land as runoff.

Not all of the water that falls on land evaporates right away or seeps into the ground. **Runoff** is water that cannot soak into the ground and instead flows across Earth's surface. Too much precipitation may cause runoff. Runoff often flows into streams, rivers, and lakes. It may also flood low-lying areas.

Precipitation that falls in cold places may become part of a glacier. A *glacier* [GLAY•sher] is a large, slow-moving mass of ice. Water can be stored in glaciers for a very long time. Eventually, though, glaciers melt. Meltwater from glaciers can form lakes, flow into oceans, or become groundwater. Melting glaciers can increase the amount of runoff in a place.

## Runaway Water

The picture shows runoff on a city street. In the space below, describe what might happen to this runoff.

_____

_____

_____

_____

_____

_____

# A Precious Resource

Can you name all the ways that you use water? Water is an important resource used by all living things. People often need to share and conserve their sources of fresh, clean water.

LEGEND

Floridan aquifer system

**Active Reading** As you read these two pages, find and underline at least three facts about aquifers.

When you turn on a faucet, water flows out. Where does it come from? People can get fresh water from rivers or lakes. They can also get fresh water from aquifers. An *aquifer* [AH•kwuh•fuhr] is a body of rock that stores groundwater. People can drill into an aquifer and pump the water to the surface.

The water in aquifers can run low if people use more than can be replaced by precipitation. Human activities can also pollute aquifers. States that share aquifers work together to find solutions to these problems. They want to make sure there is enough fresh, clean water for everyone.

The Floridan Aquifer covers about 60,000 square kilometers. Billions of liters of water are pumped out of the Floridan Aquifer each day. Large cities, such as Savannah and Orlando, get water from this aquifer.

## Where Does Your Water Come From?

Find out the source of your water at school or at home.

_____

_____

People cannot live without water. We use water for many different purposes, including recreation.

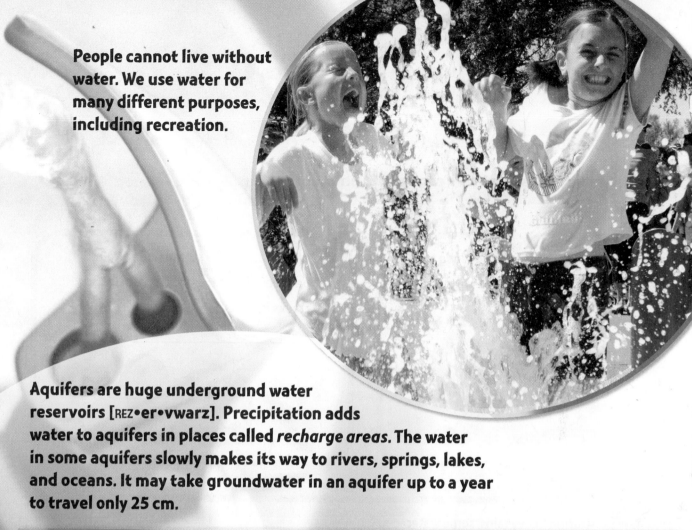

Aquifers are huge underground water reservoirs [REZ•er•vwarz]. Precipitation adds water to aquifers in places called *recharge areas*. The water in some aquifers slowly makes its way to rivers, springs, lakes, and oceans. It may take groundwater in an aquifer up to a year to travel only 25 cm.

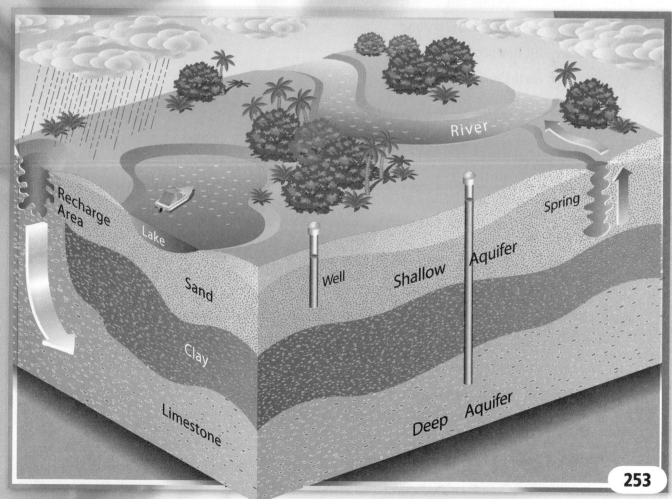

Recharge Area

Lake

Sand

Well

Shallow

Aquifer

River

Spring

Clay

Limestone

Deep Aquifer

# Sum It Up!

When you're done, use the answer key to check and revise your work.

**Write the term that matches each photo and caption.**

**1** Water can be stored for a long time in a large, slow-moving mass of ice.

_____

**2** Water can also be stored underground between the spaces in soil particles or cracks in rocks.

_____

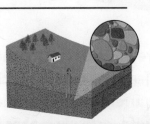

**3** During heavy rains, some water might not soak into the ground. Instead, it flows down slopes and across Earth's surface.

_____

## Summarize

**Fill in the missing words to describe the water cycle.**

The water cycle shows how water moves from Earth's surface to the 4. _____ and back again. The 5. _____ provides the energy for the water cycle. Water on the surface of the ocean heats up. During 6. _____ , it changes from a liquid to a gas. As 7. _____ rises into the atmosphere, it cools. During 8. _____ , it changes from a gas to a liquid. Billions of water droplets form a 9. _____ . When the droplets get too large for air currents to keep them up, they fall to Earth's surface as 10. _____ .

Answer Key: 1. glacier 2. groundwater 3. runoff 4. atmosphere 5. sun 6. evaporation 7. water vapor 8. condensation 9. cloud 10. precipitation

Name _____

# Word Play

**1** Use the clues to fill in the missing letters of the words.

1. g __ __ __ __ __ w __ __◯__    Water stored underground
   <br>                     10

2. __ o __ d __ __ __ __ __ __ __ __ __    The changing of water from a gas to a liquid

3. __ a __ __ __ __ __◯c __ __    The movement of water from Earth's surface to the
   <br>               7           atmosphere and back again

4. __ t __ __ __ __ p __ __ __◯    Mixture of gases that surrounds Earth
   <br>                      4

5. __ r __◯i __ __ __ __ __ t __ __ __    Water that falls from clouds to Earth's surface
   <br>           8

6. ◯u __ __ __ __    Water that flows across Earth's surface
   <br>   5

7. g◯__◯i __ __    A huge mass of frozen water that moves slowly
   <br>    9   6

8. __ r __ n __ __ __ i __ __◯__ __ __    The process in which plants return water vapor
   <br>                  3       to the atmosphere

9. ◯__ t __ __ __ __ a __ __ __    Water as a gas
   <br>  1

10. __ v __ __ o __◯t __ o __    The changing of water from a liquid to a gas
    <br>            2

**Bonus: Solve the Riddle!**

Use the circled letters in the clues above to solve the riddle.

What is water's favorite way to travel?

On a __ __ __ __ __  __ __ __ __ __
<br>     1  2  3  4  5   6  7  8  9  10

# Apply Concepts

**2** The sentences below show the steps that lead to the formation of a cloud. Number the steps to place them in the proper order.

_____ Water vapor cools and condenses around tiny particles.

_____ Water is heated by the sun.

_____ Water evaporates into the air.

_____ Billions of water droplets join together.

**3** In the picture below, show how groundwater can return to the atmosphere. Use arrows to show how the water moves and use wavy lines to show evaporation.

**4** What would happen if water could not condense in the atmosphere?

_____

_____

_____

_____

**5** In the spaces below, draw and label examples of water in the atmosphere as a solid, a liquid, and a gas. Hint: Wavy lines may be used to represent water vapor.

_____ _____ _____

_____ _____ _____

**6** Label each of the following scenes as an example of evaporation, precipitation, or condensation. Then briefly describe what happens during each process.

_____ _____ _____

_____ _____ _____

_____ _____ _____

**7** The picture shows stored water being used to irrigate crops. Circle and label the source of the water. How may this stored water be renewed?

_____

_____

**8** During an ice age, water is stored in glaciers. The picture below shows land area before and after an ice age. How are the land area and the oceans affected during an ice age?

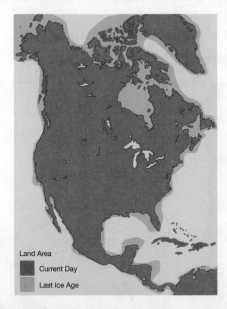

Land Area
- Current Day
- Last Ice Age

_____

_____

_____

_____

_____

_____

**Take It Home!**

Share what you have learned about water with your family. Tell them why it is important to conserve water. Set up a barrel outside to catch rainwater. Use the rainwater to wash your car or water your garden.

# What Are Types of Weather?

## Engage Your Brain!

Find the answer to the following question in this lesson and record it here.

If you are prepared, walking in the rain can be fun! What causes rain to fall?

_____

_____

_____

_____

## Active Reading

### Lesson Vocabulary

List the terms. As you learn about each one, make notes in the Interactive Glossary.

_____

_____

_____

### Cause and Effect

What causes wind to blow or rain to fall? Many ideas in this lesson are connected by a cause-and-effect relationship. A cause explains why something happens. An effect explains what happens as a result of something else. Active readers look for causes by asking themselves, Why did it happen? They look for effects by asking, What happened?

# Up in the Air

Quick! Describe today's weather. Is it cold and windy? Warm and dry? Many things you do depend on the weather. What *is* weather?

Earth's atmosphere protects living things from the sun's harmful ultraviolet rays and shields Earth from space debris. It is about 600 km (372 mi) thick, which seems very thick. However, in comparison with the rest of Earth, the atmosphere is actually quite thin.

The atmosphere is a mixture of gases. It is mostly made up of nitrogen and oxygen. The condition of the atmosphere at a given place and time is called **weather**. Weather takes place in the layer of the atmosphere closest to Earth's surface. Without the movement of gases in the atmosphere, there would be no weather.

Many factors, including air temperature, humidity, and air pressure, help us describe the weather of a place. *Air temperature* is how warm or cool the air is around us. Air temperature affects how much moisture is in the air. The air temperature also affects how we dress and what we do outside.

## Do the Math!
### Graph Data

A student recorded the temperature of the air at three times during the day: 50 °F at 8:00 a.m., 62 °F at 12:00 p.m., and 56 °F at 4:00 p.m. Graph the data.

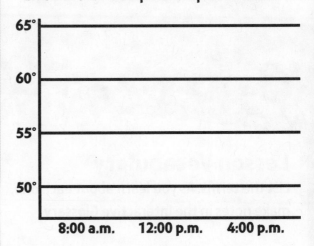

| | 8:00 a.m. | 12:00 p.m. | 4:00 p.m. |

What can you conclude?

_____

_____

**Humidity** is the amount of water vapor in the air. When the air feels dry, we have low humidity. When the air feels damp, we have high humidity. High humidity can also affect another weather factor—precipitation. *Precipitation* is water that falls back to Earth. Depending on air temperature, precipitation falls as rain, snow, sleet, or hail.

**Air pressure** is the weight of the atmosphere pressing down on Earth's surface. Air temperature and humidity both affect air pressure. Changes in air pressure usually bring changes in weather.

Weather determines whether we can go for a cool dip in a pool, whether we should be careful of strong winds, or whether we can skate on a frozen lake.

## What's the Weather?

Which of these pictures shows weather that is most like the day's weather where you live? Describe your current weather conditions.

_____

_____

_____

_____

# Under Pressure

Have you heard a meteorologist talk about high and low pressure? High and low pressure describe the air around you.

**Active Reading** As you read these pages, circle the cause of the change in air pressure as elevation changes.

You can't feel the atmosphere pressing down on you, but it is! Air pressure is the measure of the weight of the atmosphere on Earth's surface. Changes in air pressure bring changes in weather. A *barometer* is a weather instrument used to measure changes in air pressure.

Temperature, humidity, and distance above sea level all affect air pressure. Cold air is denser than warm air, which means air pressure is higher in cold areas than in warm areas. A volume of humid air is less dense than an equal volume of dry air. As a result, humid air has lower air pressure than dry air. Most air particles are found closer to Earth's surface. Air pressure decreases as elevation, or distance above sea level, increases.

In a classic barometer air presses on the liquid mercury in the pan, causing the mercury to push up inside the tube. A scale along the side of the barometer measures the height of the mercury in the tube. The average air pressure at sea level is 760 mm (29.92 in) of mercury.

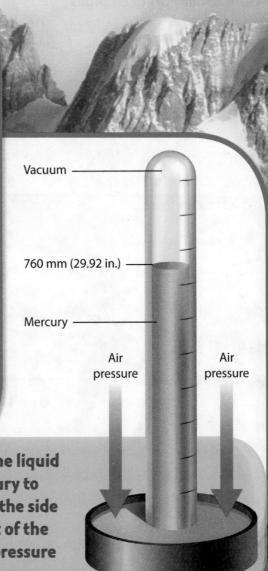

Vacuum

760 mm (29.92 in.)

Mercury

Air pressure

Air pressure

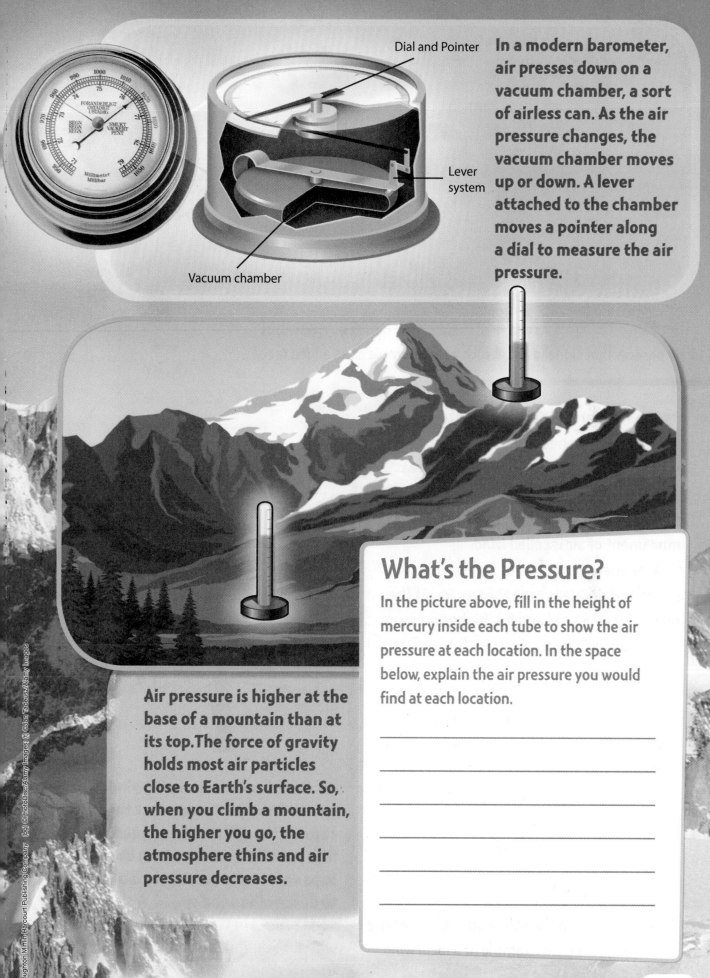

Dial and Pointer

Lever system

Vacuum chamber

In a modern barometer, air presses down on a vacuum chamber, a sort of airless can. As the air pressure changes, the vacuum chamber moves up or down. A lever attached to the chamber moves a pointer along a dial to measure the air pressure.

## What's the Pressure?

In the picture above, fill in the height of mercury inside each tube to show the air pressure at each location. In the space below, explain the air pressure you would find at each location.

_____

_____

_____

_____

_____

_____

Air pressure is higher at the base of a mountain than at its top. The force of gravity holds most air particles close to Earth's surface. So, when you climb a mountain, the higher you go, the atmosphere thins and air pressure decreases.

# When the Wind Blows

A gentle wind can be pleasant, cooling you off when it is hot outside. However, a windstorm can cause damage. What causes wind to blow?

**Active Reading** As you read these pages, circle two clue words or phrases that signal a detail such as an example or an added fact.

The sun warms Earth's surface unevenly. This uneven heating causes differences in air pressure. Air moves away from areas of higher pressure to areas of lower pressure similar to how water flows downhill. This movement of air is called *wind*.

Areas near Earth's poles receive less sunlight than areas near the tropics. At the poles, the air is cold and has higher pressure. As a result, air moves along Earth's surface from the poles toward the tropics. At the tropics, air warms, rises, and moves toward the poles. These winds, called *global winds*, blow over large areas of Earth. They move large weather systems, such as hurricanes.

Local differences in temperature can also cause winds. Earth's surface heats up at different rates. For example, the side of a mountain heats up more quickly than the valley below. As a result, a valley wind forms as air moves from the valley up the side of the mountain. This is an example of a *local wind*.

An *anemometer* measures wind speed. Wind pushes against the cups on the anemometer, causing it to spin. The rate at which the cups spin is measured and used to determine wind speed. A *wind vane* points in the direction from which the wind blows.

Local winds move short distances and can change direction. Daily changes in temperatures can cause local winds to change direction. For example, at night, the mountainside cools quicker than the valley below. The wind at night blows from the mountainside to the valley floor. In coastal areas, daily temperature changes result in local winds known as land breezes and sea breezes.

### Sea Breeze

During the day, land heats up more quickly than water. Air over the land also warms, causing the air pressure to drop. Cooler, higher-pressure air flows from over the water to the land, forming a sea breeze.

### Land Breeze

At night, land loses heat more quickly than water. As the air over land cools, the air pressure rises. Cooler, higher-pressure air flows from the land toward the sea, forming a land breeze.

▶ Draw an *L* over the low pressure and a *H* over the high pressure. Then describe the direction wind is blowing and why.

_____

_____

_____

_____

_____

# How Clouds Form

Some clouds signal precipitation. Others signal fair weather. How can you use clouds to predict weather?

**Active Reading** As you read these pages, circle the three types of clouds.

Air often has some water in it. Most of the time you can't see the water because it is an invisible gas called *water vapor*. Clouds form as water vapor cools and condenses. A cloud is made up of tiny water droplets and ice crystals; these are so small that air currents can hold them up. A water droplet can be thousands of times smaller than a raindrop!

There are three main types of clouds. Cumulus clouds are white and puffy and are common on clear, sunny days. Under the right conditions, cumulus clouds can develop into massive thunderstorm clouds. Cirrus clouds look like white streaks and are high and thin. Cirrus clouds usually signal cool, fair weather. Stratus clouds are low and gray, making the day dark and gloomy. These clouds can produce or signal incoming rain or snow.

**Producing a Cloud**

(1) The sun warms Earth's surface, causing air to rise into the atmosphere.

(2) Water vapor in the air cools and condenses around tiny specks of dust, forming water droplets.

(3) These droplets join together, forming a cloud.

## Cirrus Clouds

Thin, cold cirrus clouds are made up of ice crystals. Fast winds blow these clouds into long streamers high up in the atmosphere.

## Stratus Clouds

Stratus clouds cover the sky with a sheet of gray. Thick, wet-looking stratus clouds may produce steady, light rain or snow.

## Cumulus Clouds

Cumulus clouds usually form early in the afternoon on hot, sunny days. If these clouds grow high and thick enough, they can develop into stormy cumulonimbus clouds.

## Which Clouds Are in the Sky?

Draw the clouds you might see on a warm, windless, sunny afternoon. Write a statement to support your picture.

_____

_____

_____

_____

_____

# Some Rain, Anyone?

You might not think about rain—unless there is too much or too little of it. What causes precipitation?

**Active Reading** As you read this page, underline the cause of precipitation and circle kinds of precipitation.

Precipitation forms when water particles inside of clouds grow too large and fall to Earth's surface. Rain, snow, freezing rain, sleet, and hail are common kinds of precipitation.

Rain may start as ice crystals that melt as they fall to Earth's surface. Snow forms when water vapor changes directly into ice. Freezing rain occurs when falling, super-cooled raindrops do not freeze in the air but instead freeze when they strike objects near the ground.

Sleet is made of small lumps of ice. It forms when rain falls through a layer of freezing air. The raindrops turn to ice before hitting the ground.

Hail is made up of layers of ice. The layers form as air currents inside a thunderstorm cloud repeatedly lift and drop a hail particle. Each up-and-down trip adds ice to the particle. A ball of hail can be smaller than a pea or larger than a grapefruit!

Rain

Snow

Hail

A *rain gauge* measures rainfall. Rain fills the gauge, and the scale on the side shows how much rain fell.

Many factors affect the kinds of precipitation that falls in a place. For instance, snow falls in places with cold winters. It also falls in places with very high elevations. In contrast, hail might fall anywhere and at any time of year. It may even fall in places near the tropics!

People depend on precipitation to meet their water needs. Too much or too little precipitation can be a problem.

Too much precipitation can cause rivers to overflow. Floodwaters can damage crops and homes.

Too little precipitation is a *drought*. Droughts can cause the ground to dry out and plants and animals to die.

## Precipitation Cause and Effect

Complete the chart. Fill in the missing cause or effect.

| Cause | Effect |
|---|---|
| Snow has been melting for several weeks. Rain is predicted for the next five days. | |
| | The lake that supplies water to a city is very low. |

# Sum It Up!

When you're done, use the answer key to check and revise your work.

**Identify each weather instrument and what it measures.**

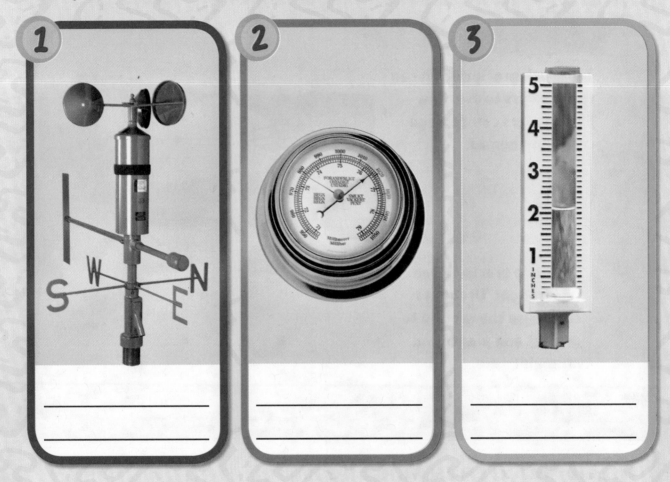

1

2

3

_____

_____

_____

_____

_____

_____

## Summarize

**Fill in the missing words to tell about weather.**

Weather is the condition of the 4. _____ at a given place and time. Factors that

affect weather include temperature and air pressure. Air moves from areas of 5. _____

air pressure to the areas of 6. _____ air pressure. This movement of air causes

7. _____ . Humidity also affects weather. Humidity is the amount of

8. _____ in the air. In the air, tiny water droplets form

9. _____ . Water falls from the sky as 10. _____ .

**Answer Key: 1.** anemometer/wind vane; wind speed/wind direction; **2.** barometer; air pressure **3.** rain gauge; amount of precipitation **4.** atmosphere **5.** high (or higher) **6.** low (or lower) **7.** wind **8.** water vapor **9.** clouds **10.** precipitation

Name _____

# Word Play

**1** Use the terms in the box to complete the crossword puzzle.

## Across

3. The layer of gases that surrounds Earth
4. The weight of the atmosphere on the surface of Earth is _____ pressure.
6. Water that falls from clouds
7. A tool that points in the direction from which the wind blows
8. The amount of water vapor in the air

## Down

1. The condition of the atmosphere at a given place and time
2. How warm or cool the air is around us
5. Air in motion

air pressure*    air temperature

atmosphere    humidity*

precipitation    weather*

wind    wind vane

\* Key Lesson Vocabulary

# Apply Concepts

**2** Identify and describe each cloud type shown below.

 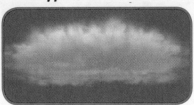 

_____   _____   _____

_____   _____   _____

_____   _____   _____

**3** At what time of day would you feel a sea breeze? A land breeze? Explain.

_____

_____

_____

_____

**4** Complete each sentence below by stating whether air pressure increases or decreases.

a. You are climbing a mountain. As you climb, air pressure is _____.

b. In the morning, the air is dry. In the afternoon, the air feels very moist. Air pressure is _____.

c. A warm day has changed to a cold afternoon. Air pressure is _____.

Take It Home!

Share what you have learned about weather with your family. Together, use Internet resources to find out how people use knowledge of global and local winds to travel and to predict weather.

**Essential Question**

# How Is Weather Predicted?

## Engage Your Brain!

Find the answer to the following question in this lesson and record it here.

How can a meteorologist use this picture to predict the weather?

_____

_____

_____

_____

_____

_____

## Active Reading

### Lesson Vocabulary
List the terms. As you learn about each one, make notes in the Interactive Glossary.

_____

_____

### Main Idea and Details
The main idea of a paragraph is the most important idea. The main idea may be stated in the first sentence, or it may be stated elsewhere. Active readers look for main ideas by asking themselves, What is this paragraph mostly about?

# Tracking the Weather

The weather forecasters on TV say, "Sunny and warm today, with rain tonight and tomorrow." How do they know?

**Active Reading** As you read this page, circle five tools used to collect weather data.

The forecasters have a lot of help! Meteorologists, or scientists who study weather, collect data from all over the world. They use automated systems at sea, on land, in the air, and in space to help track the weather.

At sea, weather buoys collect data on coastal weather conditions. These data help keep people in coastal cities safe. On land, weather-monitoring stations track weather conditions in remote locations. They can send advance notice about incoming weather. Scientists also use Doppler radar towers to observe how storm clouds are moving.

Weather balloons and weather satellites collect data from high above Earth's surface. Weather satellites can track the weather over very large areas. They also help relay data from land-based tools to meteorologists around the world.

In the United States, nearly 100 buoys like this one collect data about air temperature, air pressure, wind, and waves at sea.

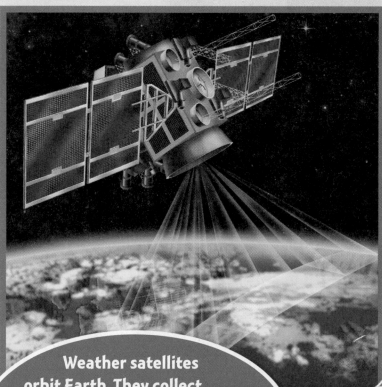

Weather satellites orbit Earth. They collect weather data, such as cloud cover, and track storms, such as hurricanes. These satellites use radio signals to transmit data back to Earth.

Scientists launch weather balloons that carry tools, called *radiosondes,* into the atmosphere. A typical radiosonde measures air temperature, air pressure, and humidity.

## Weather Wonder

Why do scientists use so many tools to collect weather data?

_____

_____

_____

_____

_____

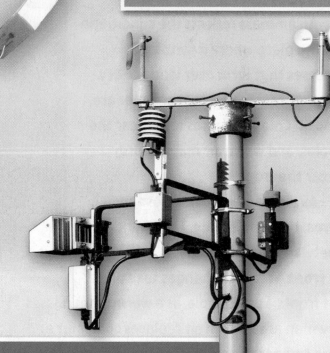

Thousands of weather-monitoring stations collect data on air temperature, air pressure, wind, humidity, and precipitation. Some weather stations use radar to track storms.

# Air Masses and Fronts

One day, it is so cool outside. The next day, it is warm enough to wear shorts. What happened to the weather?

When cold, dry freezer air meets warm, moist room air, a mini-front is formed!

**Active Reading** As you read these pages, underline the definition of an air mass. Circle four characteristics that air masses may have.

Packets of air move across Earth's surface. An **air mass** is a large body of air with the same temperature and humidity throughout.

An air mass reflects the conditions of the place where it forms. Air masses that form over land are dry. Air masses that form over water are moist. Cold air masses form near the poles, and warm air masses form near the tropics.

As air masses move across an area, they can collide. The boundary between two air masses is called a **front**. Weather changes take place at fronts. For example, as a warm front passes over an area, warm air replaces cooler air and the temperature rises. The movement of air masses and fronts explains why you might be chilly one day and warm the next. At a front, stormy conditions are common.

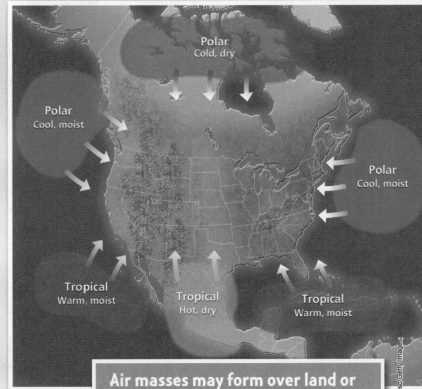

Polar
Cold, dry

Polar
Cool, moist

Polar
Cool, moist

Tropical
Warm, moist

Tropical
Hot, dry

Tropical
Warm, moist

Air masses may form over land or water. The masses that form over land near the poles will be cold and dry. The masses that form over water near the poles will be cold and moist. Which types of air masses will form near the tropics?

# Cold Front

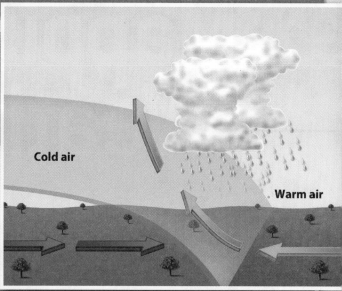

A cold front forms where a cold air mass bumps into a warmer air mass. The denser cold air pushes the warm air up. Water vapor in the air cools, and large clouds form. Thunderstorms and heavy rain often take place. Cooler temperatures follow a cold front.

**Cold air**

**Warm air**

# Warm Front

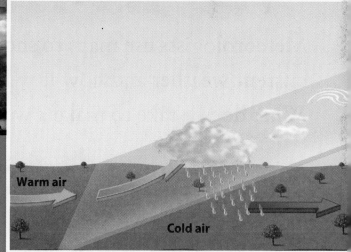

A warm front forms where a warm air mass moves over a cold air mass. A warm front forms a wider area of clouds and rain than a cold front. Steady rain or snow may fall. Warmer temperatures follow a warm front.

**Warm air**

**Cold air**

## Home Front

Identify a front inside of your home. Explain where the different air masses form, the characteristics of each one, and how the two air masses meet.

_____

_____

_____

_____

# Mapping the Weather

Meteorologists use maps to show the current weather and how it will change. What does it take to make a weather map?

Most weather forecasts are accurate within five to seven days. A *weather forecast* is a prediction about the future weather conditions of a place. Weather forecasts beyond seven days are not very accurate.

Meteorologists forecast the weather based on the local weather data and observed weather patterns. They analyze the air temperature, humidity, and air pressure data of a place. They also analyze weather patterns, such as the movement of air masses and fronts, to prepare a weather forecast. In North America, air masses and fronts generally move from west to east.

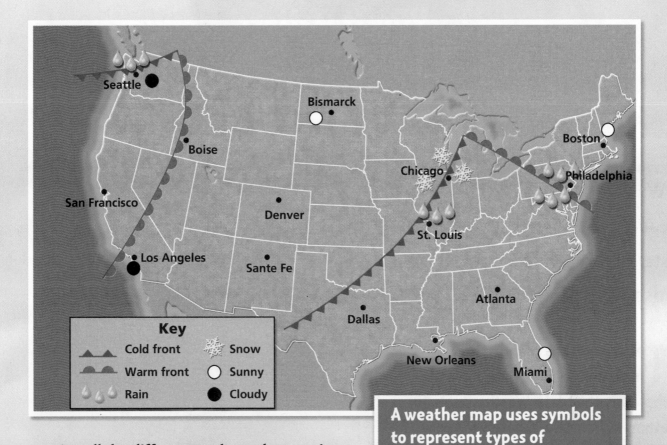

**Key**
- △ Cold front
- ◠ Warm front
- 💧 Rain
- ❄ Snow
- ○ Sunny
- ● Cloudy

Recall the different tools used to monitor the weather from Earth's surface, the oceans, and the atmosphere. These tools collect lots of weather data. Computers help us store and analyze weather data and weather patterns to make *weather maps.* Meteorologists study weather maps and use them to make weather forecasts.

A weather map uses symbols to represent types of weather. The map legend tells you what each symbol means. The triangles or half circles on a front symbol point in the direction the front is moving.

Computer programs help interpret weather information. Computer simulations help meteorologists forecast the weather.

## Read a Weather Map

Show these weather events on the map.

- Circle the name of a city where snow is falling.

- Draw a line under the names of two cities where it is sunny.

- Write a C on a cold front, and a W on a warm front.

- Draw a rectangle around the name of a city that has cloudy skies now, but will soon have rain.

# » Forewarned!

Weather forecasts help us plan each day. When severe storms strike, weather forecasts can also help save lives.

In August 2004, Hurricane Charley moved across the Atlantic Ocean and along the eastern coast of the United States. Data collected by satellites and airplanes helped meteorologists make forecasts to warn people about this storm.

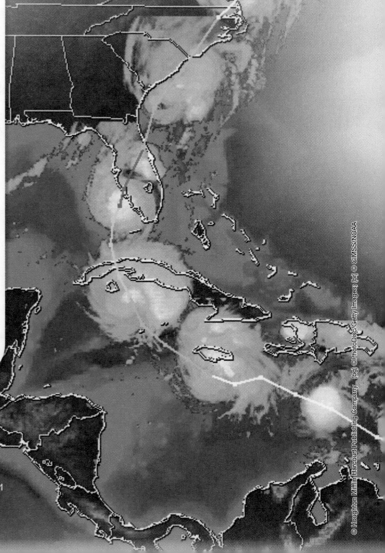

Technology has changed how we measure, analyze, forecast, and share weather data. Weather tools, for example, help us accurately measure the weather conditions of a place. Modern communication technology lets scientists share global weather data quickly and over long distances. These data can then be used to make computer models to predict weather events.

Meteorolgists work hard at predicting the strength and path of storms. In the past, meteorologists had to rely on weather ships and weather-monitoring stations on tropical islands to track hurricanes—the largest, most powerful storms on Earth. The data from these sources were limited. As a result, predicting the strength and path of these storms was very difficult.

TROPICAL DEPR
TROPICAL STORM
CATEGORY 1
CATEGORY 2
CATEGORY 3
CATEGORY 4
CATEGORY 5

Starting in the 1960s, the United States launched the first of many weather-satellite systems. For the first time, scientists were able to monitor and collect data from the uninhabited parts of Earth. As a result, the accuracy of weather forecasts and hurricane tracking improved. Today, satellites along with land- and sea-based weather tools provide information to warn people about the changing weather.

**Tropical Depression**

**Tropical Storm**

**Hurricane**

A hurricane begins as a thunderstorm near the western coast of Africa. As its winds strengthen, the storm becomes a tropical depression. When winds reach 63 km/h (39 mph), it becomes a tropical storm. A tropical storm becomes a hurricane when there are winds of 119 km/h (74 mph) or more.

## Do the Math!
### Interpret Data

Use information from the table to answer the following questions.

1. What is the wind speed and category of hurricanes that may cause extensive damage?

_____

_____

2. How much stronger is a category 5 hurricane than a hurricane that causes only minimal damage?

_____

_____

| Category | Wind Speed (km/h) | Damage |
|----------|-------------------|--------|
| 1 | 119–153 | Minimal |
| 2 | 154–177 | Moderate |
| 3 | 178–209 | Major |
| 4 | 210–249 | Extensive |
| 5 | > 249 | Catastrophic |

# Sum It Up!

When you're done, use the answer key to check and revise your work.

**Complete the details about each main idea.**

**1** Meteorologists collect weather data from all over the world. Some of the tools that they use include

_____

_____

_____

_____

**2** Air masses meet at boundaries called fronts. Weather that happens along fronts includes

_____

_____

_____

_____

**3** Meteorologists use weather maps to make forecasts. Symbols on weather maps indicate the weather. Symbols show

_____

_____

_____

_____

## Summarize

**4** Meteorologists use many tools to track and forecast the weather. Explain how a meterologist might use the three tools pictured below to predict the weather.

_____

_____

_____

**Answer Key: 1.** weather buoys, weather balloons, weather-monitoring stations, and weather satellites. **2.** thunderstorms, cloudy skies, steady rain, and windy weather. **3.** precipitation, cloud cover, and fronts. **4.** Sample answer: Weather satellites send data to computers on Earth. Meteorologists use computers to analyze the data and make weather maps.

## Word Play

Name _____

**1** Use the clues to unscramble the terms.

1. C A E N R I R U H  _ _ _ _ _ _ _ _ ⭕
   a storm with wind speeds of at least 119 km/h

2. F N O R T  _ _ _ ⭕ _
   the boundary between two different air masses

3. L O O S T I G R O E T M E  _ _ _ _ ⭕ _ _ _ _ _ _ _
   a person who studies weather and the atmosphere

4. R A I S S M A  _ _ _  _ _ ⭕ _
   a large body of air with the same temperature and humidity

5. R E W E A T H  C A E O F T S R
   _ _ _ _ _ _ _  _ _ _ _ _ _ ⭕ _
   a prediction of future weather conditions

6. L P O D P R E  D A A R R
   ⭕ _ _ _ _ _ _  _ _ _ _ _
   a tool used to see the movement of storm clouds

Solve the riddle by unscrambling the circled letters to find the missing part of the word.

What kind of radios do weather balloons carry?

RADIO_ _ _ _ _ _

# Apply Concepts

**2** Identify each weather instrument and describe what it does.

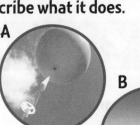

A

B

C

_____

_____

_____

_____

_____

**3** Circle the correct answer.

Which statement best describes a hurricane?

- A swirling funnel cloud

- A short-lived, local storm

- Low sheets of thick clouds

- A large storm that forms over the ocean

**4** Where does a cold, moist air mass form? What type of weather will it cause?

_____

_____

_____

_____

**5** Identify the type of front shown in the picture. Explain your answer.

_____

_____

_____

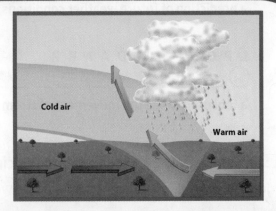

Cold air

Warm air

**Take It Home!**

Work with a family member to research how severe weather affects electrical energy generation, distribution, and use. Describe what experts recommend people do to conserve energy during severe weather.

# Stormy Weather:
## Beaufort Wind Scale

If you were a sailor on a ship, being able to measure wind speed would be very important. In the past, wind speed was estimated by observating its effect on things. Today, we use tools to measure wind speed. Read on to find out about ways to measure wind speed.

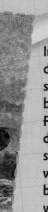

In 1805, Sir Francis Beaufort developed a scale to classify wind speed. This scale assigned levels based on sailors' observations. For example, a Force 3 wind describes a gentle breeze in which ships move steadily across the water. Force 6 describes a strong breeze that produces large waves, whitecaps, and spray. And Force 11 describes a violent storm.

You can observe a flag to see how wind blows. A windsock shows the relative direction and speed of winds. The windsock droops during low wind speed. It flies straight out from the pole during high wind.

Use the text and information from reference materials to complete the Beaufort Wind Scale table.

| Beaufort Wind Force | Average Wind Speed (km/h) | Description | Beaufort Wind Force | Average Wind Speed (km/h) | Description |
|---|---|---|---|---|---|
| 0 | 0 | Calm | | 56 | Near Gale |
| | 3 | Light Air | | | Gale |
| | 9 | Light Breeze | | 82 | Severe Gale |
| | | Gentle Breeze | | | Storm |
| | 24 | Moderate Breeze | | 110 | |
| | | Fresh Breeze | 12 | 124 | Hurricane |
| 6 | 44 | | | | |

# S.T.E.M.
continued

Today, wind speed is measured using anemometers.

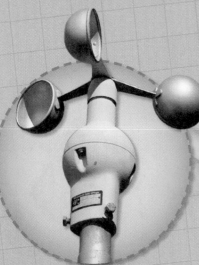

This anemometer uses cuplike devices to measure wind speed. The faster the wind blows, the faster the cups spin. The cups are attached to sensors that measure the actual wind speed.

This digital anemometer uses spinning fans to generate magnetic pulses. Then, the instrument translates these pulses into measurements of the wind speed.

An ultrasound anemometer has pairs of sound speakers and microphones. Electronic circuits measure the time it takes for sound to travel from each speaker to its microphone. The anemometer uses the data collected to determine wind speed as well as wind direction.

## Design Your Future

Use observations to design your own scale to measure something such as temperature, cloud cover, or amount or strength of rainfall. Write the process for using the scale, and then try it out.

_____

_____

_____

## Build On It!

Rise to the engineering design challenge—complete **Design It: Build a Wind Vane** on the Inquiry Flipchart.

Name _____

Essential Question

# How Can We Observe Weather Patterns?

## Set a Purpose

**Why is it helpful to observe the weather?**

_____

_____

_____

_____

## Think About the Procedure

**Why should the location for your weather station be sheltered from the sun?**

_____

_____

_____

_____

**Why would it be useful to measure the weather conditions at the same time every day?**

_____

_____

_____

_____

## Record Your Data

| Day | Weather Observations |
|-----|----------------------|
|     |                      |
|     |                      |
|     |                      |
|     |                      |
|     |                      |
|     | **Weather Predictions** |
|     |                      |
|     |                      |
|     |                      |

## Draw Conclusions

How can we observe weather patterns?

_____

_____

_____

_____

## Analyze and Extend

1. Describe weather patterns in
   your data.

_____

_____

_____

_____

2. Which weather conditions were
   most likely to change before the
   weather changed?

_____

_____

_____

3. What were your weather predictions?
   On which weather pattern did you
   base your predictions?

_____

_____

_____

4. Were your predictions accurate?
   Explain.

_____

_____

_____

5. What would have made your weather
   predictions more accurate?

_____

_____

_____

_____

_____

6. Think of other questions you would
   like to ask about weather patterns
   and predictions.

_____

_____

_____

**288**

# 8 THINGS YOU SHOULD KNOW ABOUT N. Christina Hsu

**1** Dr. Hsu is an atmospheric scientist. She studies how Earth's atmosphere changes, and how these changes affect Earth's surface.

**2** Dr. Hsu earned a Ph.D. degree in atmospheric science from the Georgia Institute of Technology.

**3** Today, Dr. Hsu works for NASA—the U.S. agency that explores space and studies Earth from space.

**4** Dr. Hsu studies aerosols, which are tiny particles that hang in the air. Aerosols include solids, such as smoke and soot, and liquids, such as tiny water droplets.

**5** Dr. Hsu studies aerosols because water vapor condenses on them to form water droplets. She is interested in the source, amount, and distribution of these particles in the atmosphere.

**6** Dr. Hsu uses satellites to measure and track the movement of aerosols.

**7** Dr. Hsu studies the effects of aerosols blocking sunlight.

**8** In 2007, Dr. Hsu received an award for exceptional achievement from NASA's Goddard Space Flight Center.

# Now You Be an Aerosol Detective!

Each clue describes a source of aerosol particles. Match each clue with the picture that illustrates it.

**1.** It may be quiet for years, then it releases smoke and ash with a *boom*!

**2.** Blustery winds launch sandy aerosols every day from dry places such as this one.

**3.** People are the source of this air pollution.

**4.** Tiny water droplets are aerosols, too. They often come from this source.

**5.** One little match can spark one of these.

## Think About It!

How might human activities add aerosols to the atmosphere?

_____

_____

_____

# Unit 5 Review

## Vocabulary Review

Use the terms in the box to complete the sentences.

> air mass
> air pressure
> atmosphere
> condensation
> humidity
> precipitation
> runoff
> weather

1. The condition of the atmosphere at a certain place and time

   is _____.

2. The amount of water vapor in the air

   is _____.

3. The weight of the atmosphere pressing down on Earth's surface

   is _____.

4. A large body of air with the same temperature and humidity

   throughout is an _____.

5. The mixture of gases that surround Earth is

   the _____.

6. The process by which a gas changes into a liquid
   is _____.

7. Water that falls from clouds to Earth's surface

   is _____.

8. Water that cannot soak into the ground and instead flows across

   Earth's surface is _____.

# Science Concepts

Fill in the letter of the choice that best answers the question.

**9.** Deanna measured the temperature and humidity every afternoon for four days. She recorded the results in this table.

| Day | Temperature (°C) | Relative Humidity (%) |
|---|---|---|
| Monday | 28 (82 °F) | 90 |
| Tuesday | 27 (81 °F) | 79 |
| Wednesday | 24 (75 °F) | 70 |
| Thursday | 28 (82 °F) | 69 |

Which day could Deanna conclude was hottest and **most** humid?

(A) Monday          (C) Wednesday

(B) Tuesday          (D) Thursday

**10.** Carl reads the weather forecast on the Internet. It says that a cool, wet air mass is moving toward the town where he lives. What type of weather should Carl expect?

(A) cool temperatures, sun, and clear skies

(B) warm temperatures, sun, and clear skies

(C) warm temperatures, sun, and decreasing cloudiness

(D) cool temperatures, increasing cloudiness, and precipitation

**11.** Oceans get fresh water from precipitation and rivers. However, ocean water levels do not change very much as a result. Why are these levels not greatly affected?

(A) Water is constantly seeping into the ocean floor.

(B) Water is constantly evaporating over the ocean's surface.

(C) Water is constantly flowing back into rivers from the oceans.

(D) Water is constantly deposited back on land by ocean wave action.

**12.** Which of the following sequences shows how water may move from an ocean to land and back to an ocean?

(A) precipitation → runoff → cloud formation → groundwater

(B) evaporation → cloud formation → precipitation → runoff

(C) groundwater → cloud formation → precipitation → runoff

(D) cloud formation → precipitation → evaporation → runoff

**13.** Scientists study many factors that help them predict weather. Which factor **most** directly affects the movement of air?

(A) humidity          (C) precipitation

(B) air pressure          (D) temperature

**14.** This diagram shows the water cycle.

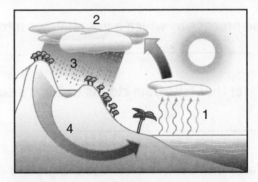

At which point in the cycle does precipitation take place?

(A) 1          (C) 3

(B) 2          (D) 4

**15.** Sarah looks at a barometer to record a reading. What is Sarah measuring?

(A) air pressure          (C) precipitation

(B) humidity          (D) temperature

**16.** This diagram shows the pattern of air movement in a coastal area.

Which type of wind is illustrated in the diagram?

Ⓐ sea breeze

Ⓑ land breeze

Ⓒ valley breeze

Ⓓ coastal breeze

**17.** This picture shows how a puddle changes over the course of a day.

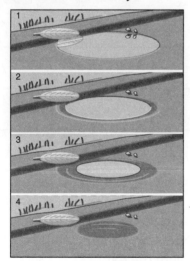

Which process is taking place?

Ⓐ runoff

Ⓑ evaporation

Ⓒ precipitation

Ⓓ condensation

**18.** Taro is studying the water cycle. He knows that energy is needed for matter to move and change state. What is the main source of energy for the water cycle?

Ⓐ clouds

Ⓑ the sun

Ⓒ the oceans

Ⓓ chemical reactions

**19.** Jerry notices that the air pressure is rising. Based on this observation, which type of weather does Jerry expect?

Ⓐ fair weather

Ⓑ windy weather

Ⓒ stormy weather

Ⓓ unstable weather

**20.** The following diagram shows a location where two air masses meet.

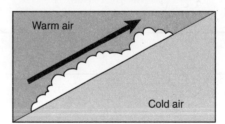

Warm air

Cold air

What is the weather like at this type of air boundary?

Ⓐ clear and cold

Ⓑ clear and warm

Ⓒ cloudy and rainy

Ⓓ windy and cold

UNIT 5

# Apply Inquiry and Review the Big Idea

Write the answers to these questions.

**21.** This diagram shows the atmosphere on a day in late winter. Precipitation is falling.

Which type of precipitation is **likely** to form in the freezing cold layer of air? Explain how you know.

_____

_____

_____

_____

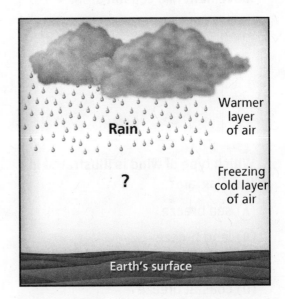

Warmer layer of air

Rain

Freezing cold layer of air

?

Earth's surface

**22.** Hurricanes are one type of severe storm. Explain why predicting hurricanes is important.

_____

_____

_____

_____

**23.** A weather forecaster says that a front is approaching. She says that the weather will be warmer the next day, with increased cloudiness and late day rain. What type of front is headed for the area? How were the data gathered to make this prediction?

_____

_____

_____

# Earth and Space

## Big Idea

Objects in space including Earth and its moon move in regular observable patterns.

# I Wonder Why

People have studied space for hundreds of years. How has modern space exploration changed our lives? *Turn the page to find out.*

**Here's Why** Space technology has led to many discoveries about our universe. In addition, technology originally invented to explore space has solved many problems here on Earth.

In this unit, you will explore the Big Idea, the Essential Questions, and the Investigations on the Inquiry Flipchart.

Levels of Inquiry Key ■ DIRECTED ■ GUIDED ■ INDEPENDENT

Track Your Progress

**Big Idea** Objects in space including Earth and its moon move in regular observable patterns.

## Essential Questions

Now I Get the Big Idea!

**Science Notebook**
Before you begin each lesson, be sure to write your thoughts about the Essential Question.

# How Do the Sun, Earth, and Moon Interact?

## Engage Your Brain!

Find the answer to the following question in this lesson and record it here.

Why is only part of Earth's surface visible?

_____

_____

_____

_____

## Active Reading

### Lesson Vocabulary

List the terms. As you learn about each one, make notes in the Interactive Glossary.

_____

_____

_____

_____

### Cause and Effect

Some ideas in this lesson are connected by a cause-and-effect relationship. Why something happens is a cause. What happens as a result of something else is an effect. Active readers look for effects by asking themselves, What happened? They look for causes by asking, Why did it happen?

# Night and Day

How can it be morning where you live and be nighttime in India at the same time? You cannot feel it, but Earth moves in space.

**Active Reading** As you read this page, draw one line under a cause of night and day. Draw two lines under an effect of night and day.

People once thought that the sun moved around Earth. After all, the sun seems to rise, to move across the sky, and to set each day. Today we know what makes it seem like the sun moves around Earth. Earth **rotates**, or turns like a top. Earth rotates around an imaginary line, called an **axis**. Earth's axis runs through it from the North Pole to the South Pole. Once every 24 hours, or once a day, Earth rotates about its axis.

Earth's rotation causes day and night. As it rotates, one side of Earth faces the sun. This part of Earth has daytime. The other side of Earth faces away from the sun and has nighttime. As Earth's rotation continues, parts of Earth cycle between day and night.

Each planet rotates at a different rate, so the length of a day is different. For example, Venus rotates so slowly that one day on Venus is equal to 225 days on Earth!

## Do the Math!
### Use and Represent Numbers

Find the difference between a day on Earth and a day on other planets. (1 Earth day = 24 hours)

Length of Day:

Mercury: 59 Earth days

_____

Jupiter: 9 Earth hours, 55 minutes

_____

Neptune: 16 Earth hours, 6 minutes

_____

Night

Day

Earth rotates on its axis from west to east. As a result, the sun appears to rise in the east and set in the west.

# The Sun-Earth-Moon System

Earth is not alone in space. You can easily spot two other bodies in the sky—the sun and the moon. How do they all move together?

**Active Reading** As you read these pages, underline the main idea, and circle a sentence that supports it.

The sun, Earth, and the moon form a system in space. This system is held together by gravity. *Gravity* is a force that pulls objects toward each other. Gravity pulls Earth toward the sun, holding Earth in orbit around it. An **orbit** is the path that an object takes around another object in space. Earth *revolves*, or travels around the sun. It takes Earth about 365 days to complete one revolution.

While Earth revolves around the sun, the moon revolves around Earth. Earth's gravity pulls on the moon. Like Earth, the moon also turns on its axis. It takes about a month for the moon to complete one rotation. During the same period of time, the moon makes one complete revolution around Earth. As a result, the same side of the moon always faces Earth.

## Sun

The sun is so large that about 1 million Earths could fit inside it. The sun's gravity holds the Earth-moon system in place.

The sun, the moon, and Earth all have distinct characteristics. The sun has the largest diameter of all bodies in the solar system. An object's *diameter* is the distance from one side, through its center, to the other side.

| | Makeup | Diameter | Age |
|---|---|---|---|
| **Sun** | hot, glowing gases; mostly helium and hydrogen | 1,391,000 km (864,400 mi) | about 4.6 billion years old |
| **Earth** | rocky surface with large oceans; thick atmosphere of nitrogen and oxygen; life forms | 12,756 km (7,926 mi) | about 4.5 billion years old |
| **Moon** | rocky surface; no atmosphere or water; extreme cold and heat; no known life forms | 3,475 km (2,159 mi) | at least 4.5 billion years old |

Moon

Earth

## How Do They Move?

The arrows in the picture show the two types of movements that Earth makes in space. Label each arrow with the movement it shows. Then, explain how Earth moves.

Earth spins quickly—more than 1,600 km/hr (1,000 mi/ hr) at its equator. As Earth spins, it also speeds around the sun at more than 107,000 km/hr (67,000 mi/hr). Earth and the moon are relatively close to one another. They are about 382,000 km (237,400 mi) apart. In contrast, Earth is about 150 million km (93 million mi) from the sun.

_____

_____

_____

_____

_____

_____

# Seasons

When it is summer in the United States, it is winter in Chile. How can two places have a different season at the same time of year?

**Active Reading** As you read this page, underline the cause of the seasons.

Earth rotates on its tilted axis. As Earth revolves around the sun, the direction of its tilted axis doesn't change. The tilt of Earth's axis and its orbit cause the seasons.

Earth is divided into halves called *hemispheres*. The Northern Hemisphere extends from the equator to the North Pole. The Southern Hemisphere extends from the equator to the South Pole. In June, the Northern Hemisphere is tilted toward the sun and gets more direct rays of sunlight. It has more hours of daylight and warmer weather. It is summer there.

In June, in the Southern Hemisphere, the opposite season takes place. Why? The Southern Hemisphere is tilted away from the sun and gets less direct sunlight. It has fewer hours of daylight and cooler weather. It is winter there.

In December, the Northern Hemisphere is tilted away from the sun. As a result, it is winter there. At the same time, the Southern Hemisphere is tilted toward the sun and has summer.

## me Sweet Home

ch season is it where you live?
w a picture of the sun and Earth
he correct positions to show the
son. Include the tilt of Earth's axis
our picture.

# Seasons in the Northern Hemisphere

When the Northern Hemisphere is tilted away from the sun, that part of Earth has winter. When the Northern Hemisphere is tilted toward the sun, it has summer.

Winter

Fall

Spring

Summer

# Patterns in the Sky

The Big Dipper is a part of a star pattern in the night sky. To Ancient Greeks, the pattern looked like a giant bear.

**Active Reading** As you read these pages, draw a circle around words or phrases that provide details about constellations.

People have looked at the stars for thousands of years. A star pattern, or **constellation**, is a group of stars that seems to form a picture in the night sky. The early Greeks named constellations after animals or people from stories called *myths*. The Big Dipper is part of a constellation called *Ursa Major*, or Great Bear. Orion is a constellation named after a hunter in a Greek myth.

As Earth rotates on its axis, constellations seem to move across the night sky. Like the sun, constellations seem to rise in the east and set in the west. Stars above the North Pole, however, seem to move in a circle.

The positions of the constellations seem to change with the seasons, because we see different parts of space as Earth revolves around the sun. The stars in the constellations do change a little over time. However, it might take millions of years for a constellation to change its shape!

For thousands of years, people have seen pictures in the stars. They connect the stars to make a pattern or shape.

These pictures show stars seen from the same location during summer (at left) and winter (at right). The constellations seem to change their places in the sky.

## Connect the Stars

Connect the stars to draw a constellation. Use all or some of the stars. What is the name of your constellation?

_____

_____

# Our Place in Space

At one time, people thought Earth was the center of the universe. How did we learn that this isn't true?

Long ago, astronomers believed Earth was the center of the universe. Daily observations seemed to confirm this belief. When people looked at the sky, they saw the sun, the moon, planets, and stars in motion. Naturally, they concluded that Earth was at the center of the universe. It took hundreds of years, new technology, and new observations for this idea to change.

In the 1500s, a Polish astronomer named Nicolaus Copernicus designed a new *model*, or system, of the universe. Based on new observations about the motion of the planets, he suggested that Earth and the planets revolved around the sun. Then, in the 1600s, scientists gathered more evidence to support this sun-centered model of the solar system.

Using a telescope he made, Galileo Galilei was the first to see moons orbiting Jupiter. His observation showed that all objects in space did not orbit Earth. Around this time, Johannes Kepler correctly described the shape of the planets' orbits around the sun. His calculations showed that the planets revolved around the sun in elliptical [ee▪LIP▪tih▪kuhl] orbits. All these scientists' observations changed our idea about Earth's place in space.

Earth

When people measured time using sundials, the changing shadow cast by the sun seemed to confirm that the sun revolved around Earth. We now know that the sun doesn't revolve around Earth. Earth revolves around the sun!

## What Do You Know?

Describe what you know about the sun-Earth-moon system that astronomers did not know long ago.

_____

_____

_____

_____

_____

**Jupiter**

**Mars**

**Saturn**

**Venus**

**Mercury**

**Sun**

**Moon**

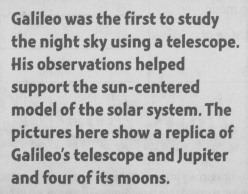

Galileo was the first to study the night sky using a telescope. His observations helped support the sun-centered model of the solar system. The pictures here show a replica of Galileo's telescope and Jupiter and four of its moons.

When you're done, use the answer key to check and revise your work.

**Read the summary statements below. Each one is incorrect. Change the part of the summary in blue to make the statement correct.**

## Summarize

| | |
|---|---|
| 1. Day and night are caused by Earth's revolution around the sun. | _____ _____ |
| 2. The discovery of moons around Jupiter proved that all objects in space revolve around Jupiter. | _____ _____ _____ _____ |
| 3. Earth's seasons are caused by Earth's revolution and rotation in space. | _____ _____ |
| 4. During winter in the Northern Hemisphere, there are more hours of daylight and it is warmer. | _____ _____ _____ _____ |
| 5. When it is spring in the Northern Hemisphere, the season is summer in the Southern Hemisphere. | _____ _____ _____ |
| 6. Constellations appear to move across the night sky because of Earth's tilt on its axis. | _____ _____ |

Name _____

## Word Play

**1** Unscramble letters to fill in the blanks with the words from the box below. Use the hints to help you unscramble the letters.

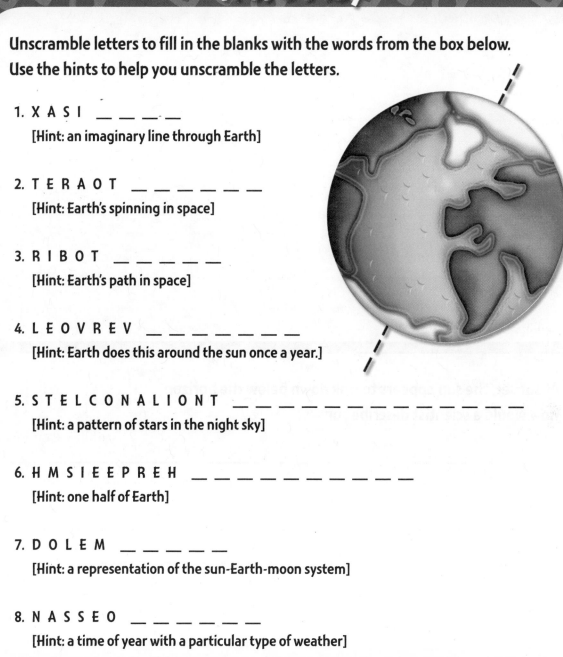

1. X A S I   __ __ __ __
   [Hint: an imaginary line through Earth]

2. T E R A O T   __ __ __ __ __ __
   [Hint: Earth's spinning in space]

3. R I B O T   __ __ __ __ __
   [Hint: Earth's path in space]

4. L E O V R E V   __ __ __ __ __ __ __
   [Hint: Earth does this around the sun once a year.]

5. S T E L C O N A L I O N T   __ __ __ __ __ __ __ __ __ __ __ __ __
   [Hint: a pattern of stars in the night sky]

6. H M S I E E P R E H   __ __ __ __ __ __ __ __ __ __
   [Hint: one half of Earth]

7. D O L E M   __ __ __ __ __
   [Hint: a representation of the sun-Earth-moon system]

8. N A S S E O   __ __ __ __ __ __
   [Hint: a time of year with a particular type of weather]

| model | revolve | orbit* | hemisphere |
|-------|---------|--------|------------|
| axis* | constellation* | rotate* | season |

* Key Lesson Vocabulary

# Apply Concepts

**2** Draw a picture of the sun and Earth. Draw lines to show Earth's axis and rays from the sun. Label which side of Earth has day and which side has night.

**3** At sunset, the sun appears to sink down below the horizon. How would a scientist describe sunset?

_____

_____

_____

_____

**4** The constellation Orion is seen in the night sky during winter in the Northern Hemisphere. During summer, Orion cannot be seen. Why is Orion only seen during part of the year?

_____

_____

_____

_____

_____

_____

**5** Imagine you are going on a ride in a spacecraft next to Earth. Your trip takes one whole year. Describe Earth's tilt in the Northern Hemisphere during your trip. What happens as a result of the tilt?

_____

_____

_____

_____

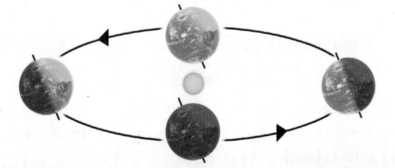

**6** Suppose you are an astronomer who lived at the same time as Galileo. Write a letter to a friend explaining Galileo's discoveries, his ideas about a sun-centered universe, and the conclusions he made about them.

_____

_____

_____

_____

_____

_____

_____

_____

_____

_____

**Take It Home!**

With an adult, observe constellations outside on a clear night. Draw a picture of a constellation you observe. What do you think the night sky will look like in three months?

# Meet the Climate Scientists

### Milutin Milankovitch

During an ice age, ice sheets cover much of Earth. Why do ice ages happen? Serbian scientist Milutin Milankovitch [mih•LOO•tin mih•LAHNG•koh•vich] spent his career trying to find out. Milankovitch learned that Earth's orbit changes in cycles lasting thousands of years. He determined that these changes affect the amount of sunlight reaching Earth. As a result, during cooler periods, ice ages occur. Today, data from the ocean floor supports Milankovitch's ideas. These climate patterns are called Milankovitch cycles in his honor.

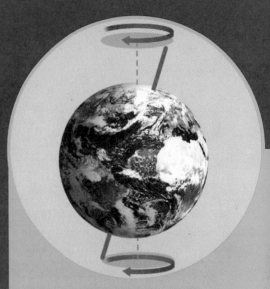

The direction of Earth's axis changes over time as part of a cycle that lasts about 23,000 years. This change affects Earth's temperature.

### Dr. Maureen Raymo

Dr. Maureen Raymo is an earth scientist. She studies how Earth's climate has changed over long periods of time. Like Milankovitch, Dr. Raymo studies the relationship between changes in Earth's orbit and climate. During an ice age, much of Earth's water is stored in glaciers. This affects sea level. Dr. Raymo has been able to find evidence of ancient changes in climate by studying rocks and sediment on the ocean floor. Through her research, she has been able to describe the sea level and water flow direction in ancient oceans.

# The Road to a New Hypothesis

Use the information below to make a timeline of the events that led Milutin Milankovitch to develop his hypothesis.

**1930** Milutin Milankovitch publishes his hypothesis. He bases it on improved methods of calculating differences in Earth's orbit, axis direction, and axis tilt.

**1864** James Croll explains ice ages as a result of changes in Earth's axis and the shape of its orbit around the sun.

**1960s** Continued research shows that Milankovitch's hypothesis explains some climate trends.

**1754** Jean le Rond d'Alembert calculates how the direction in which Earth's axis is pointed changes over time.

**1824** J. A. Adhemar studies d'Alembert's ideas and suggests that the change in axis direction is responsible for ice ages.

**Today** Dr. Raymo finds evidence in rocks and sediment on the ocean floor that supports Milankovitch's hypothesis.

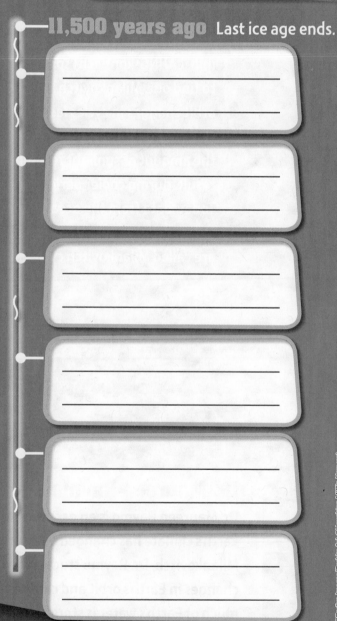

Milankovitch cycles predict ice ages as a result of Earth's motion in space.

**11,500 years ago** Last ice age ends.

_____
_____

_____
_____

_____
_____

_____
_____

_____
_____

_____
_____

# Think About It!

Where should the following event be placed on the timeline?
**Scientists find data that conflict with Milankovitch's hypothesis, which falls into disfavor.**

_____

**Essential Question**

# What Are Moon Phases?

## Engage Your Brain!

Find the answer to the following question in this lesson and record it here.

What do you observe about the moon in the night sky?

_____

_____

_____

_____

## Active Reading

### Lesson Vocabulary

List the terms. As you learn about each one, make notes in the Interactive Glossary.

_____

_____

_____

### Sequence

Many ideas in this lesson are connected by a sequence, or order, that describes the steps in a process. Active readers stay focused on sequence when they mark the transition from one step in a process to another.

# Our Moon

Neil Armstrong was the first person to walk on Earth's moon. He said of the moon, "The surface is fine and powdery. I can pick it up with my toe."

The moon is Earth's satellite. A satellite is an object that moves around another larger object in space. Earth's moon is the largest and brightest object in the night sky. It looks large because it is close to Earth. But the moon is small compared to Earth. It is only about one-fourth the size of Earth. The moon has no air, wind, or liquid water. We see the moon because light from the sun reflects from it and back to Earth.

The pull of Earth's gravity keeps the moon in its orbit around Earth. We see only one side of the moon from Earth. That is because the moon takes the same amount of time to rotate once as it does to orbit Earth once.

We can see the moon at night (small photo) and sometimes during the day.

# Moon and Earth

Compare the moon and Earth. How are they alike? How are they different?
Complete the Venn diagram below.

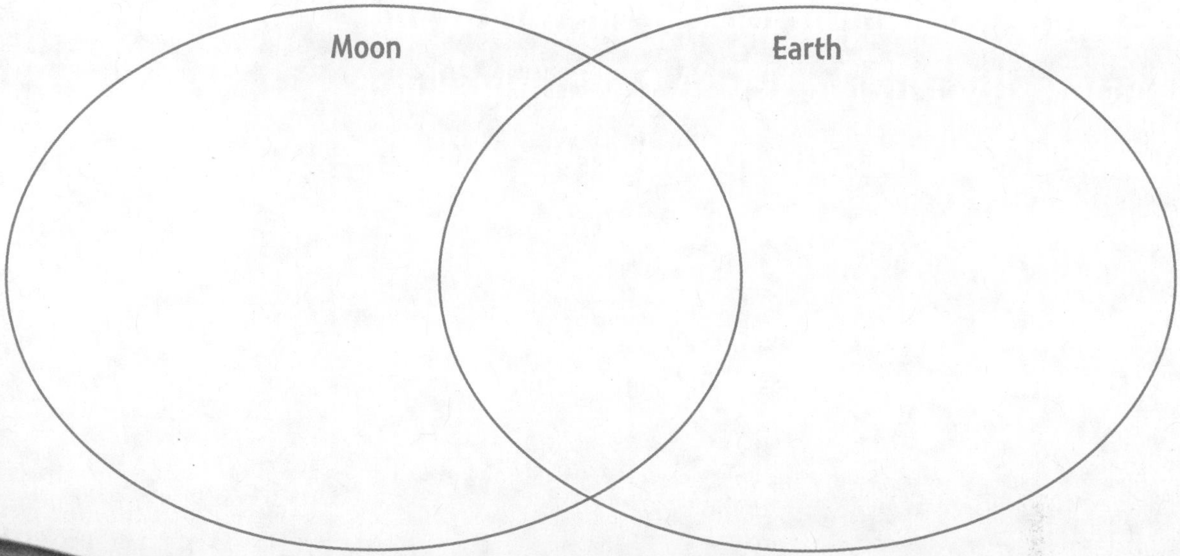

Moon         Earth

Rocks and chunks of debris from space slammed into the moon and formed its many craters. Craters, or pits in the ground, cover the moon's rocky surface.

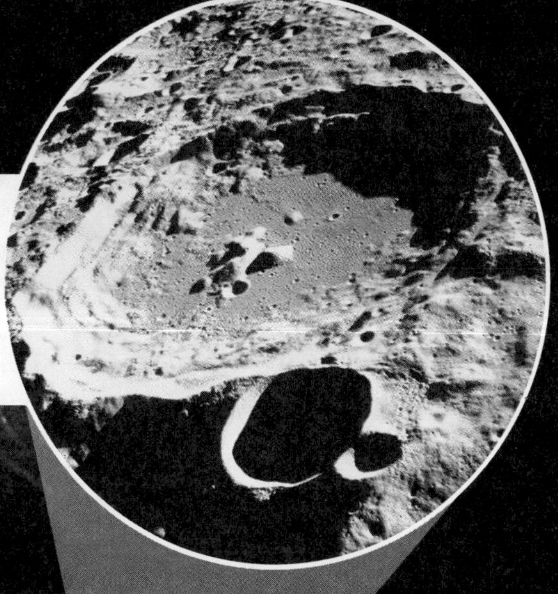

There are mountains and large, flat plains. The plains on the moon's surface are called *maria* [mah•REE•uh], a Latin word meaning "seas."

# Moon Phases

One night, you might look at the moon and see a tiny sliver in the sky. A few nights later, you might see a bright, round circle. What makes the moon look so different?

**Active Reading** As you read the last paragraph, write numbers next to the sentences to show the sequence of moon phases.

As Earth orbits the sun, the moon also orbits Earth. The moon reflects light from the sun. That is the light we see from Earth. As the moon travels in its orbit, different amounts of the moon's lit side can be seen from Earth.

**First Quarter**

**New Moon**

During the new moon phase, the moon is between Earth and the sun. We can't see the moon at all. During a first quarter moon, we see one-half of the moon's lit side.

The moon's shape does not change. The changes in the appearance of the moon's shape are known as **moon phases**.

You know that sunlight reflects from the moon to Earth. Yet the sun lights only half of the moon at any time. The motions of Earth and the moon are responsible for the phases you see. As the moon revolves around Earth, the amount of the lit part that we see from Earth changes. These different amounts of the moon's lighted side are the different phases of the moon.

Each phase of the moon has a different shape. It takes about 1 month for the moon to complete all of its phases. Then the cycle repeats.

During the new moon phase, we can't see the moon. That is because the lit part of the moon faces away from Earth. As the moon moves in its orbit around Earth, we see more of the moon's lit part. We see a full moon when all of the lit part of the moon faces Earth. Then we see less and less of the lit part again.

# Do the Math!
## Estimate Fractions and Percentages

What fraction and percent of the moon's lit side is seen during each phase? Complete the table.

|  | Full moon | First quarter | New moon | Third quarter |
|---|---|---|---|---|
| Fraction |  | $\frac{1}{2}$ |  |  |
| Percent |  | 50% |  |  |

Full Moon

Third Quarter

The lit portion grows larger until we see a full moon. This happens when Earth is between the moon and the sun. As the moon continues in its orbit, we see less of its lit portion. When it is half lit again, it is a third quarter moon.

# Lunar and Solar Calendars

For thousands of years, people used the phases of the moon to make calendars and track time. These are called lunar calendars. Earth's orbit around the sun also has been used to make calendars and track time. These are called solar calendars.

## The Chinese Zodiac Calendar

The Chinese zodiac calendar is based in part on the phases of the moon. Twelve animals stand for cycles of time on the calendar. Some of these animals are the tiger, rabbit, dragon, and snake. Each year is also given an animal name. For example, in 2026, it will be the "Year of the Horse." The year 2027 will be the "Year of the Sheep".

**Chinese New Year comes sometime between late January and early February. It is celebrated with fancy dragon costumes.**

The Aztec calendar is based on Earth's orbit around the sun. Each part of the calendar has colorful animals or symbols. These symbols marked important times of the year, such as when to plant crops.

## APRIL

| Sunday | Monday | Tuesday | Wednesday | Thursday | Friday | Saturday |
|--------|--------|---------|-----------|----------|--------|----------|
| | | | 1 | 2 | 3 | 4 |
| 5 | 6 | 7 | 8 | 9 | 10 | 11 |
| 12 | 13 | 14 | 15 | 16 | 17 | 18 |
| 19 | 20 | 21 | 22 | 23 | 24 | 25 |
| 26 | 27 | 28 | 29 | 30 | | |

## New Year's Day

In the United States, New Year's Day is always January 1. In China, it is on the day of the new moon. Why do you think New Year's Day always falls on a different day each year in China?

_____

_____

_____

Our modern calendar is based on Earth's orbit around the sun. Each month is based roughly on the moon's phases. Once in a while, there are two full moons in one month.

When you're done, use the answer key to check and revise your work.

**The idea web below summarizes the lesson. Complete the web.**

## Summarize

1.

2.

rocky surface

3.

The Moon's Features

Phases of the Moon

New Moon

6.

4.

5.

Answer Key: 1–3. Sample answers: no air or liquid water; craters; mountains and flat plains; revolves around Earth 4. First Quarter Moon 5. Full Moon 6. Third Quarter Moon

Name _____

# Word Play

**1** Look at the picture and word clues. Write the answer to each clue on the blanks.

**1.**

The picture shows a first

__ ◯ __ ◯ __ __ __ moon.
   1     2

**2.**

People use this to track time.

__ __ ◯ __ ◯ __
     3     4

**3.**

These are pictures of some moon

__ __ __ __ ◯◯ .
        5  6

**4.**

An object that moves around another larger object in space is a

__ ◯◯ __ __ __ __ __ __ .
  7  8

Look at the letters in circles. Match the letter with the number below each space to solve the riddle.

**What kind of cartoons does the moon watch?**

__ __ __ __ __ __ __ __ __ __
3  1  4  7  2   8  1  4  5  6

# Apply Concepts

**2** Draw a picture of the sun and the moon. Add lines to show light rays from the sun. Shade the part of the moon that is dark.

**3** Look at the calendar. One of the moon's phases is missing for January 10th. Draw and label the missing moon phase in the space below.

_____

**4** Explain why you drew the moon the way you did in Question 3.

_____

_____

_____

Take It Home!

With an adult, use a pair of binoculars to observe the moon. Can you see craters? Draw a picture of what you see.

Name _____

Essential Question

# How Does the Moon Move Around Earth?

## Set a Purpose

What do you think you will learn from this activity?

_____

_____

_____

## Think About the Procedure

How does the moon have to move for its marked side to always face Earth?

_____

_____

_____

The student holding the flashlight also moves. Why? How is this different from what we know about the sun?

_____

_____

_____

_____

## Record Your Data

In the space below, draw the position of the marked side of the moon with respect to Earth and the sun. Show the shaded and lit portions of the moon.

**Position 1**

**Position 2**

**Position 3**

**Position 4**

## Draw Conclusions

Where does the moon get its light?

_____

_____

What happens to the visible part of the
moon as it moves through its orbit?

_____

_____

_____

The moon turns as it orbits Earth. When
does the moon complete a full rotation?

_____

_____

_____

## Analyze and Extend

1. Draw the moon phase that takes place
   when the moon is between Earth and
   the sun. Describe how this moon phase
   would look from Earth.

   ┌─────────────────────────────┐
   │                             │
   │                             │
   │                             │
   │                             │
   │                             │
   │                             │
   │                             │
   └─────────────────────────────┘

   _____

   _____

2. Why does the amount of sunlight on
   the moon seem to change?

   _____

   _____

   _____

   _____

3. A friend thinks that Earth's shadow
   causes moon phases. Use evidence
   from this investigation to explain why
   your friend's idea is incorrect.

   _____

   _____

   _____

   _____

   _____

4. The same friend also thinks that the
   moon has a dark side where the sun
   never shines. What evidence would
   you use to explain why your friend's
   idea is incorrect?

   _____

   _____

   _____

   _____

5. What other questions would you like
   to ask about moon phases?

   _____

   _____

   _____

**Essential Question**

# What Are the Planets in Our Solar System?

## Engage Your Brain!

Find the answer to the following question in this lesson and record it here.

How is Jupiter different from Earth?

_____

_____

_____

_____

## Active Reading

### Lesson Vocabulary

List the terms. As you learn about each one, make notes in the Interactive Glossary.

_____

_____

### Compare and Contrast

Many ideas in this lesson are connected because they describe comparisons and contrasts—how things are alike and how they are different. Terms that signal comparisons include *alike, also, same as,* and *similar to.* Terms that signal contrasts include *but, however,* and *on the other hand.* Active readers focus on comparisons and contrasts when they ask, How are these things alike? How are these things different?

# In Our Corner of Space

You are familiar with Earth, the sun, and the moon. What other objects are part of the solar system?

**Active Reading** As you read this page, circle the names of smaller objects in the solar system.

Earth and millions of other objects make up our solar system. A **solar system** is made up of a star and the planets and other bodies that revolve around it. The sun is the star at the center of our solar system.

Our solar system has eight planets—Mercury, Venus, Earth, Mars, Jupiter, Saturn, Uranus, and Neptune. A **planet** is a large round body that revolves around a star in a clear orbit.

The solar system has smaller objects, too. Dwarf planets, such as Pluto, are nearly round bodies whose orbits cross those of other bodies. An asteroid is made of rock and metal. Most asteroids are in the *asteroid belt* between Mars and Jupiter. A *comet* is a ball of rock and frozen gases. Astronomers think that trillions of comets orbit the sun in areas at the edge of the solar system.

Distances in the solar system are measured using the *astronomical unit*, or AU. One AU is the distance between Earth and the sun—about 150 million km.

Asteroids are large rocks left over from when the solar system was formed. Most asteroids have an irregular shape. The largest known asteroid had a diameter of almost 1,000 km (620 mi).

Mars

Earth

Venus

Mercury

The *inner planets* are those closest to the sun—Mercury, Venus, Earth, and Mars. Earth is the largest and densest of the inner planets.

Images not to scale

**Neptune**

**Uranus**

**Saturn**

**Jupiter**

The *outer planets* are those farthest from the sun—Jupiter, Saturn, Uranus, and Neptune. These planets are the largest in our solar system. In fact, Jupiter is larger than all of the other planets combined.

As a comet approaches the sun, the sun's heat turns the comet's frozen parts into gas. This gas may look like a fiery tail streaming away from the sun. Comets are less than 10 km (6.2 mi) across but can have tails that are up to 100,000 km (62,137 mi) long.

## Compare Planets and Dwarf Planets

In the space below, compare planets and dwarf planets.

_____

_____

_____

# Planets
# Near and Far

The solar system's planets are divided into two groups. How and why are the planets in each group different?

After the sun had formed, a cloud of rock, dust, and gas remained around it. The planets in the solar system were formed from these leftover materials.

The part of the cloud closest to the sun was also the warmest. In this area, rock and metal bits clumped together to form the rocky bodies that became the inner planets. These planets developed small diameters and thin atmospheres.

The outer solar system was much colder. Gases formed icy particles in the extreme cold. The cold gases and icy particles clumped together to form huge balls of gas and ice that became the outer planets.

Mars

Earth

Venus

Mercury

## Inner Planets

The inner planets are the smallest and warmest planets in our solar system. They have hard surfaces made of rock. The inner planets revolve around the sun more quickly than the outer planets. They are the only planets where probes from Earth have landed.

Images not to scale

Neptune

Uranus

Saturn

Jupiter

Images not
to scale

## Outer Planets

The outer planets are giant
balls of gases. These planets
are larger and less dense
than the inner planets. They
rotate quickly, which makes
for a short day, but take a
long time to revolve once
around the sun. Unlike the
inner planets, the outer
planets have rings.

Jupiter

Mercury

Compared to the outer planets,
the inner planets are small balls
of rock that have relatively large,
solid cores. The outer planets are
huge balls of gas; some are thought
to have very small, solid cores.

## Do the Math!
### Calculate Diameter

Draw lines on the pictures of Jupiter
and Mercury on this page to show their
diameters.

If Jupiter's diameter is 142,984 km
(88,846 mi) and Mercury's diameter is
4,879 km (3,032 mi), how much bigger
is Jupiter's diameter than Mercury's?

_____

_____

_____

# The Inside Track

The inner planets are Earth's closest neighbors. Sometimes, these planets look like bright stars in the night sky. How are the inner planets alike and different?

**Active Reading** As you read these pages, draw a star next to words or phrases that identify characteristics shared by all of the inner planets.

The inner planets are alike in some ways. They are all small and rocky. They have few moons—or none at all. Still, each planet is unique. Mercury has a thin atmosphere of carbon dioxide with a surface like our moon. Venus has a thick carbon dioxide atmosphere, which makes it boiling hot. Drops of acid fall from Venus's clouds. Mars is dry and freezing cold. Huge dust storms blow across Mars's surface. Only Earth has water, soil, and air to support life.

Images taken by the *Venus Express* probe show one of the more than 1,600 volcanoes on Venus's surface. For a long time, it was hard to study Venus's surface because of the thick clouds hiding it. These same clouds trap heat on Venus, making it the hottest planet.

**Venus**

Mercury is the smallest planet in our solar system. Images taken by the *Messenger* space probe show the deep craters on Mercury's surface. Rocky objects slammed into Mercury, leaving deep scars.

**Mercury**

Images not to scale

The Mars *Rover Spirit* has sent images of Mars's surface back to Earth. Mars's surface has mountains, wide plains, canyons, and volcanoes. Its surface looks red because of the iron oxide in its soil.

**Mars**

**Earth**

Satellite images of Earth show large green areas. Earth is the only planet with visible life, a large supply of liquid water, and an atmosphere most made of nitrogen, oxyg and carbon dioxide.

## Survivor—Mars!

Suppose you have the chance to go to Mars. Think about what Mars is like. Make a list of things you would need to survive on Mars, and explain your choices.

_____

_____

_____

_____

Images not to scale

# The Outside Track

The outer planets are so far away that even the fastest space probes take many years to reach them.

**Active Reading** As you read these pages, underline the sentence that contains the main idea.

**A**stronauts and probes will never land on Jupiter, Saturn, Uranus, or Neptune—the outer planets. The outer planets are very different from the inner planets. These huge planets do not have solid surfaces. They are *gas giants*, made up mostly of gases.

All the outer planets have many moons and are surrounded by rings made of dust, ice, or rock. Jupiter and Saturn are the largest planets in our solar system. Uranus and Neptune are smaller and are the coldest planets.

Jupiter has at least 63 moons. Astronomers think that Europa, one of Jupiter's moons, has an icy surface that covers a cold, slushy ocean. Jupiter's atmosphere is in constant motion. Its Great Red Spot is a swirling storm that has raged for more than 300 years.

**Jupiter**

Images not to scale

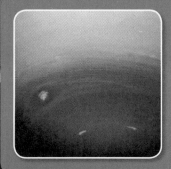

At about 30 AU, Neptune is the planet farthest from the sun. From space, its atmosphere looks blue; sometimes, high white clouds of methane ice crystals blow across Neptune. Physical changes inside Neptune are thought to slightly increase its temperature.

**Neptune**

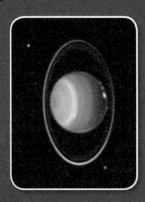

Uranus tilts so far on its axis that it looks as if it's revolving around the sun on its side. Methane gas in its atmosphere gives Uranus its blue color. Uranus is very cold—its temperature is about –215 °C (–355 °F).

**Uranus**

▶ Circle a feature on each planet that may help you identify it.

**Saturn**

Saturn has thousands of rings. Scientists think that these rings are leftover pieces of comets, asteroids, or moons that broke up long ago. Saturn's atmosphere has winds that can blow at speeds of 1,800 km/hr (1,118.5 mi/hr), which is many times faster than Earth's strongest hurricane wind.

Images not to scale

# The Right Spot

Living things like those found on Earth do not exist elsewhere in the solar system, which makes Earth a unique place.

Out of the eight planets in our solar system, only Earth has life as we know it. Why? Scientists think it is because Earth is the only planet within the solar system's life zone. The *life zone* is the region of space where the temperature range allows life to thrive.

Our solar system's life zone begins just outside Venus's orbit and ends before the orbit of Mars. If Earth were outside this zone, it would be either too hot or too cold for life to exist on our planet. Earth sits near the center of the life zone.

Our moon is also within the life zone, yet it has no life. Why? The moon doesn't have an atmosphere or liquid water. Earth's atmosphere does many things to support life. It traps solar energy to keep Earth's temperature comfortable. It contains the gases that most living things need. It also protects living things from harmful solar radiation.

Earth's average temperature is about 13 °C (55 °F). Earth's oceans help maintain this temperature. The oceans store and distribute heat from the sun. Ocean currents carry heat away from the equator and toward the poles. Without the oceans to store and distribute heat from the sun, some places on Earth would be extremely cold or extremely hot.

Venus and Earth are sometimes called sister planets, but Earth supports life and Venus does not. It's all because of Earth's position within the solar system's *life zone*.

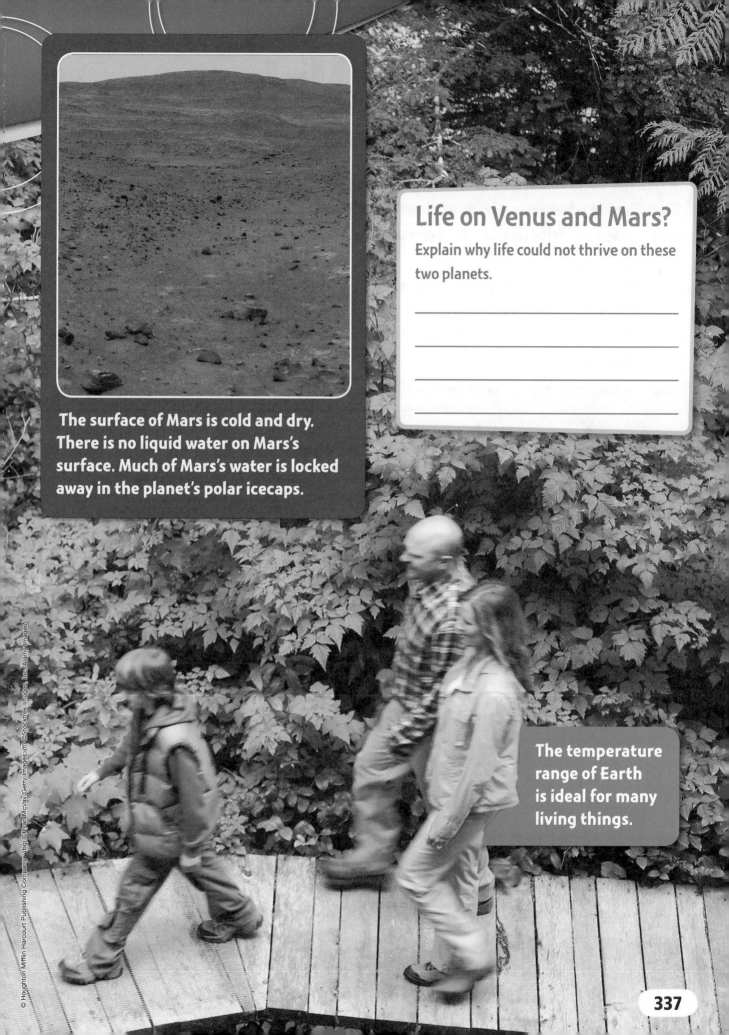

The surface of Mars is cold and dry. There is no liquid water on Mars's surface. Much of Mars's water is locked away in the planet's polar icecaps.

## Life on Venus and Mars?

Explain why life could not thrive on these two planets.

_____

_____

_____

_____

The temperature range of Earth is ideal for many living things.

# Sum It Up!

When you're done, use the answer key to check and revise your work.

**Write the correct word to complete the sentences in the four outer boxes. Then decide whether each set of clues describes the inner planets or the outer planets. Write the correct type of planet in the middle box.**

1. Each planet in this group has many _____ orbiting it.

2. These distant planets are sometimes called _____ .

5. _____

3. Only the planets in this group have _____ around them.

4. Because of their distances from the sun, these planets have lower _____ .

6. Probes have landed on these planets because their surfaces are _____ .

7. Some planets in this group have one or two _____ . Others have none.

10. _____

8. None of the planets in this group has _____ around it.

9. These planets' _____ are smaller than those of the planets in the other group.

Answer Key: 1. moons 2. giants 3. rings 4. temperatures 5. Outer Planets 6. hard 7. moons 8. rings 9. diameters 10. Inner Planets

Name _____

## Word Play

**1** Unscramble the names of each planet and write them on the lines. Then draw a line between each planet's name and the clue that describes it.

 Npueten _____

 yrecruM _____

 sraM _____

 Stnuuar _____

 Etrah _____

sUrnau _____

 ripuJte _____

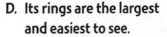 nesVu _____

A. It is the largest planet in the solar system.

B. Its tilt is so great that it seems to revolve on its side.

C. It is the closest planet to the sun.

D. Its rings are the largest and easiest to see.

E. It looks red because of the iron oxide in its soil.

F. Liquid water covers most of its surface.

G. Thick clouds of carbon dioxide make it the hottest planet in the solar system.

H. It is the coldest and windiest planet in the solar system.

# Apply Concepts

**2** Circle the planet that does not belong with the group. Then explain your choice on the lines below.

 Venus

 Mercury

 Mars

 Neptune

_____

_____

**3** Suppose that scientists discover a planet orbiting a star within its life zone. What else might scientists want to know before concluding that this planet could support Earth-like life forms?

_____

_____

_____

_____

_____

_____

**4** Draw a picture of a our solar system. Then identify objects found in the solar system. What are planets?

_____

_____

_____

**Take It Home!**

With a family member, explore NASA's websites to learn more about efforts to detect water on the surface of the moon and Mars. Make a poster or write a report to share your findings with your class.

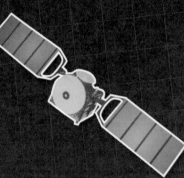

# Space Exploration

Typically, engineering design problems have many solutions. An engineer often needs to find a balance among many trade-offs to get the best solution. A *trade-off* is the giving up of one design feature to make another design feature better. The charts below show trade-off analyses for spacecraft with and without crew. The benefits and drawbacks of some major design features of each kind of mission are shown. You decide which one should blast off.

## Spacecraft with Crew

| Design Feature | Benefit | Drawback |
| --- | --- | --- |
| living space for crew | people onboard to fix problems and run difficult science experiments | greater cost to build and to fuel; increased weight during liftoff (must store air, food, and water) |
| heat shield for reentry to Earth's atmosphere | safe return of crew; reusable ship | more fuel needed; less space for everything else |

## Spacecraft without Crew

| Design Feature | Benefit | Drawback |
| --- | --- | --- |
| smaller, lighter | less fuel needed; costs less to launch | less room for instruments |
| no living space for crew | no need to store air, food, water | no one to fix problems or watch experiments |
| large energy suppy to last many years in space | can learn about faraway objects | spacecraft doesn't return to Earth; it cannot be reused |

## You Decide

Which type of spacecraft works best for space exploration? Use information from the chart to explain your answer.

_____

_____

# Analyze Trade-offs

Engineers think about trade-offs before designing
a spacecraft. Sometimes, the trade-offs lead them to
conclude that a particular solution is not worth trying.

Suppose a crew wants new space suits. Use the features and
trade-offs of the old and new space suits to answer the questions below.

| Old Space Suit | | New Space Suit | |
|---|---|---|---|
| Design Feature | Trade-off | Design Feature | Trade-off |
| thick space suit protects astronaut against extreme temperatures and debris | hard to move around in | thinner space suit lighter and easier to move around in | may not protect as well as the old suit against extreme temperatures or debris |
| sturdy material and strong joints | difficult to put on quickly | has newer technologies built in | all technologies may not have been tested in space |

What is the most important feature of a space suit?

_____

Do you think the benefits of the new space suit outweigh its trade-offs? Why or why not?

_____

_____

_____

# Build On It!

Rise to the engineering design challenge—complete **Design It: Build a Sundial**
on the Inquiry Flipchart.

© Houghton Mifflin Harcourt Publishing Company  (l) ©NASA; (r) ©NASA

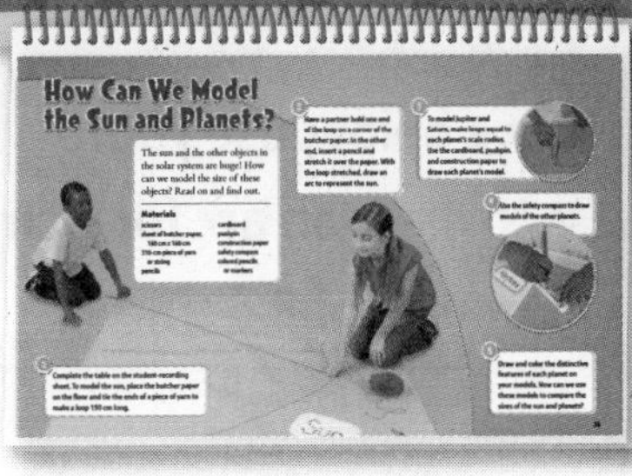

Inquiry Flipchart page 36

Lesson 5
INQUIRY

Name ______________________________

Essential Question

# How Can We Model the Sun and Planets?

## Set a Purpose

**What do you think you will learn from this activity?**

______________________________

______________________________

______________________________

## Think About the Procedure

**The word *scale* has several meanings. What does it mean to make a *scale model* of the sun and planets?**

______________________________

______________________________

______________________________

**You know that diameter is any line that passes through the center of a circle and connects two points on its circumference. Based on Step 1 of the activity, how would you define *radius*?**

______________________________

______________________________

______________________________

## Record Your Data

**Complete the chart below. To find the missing values, divide the scale diameter of each object by 2.**

| Object | Actual Diameter (km) | Scale Diameter (cm) | Scale Radius (cm) |
|---|---|---|---|
| Sun | 1,391,900 | 300.0 | |
| Mercury | 4,880 | 1.0 | |
| Venus | 12,104 | 2.6 | 1.3 |
| Earth | 12,756 | 2.8 | |
| Mars | 6,794 | 1.5 | 0.75 |
| Jupiter | 142,984 | 32.0 | |
| Saturn | 120,536 | 25.0 | 12.5 |
| Uranus | 51,118 | 10.0 | |
| Neptune | 49,532 | 9.8 | 4.9 |

## Draw Conclusions

Which planet has the smallest diameter?

_____

_____

Earth is the largest inner planet. What is Earth's diameter? How does it compare to the diameter of the outer planets?

_____

_____

_____

Jupiter is the largest planet in the solar system. How does Jupiter's diameter compare to the sun's diameter?

_____

_____

## Analyze and Extend

1. Why would a scientist want to model the size of the sun and planets?

_____

_____

_____

2. A section of the circumference of a circle is called an *arc*. In this investigation, why did you use an arc to model the sun and not the planets?

_____

_____

_____

3. In the space below, use your compass to draw an arc for a circle with a diameter of 8.6 cm.

4. If the circle in item 3 were a model of a new planet in the solar system, based on its size alone, to which group of planets would it belong? Explain.

_____

_____

_____

5. Think of other questions you would like to ask about objects in the solar system. Write your questions here.

_____

_____

_____

_____

**344**

© Houghton Mifflin Harcourt Publishing Company   HMH Credits

Name _____

## Vocabulary Review

Use the terms in the box to complete the sentences.

axis
constellation
moon phase
orbit
planet
rotate
solar system

1. A change in the appearance of the moon's shape is known

   as a(n) _____.

2. When things turn like a top, they _____.

3. Earth turns around an imaginary line called

   a(n) _____.

4. The path that one object takes around another object in space

   is its _____.

5. A star and the planets and other objects that revolve around it

   make up a(n) _____.

6. A large round body that revolves around a star in a clear orbit

   is a(n) _____.

7. A group of stars that seems to form a pattern in the night sky

   is a(n) _____.

# Science Concepts

Fill in the letter of the choice that best answers the question.

**8.** The picture below is a two-dimensional model of how Earth moves in space.

How long does it take for Earth to complete one full movement?

(A) 1 day     (C) 1 month

(B) 1 week     (D) 1 year

**9.** A fourth grader in the United States does an experiment in her science class. At the same time, a fourth grader in China is asleep. Why is it daytime in the United States while it is nighttime in China?

(A) Earth's rotation

(B) Earth's revolution

(C) the moon's revolution

(D) Earth's path as it orbits the sun

**10.** In the United States, an August day is usually hotter than a January day. Why is this true?

(A) The sun gives off more heat in the summer.

(B) Earth is closer to the sun in summer and farther away in winter.

(C) Earth's rotation slows down in the summer and speeds up in winter.

(D) Earth's North Pole tilts toward the sun in summer and away from it in winter.

**11.** Which characteristic do all the inner planets in our solar system have?

(A) rings

(B) many moons

(C) lower densities

(D) relatively large cores

**12.** Ashley notices changes in the moon over the course of a month. Which of the following sequences could Ashley have seen?

(A)

Full moon   New moon   Third quarter moon   First quarter moon

(B)

New moon   First quarter moon   Full moon   Third quarter moon

(C)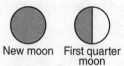

New moon   First quarter moon   New moon   Third quarter moon

(D)

Full moon   New moon   First quarter moon   Third quarter moon

**13.** Some constellations are visible from different places on Earth only during part of the year. Why are these constellations not visible from every location on Earth year-round?

(A) because of the sun's rotation

(B) because of the moon's revolution

(C) because of Earth's rotation

(D) because of Earth's revolution

14. The table below contains data showing how long it takes each planet to make one complete rotation and revolution. The numbers are in Earth days.

| Planet | Time needed to make one complete rotation (Earth days) | Time needed to make one complete revolution (Earth days) |
|---|---|---|
| Mercury | 58.6 | 87.96 |
| Venus | 243.0 | 224.7 |
| Earth | 1.0 | 365.26 |
| Mars | 1.02 | 687.0 |

According to the data table, which one of these statements is correct?

(A) Earth takes less time to orbit the sun than does Mars.

(B) Venus takes more time to orbit the sun than does Mars.

(C) Venus takes less time to orbit the sun than does Mercury.

(D) Mercury takes more time to orbit the sun than does Earth.

15. Each planet in the solar system has its own characteristics. Which set of characteristics describes Mars?

(A) boiling hot; thick clouds

(B) iron oxide in soil; fourth planet from the sun

(C) made of frozen gases; stormy atmosphere

(D) similar size to Earth; atmosphere rich in carbon dioxide

16. The same side of the moon always faces Earth. Why is this?

(A) Half the moon faces the sun.

(B) The moon does not rotate like Earth does.

(C) The moon's revolution and rotation are about the same length.

(D) Earth blocks part of the sunlight that shines on the moon's surface.

17. Pluto was once classified as a planet. Now it is classified as a dwarf planet. What is one reason for this change?

(A) Pluto is too big to be a planet.

(B) Pluto has a core that is too small.

(C) Pluto's orbit crosses the orbit of another body.

(D) Pluto is too far from the sun to be in the solar system.

18. Which of the following correctly lists the planets of the solar system in order of distance from the sun?

(A) Jupiter, Saturn, Uranus, Neptune, Mercury, Venus, Earth, Mars

(B) Mercury, Venus, Earth, Mars, Jupiter, Saturn, Uranus, Neptune

(C) Mars, Venus, Earth, Mercury, Jupiter, Saturn, Uranus, Neptune

(D) Venus, Mercury, Earth, Saturn, Jupiter, Neptune, Mars, Uranus

# Apply Inquiry and Review the Big Idea

Write the answers to these questions.

19. The diagram below shows Earth, the moon, and the sun.
This diagram is not drawn to scale.

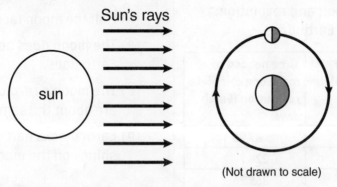

Sun's rays

sun

(Not drawn to scale)

Use the diagram to explain why you can see the moon from Earth.

_____

_____

_____

20. Scientists classify the planets in our solar system into two groups—
inner planets and outer planets. The planets in each group share several
characteristics. List four ways in which the inner planets are similar. Then
list four ways that the outer planets are similar.

Inner Planets: _____

_____

Outer Planets: _____

_____

21. Astronomers before Copernicus and Galileo knew about Earth's moon.
They also knew about the planets Mars, Jupiter, and Saturn. Do you think
they knew about the moons of Mars, Jupiter, and Saturn? Explain your answer.

_____

_____

_____

# UNIT 7

# Properties of Matter

## Big Idea

The physical properties of matter can be used to identify it even if it has changed states or has been mixed with other matter.

## I Wonder Why

Snow, steam, and water vapor are all forms of the same type of matter—water. How do they differ? *Turn the page to find out.*

**Here's Why** Everything around you is matter. Color, mass, and volume are physical properties of matter. Snow, steam, and water vapor are all water in different states, or phases, of matter. In each of these states, water has distinct physical properties.

In this unit, you will explore the Big Idea, the Essential Questions, and the Investigations on the Inquiry Flipchart.

Levels of Inquiry Key ■ DIRECTED ■ GUIDED ■ INDEPENDENT

Track Your Progress

**Big Idea** The physical properties of matter can be used to identify it even if it has changed states or has been mixed with other matter.

## Essential Questions

○ Now I Get the Big Idea!

**Science Notebook**

Before you begin each lesson, be sure to write your thoughts about the Essential Question.

**Essential Question**

# What Are Physical Properties of Matter?

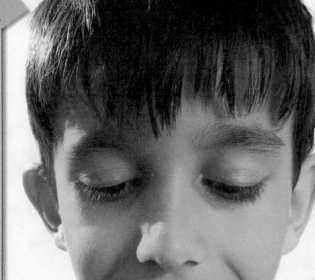

## Engage Your Brain!

Find the answer to the following question in this lesson and record it here.

How is the chocolate shell on the outside of the bar different from the ice cream on the inside?

_____

_____

_____

_____

_____

## Active Reading

### Lesson Vocabulary

List the terms. As you learn about each one, make notes in the Interactive Glossary.

_____   _____

_____   _____

_____

### Main Idea and Details

Detailed sentences give information about a topic. The information may be examples, features, characteristics, or facts. Active readers stay focused on the topic when they ask, What fact or information does this sentence add to the topic?

# Use Your Senses

## See

You can see shapes in the sandwich. What other property can you see?

_____

You can use your senses to describe a sandwich. What does it look, taste, and smell like?

## Hear

When you bite into a sandwich, you might hear the crunch of the crust.

## Matter

Is this sandwich made of matter? Anything that takes up space and has mass is **matter**. A characteristic of matter that you can observe or measure directly is a **physical property**.

The amount of matter in an object is its **mass.** You use a pan balance to measure mass. Less massive objects are measured in grams (g). More massive objects are measured in kilograms (kg).

## Taste

You can taste sweet, sour, salty, and bitter. Which would you taste in this sandwich?

_____

_____

## Smell

You may smell mustard, onion, or pepper. You may even smell the fresh bread.

## Feel

The bread feels soft. The dressing may feel oily. Salt and pepper feel grainy.

You start by placing the object to be measured on one side of the balance. You add known masses to the other pan until the sides balance. You add up the masses to find the mass of the object.

# Describe That!

You can use all the words you see here to describe matter. You can use your senses to find an object's hardness, color, taste, size, shape, odor, or texture.

**Active Reading** As you read these two pages, circle words or phrases that signal a detail about physical properties.

## Hardness

A walnut shell is hard. The grapes are soft. Hardness describes how easily something can bend or dent.

## Size

A silver dollar takes up more space than other coins. Pennies are larger than dimes.

## Color

The words we use for color describe the way light bounces off an object. What colors do you see below?

_____

## Taste

Crackers are salty. Candy can taste sweet or sour. Can you think of something that tastes bitter?

_____

► List five properties that describe this banana.

_____

_____

_____

_____

## Texture

Texture describes what something feels like. The pinecone has a rough texture. The leaf feels smooth.

## Odor

These shoes are stinky! Perfume has a nice smell. How can odor tell you if milk has gone bad?

_____

## Shape

Objects can be long, short, flat, tall, or irregular like these keys. Shape describes an object's form. How can you describe the MP3 player?

_____

# Pump Up the Volume!

You can measure mass with a pan balance. What is another property of matter that we can use tools to measure?

**Active Reading** As you read these two pages, underline the definition of *volume*. Circle units used to measure volume.

## Volume

**Volume** is how much space an object takes up. The beaker on the left measures the volume of water in milliliters (mL). The beaker on the right measures the volume of an object with an irregular shape plus the volume of the water. To find the volume of just the orange, you must use subtraction:

$$\left\{ \begin{array}{l} \text{volume of water and orange} \\ -\ \text{volume of water} \\ \hline \text{volume of orange} \end{array} \right\}$$

# Do the Math!

## Measure the Volume of Objects

**A**

2 cm

5 cm    4 cm

**B**

3 cm

3 cm    3 cm

## Find It!

The volume of a rectangular solid is found by multiplying the width by the length by the height. Find the volume for each box. The units are cubic centimeters.

Volume of Box A:

Volume of Box B:

To find the volume of both boxes together, you add their individual volumes.

A+B =

## Displacement

The dog in this tub takes up space. To make room for him, water was pushed out of the tub.

# Don't Be So Dense!

Why does the hook sink? Why doesn't it float? You must use mass and volume to find the answers.

Density is a physical property of matter. It tells how much space (volume) a certain amount (mass) of matter takes up. In other words, **density** is the amount of matter present in a certain volume of a substance.

Density indicates how close together the particles in an object are. The density of a substance is always the same, no matter how much of the substance there is. A small piece of an eraser, for example, has the same density as a whole eraser.

## This Part Floats

Objects that are less dense than water float. This fishing float is made of plastic.

## This Part Sinks

The hook and weights are metal. The density of metal is greater than water.

► Name three objects that are more dense than water.

_____

_____

foam

sand

pumice

obsidian

## Different Densities

The density of the foam balls is different than the density of sand. Which is less dense? How do you know?

_____

_____

_____

_____

## More About Density

These rocks have different properties. One rock is more dense than the other. Which rock has particles that are closer together? Which rock has the greater density?

_____

_____

_____

# Let's Sort Things Out

## Shape

Study this example. Then sort using the other properties!

round

rectangular

other

## Mass

## Texture

Imagine going into a store or a library and finding that nothing is organized. How would you find anything? How can you find your homework in a messy backpack? Organizing makes life easier. Sorting things helps us find things faster.

We can use properties to sort everything, including food, books, and clothes. The items shown are at the bottom of a closet. Sort them by each of the properties listed.

▶ Name another property you could use to sort these items.

_____

Color ⬭──────────────────────────

Odor ⬭──────────────────────────

Hardness ⬭──────────────────────────

# Sum It Up!

When you're done, use the answer key to check and revise your work.

**Use the information in the summary to complete the graphic organizer.**

## Summarize

All matter has physical properties. Physical properties can also be called characteristics. Some properties can be described by using your senses. You can feel hardness and see shape or color. You can feel texture and smell odor. Other properties can be measured using tools. You can measure volume with a graduated cylinder. You can measure mass with a pan balance. All matter has density. To measure an object's density, you must know its mass and volume.

[1] Main Idea: All matter has _____.

[2] Detail: Some properties can be

_____

_____

_____.

[3] An example of one of these properties is

_____

_____

_____.

[4] Other properties must be

_____

_____

_____.

[5] An example of one of these properties is

_____

_____

_____.

[6] To find an object's density, you divide its

_____

_____

_____.

[7] by its

_____

_____

_____.

Answer Key: 1. physical properties. 2. described by using your senses 3. Sample answers: hardness, color, shape, texture, and odor. 4. measured 5. Sample answers: mass, volume 6. mass 7. volume

Name _____

## Word Play

**1** Which word describes each photo best? Use each word only once.

| | | |
|---|---|---|
| mass | volume | density |
| hard | size | shape |
| texture | odor | taste |

_____  _____  _____

_____  _____  _____

 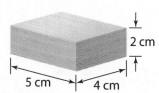 

_____  _____  _____

# Apply Concepts

2

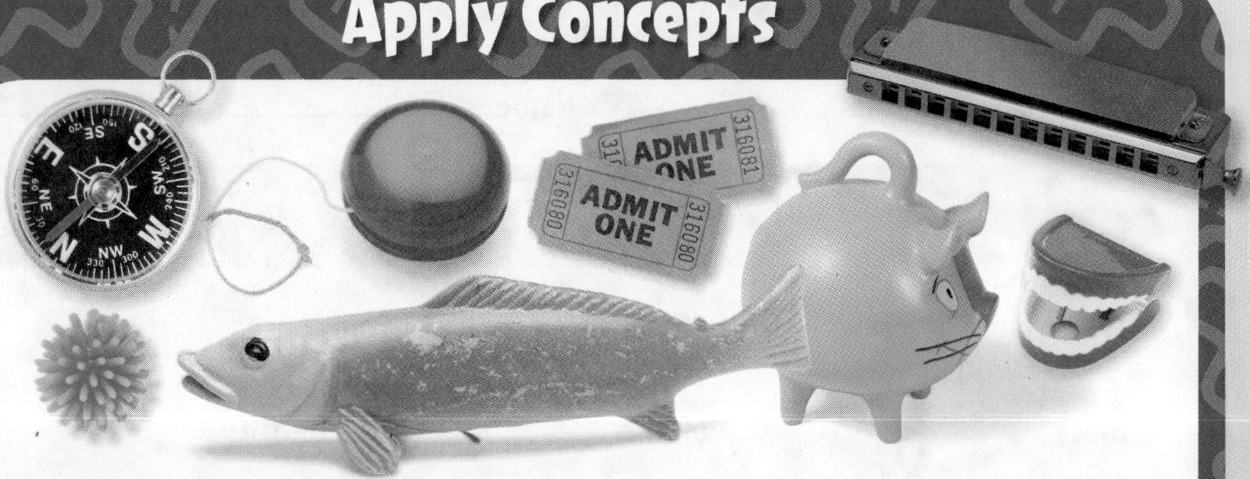


Use the chart below to sort the objects into two groups. Label the groups at the top of the chart.

| | |
|---|---|
| | |
| | |

What properties did you use to sort the objects?

______________________________________________

______________________________________________

Can you sort the same objects into three groups?
Don't forget to label the groups at the top of your chart.

| | | |
|---|---|---|
| | | |
| | | |

Did you use the same properties to sort the objects the second time?

______________________________________________

**3** Look at each pair of objects. Tell which one has the greater mass, volume, or density.

greater mass?

greater volume?

greater density?

_____   _____   _____

**4** Choose a type of matter that you had for breakfast today. List as many physical properties as you can to describe it. Trade your list with a partner, and see if you can identify the matter your partner chose based on its properties.

_____

_____

_____

_____

_____

_____

**5** Work with a group to make a list of ten favorite television shows, songs, or movies. Tell how you can sort them into groups.

_____

_____

_____

_____

_____

_____

**6** How could you use physical properties to sort the objects in a desk drawer?

_____

_____

_____

_____

_____

_____

_____

_____

**Take It Home!**

Share with your family what you have learned about properties of matter. With a family member, name properties of matter you observe at mealtime or in different places in your home.

Name _____

Essential Question

# How Are Physical Properties Observed?

## Set a Purpose
**What skills will you learn from this investigation?**

_____

_____

_____

_____

_____

_____

## Think About the Procedure
**How can you find the mass of an object?**

_____

_____

_____

_____

_____

_____

_____

**Why do you add up the masses on the other pan?**

_____

_____

_____

## Record Your Data
**Make a table in which you record your results.**

## Draw Conclusions

What are three ways that you can sort the objects?

_____

_____

_____

_____

_____

## Analyze and Extend

1. Why did you have to use a tool to help you observe an object's mass?

_____

_____

_____

_____

2. What other tool could you use to sort items? What information can you get with this tool?

_____

_____

_____

_____

3. How can sorting objects help you in everyday life?

_____

_____

_____

_____

_____

4. Did all the groups in your class sort objects in the same way? What are some ways they used?

_____

_____

_____

_____

_____

5. What other questions would you like to ask about sorting objects by physical properties?

_____

_____

_____

_____

# Ask a Materials Scientist

Did you know that these objects are all made from recycled plastic? Materials scientists think of new ways to use old materials.

## Now It's Your Turn!

What material would you like to invent or improve? What would the material do?

_____

_____

_____

_____

_____

_____

**Q.** What does a materials scientist do?

**A.** We invent new materials or improve existing materials. We might work to develop new types of paint, plastic, fabric, cardboard, or any other material you can name.

**Q.** What is an example of a material that materials scientists helped develop?

**A.** Artificial fleece is one example. We can make fleece from recycled plastic bottles that are cut apart, treated with chemicals, and then woven into fibers.

**Q.** How has your work changed in recent years?

**A.** More than ever before, scientists are working in teams. A materials scientist might work closely with experts in life science, physical science, or computer science. Everyone shares his or her knowledge and skills to reach a common goal.

Materials scientists study properties of matter. These scientists test materials to find out how strong they are and whether they stretch, bend, or resist heat.

# Introducing the New...

Which material described below would you use to make a frying pan? Give reasons for using or not using each one.

Wood is strong, hard, and can last many years. You can cut, chop, or glue it. Wood burns.

_____

_____

Plastic is strong and lightweight. It can be flexible or keep its shape. Plastic burns.

_____

_____

Metal can be heated to a high temperature without burning or changing shape.

_____

_____

Glass is strong and holds its shape. It can be heated without burning or changing shape.

_____

_____

## Think About It!

Hook-and-loop fastener is a type of two-layer tape often used to fasten things, such as shoes. The hooks on one layer stick to the loops on the other layer. How could you make this material better?

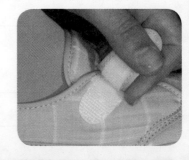

_____

_____

Name _____

**Essential Question**

# What Is Conservation of Mass?

The **law of conservation of mass** says that you cannot make or destroy matter. You can change matter into a new form. However, the new form will have the same amount of mass as the old form.

## Set a Purpose

What do you expect to show in this experiment?

_____

_____

_____

_____

_____

## Think About the Procedure

How can you change the object?

_____

_____

_____

_____

_____

## Record Your Data

Make a table in which you record your results.

Was the mass of the whole object the same as the mass of the object broken apart?

_____

_____

_____

## Draw Conclusions

How is this investigation a good example of the law of conservation of mass?

_____

_____

_____

_____

_____

_____

_____

_____

## Analyze and Extend

1. Write the law of conservation of mass in your own words. Can you think of another example of this law?

_____

_____

_____

_____

_____

_____

2. Scientists often have to be creative when planning investigations. What is another way that you could show the law of conservation of mass?

_____

_____

_____

_____

_____

_____

_____

_____

_____

3. What other questions would you like to ask about the law of conservation of mass?

_____

_____

_____

_____

_____

_____

_____

**Essential Question**

# What Are the States of Water?

## 🧠 Engage Your Brain!

Find the answer to the following question in this lesson and record it here.

How is the snow in this picture like an ice cube?

_____

_____

_____

_____

## Active Reading

### Lesson Vocabulary

List the terms. As you learn about each one, make notes in the Interactive Glossary.

_____ _____

_____ _____

_____ _____

_____

### Compare and Contrast

Many ideas in this lesson are connected because they explain comparisons and contrasts—how things are alike and how they are different. Active readers stay focused on comparisons and contrasts when they ask themselves, How are these things alike? How are they different?

# Solids, Liquids, and Gases

Matter exists in different forms. The air around us is a gas. The water we drink is a liquid. Your book is a solid.

**Active Reading** As you read these two pages, underline the contrasting characteristics of each state of matter.

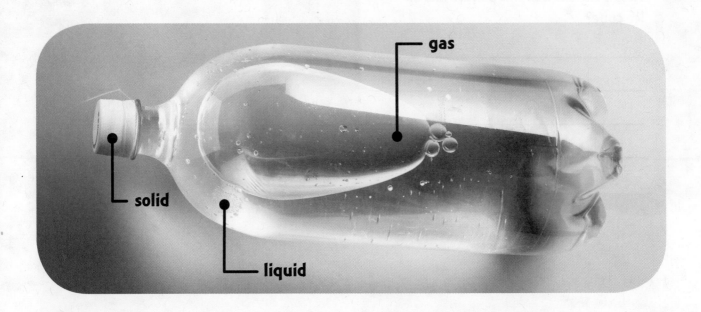

gas

solid

liquid

Solids, liquids, and gases are three **states of matter**. Most matter on Earth is classified as one of these forms.

A **solid** has a definite volume and shape. Your desk, book, pencil, and chair are all solids. Solids stay solid unless something, such as heat, changes them.

A **liquid** has a definite volume but not a definite shape. A liquid takes the shape of whatever container holds it. Water, shampoo, and fruit juice are liquids.

A **gas** doesn't have a definite volume or shape. It expands to take up all the space in a container. If you blow up a balloon, you can see that air spreads out to fill the space. The air we breathe is a mixture of gases.

► Label each item as a solid, a liquid, or a gas.

helmet

sweat

breath

teeth

outside of bottle

water inside bottle

bone

muscle

outside of ball

inside of ball

You are nearly 70% water! The rest of your body is made of gases such as oxygen and solids such as fats.

# Water's Forms

Water can be a solid, a liquid, or a gas. This ice cube is solid water. It melts into a liquid. When water is a gas, it is called water vapor.

Water is made of tiny particles. We can learn what state water is in by knowing how fast the particles in it move.

## Solid

The particles in solids vibrate in place. The particles in the solid form of most substances are closer than those in the liquid form. Water is an exception—the water particles in ice are farther apart than in liquid water.

## Liquid

Liquid water has a definite volume but not a definite shape. Pouring water from a glass into a bowl changes its shape, but not its volume.

The particles in liquids move around more than particles in solids do. The particles slide past one another.

## Gas

The air around the ice cube has water vapor in it. We can't see the water vapor, but it's there. A gas doesn't have a definite volume or shape.

Particles in a gas are far apart. They are much farther apart than the particles in a liquid. They move very quickly in all directions.

▶ Use what you have learned to fill in the chart.

|  | Physical Properties | How We Use It |
|---|---|---|
| ice |  |  |
| liquid water |  |  |
| water vapor | no definite volume or shape | steam cleaning |

## Freezing

At a certain temperature, water can freeze as heat energy is removed. Particles slow down and begin to lock into place. Water changes from a liquid to a solid. A **change of state** occurs when matter changes from one state to another.

## Melting

Adding heat energy causes ice to melt. Particles speed up until they overcome the attractions that hold them in place. Water melts when it changes from a solid to a liquid.

# Water Changes Form

Anything made out of snow will melt if it gains enough heat energy. Energy from the sun causes the snow to change to a liquid.

**Active Reading** As you read these two pages, compare changes of state. Draw a circle around changes that happen when heat is added.

## Evaporation

When heat energy is added to water, its particles speed up. Particles that gain enough energy enter the air as water vapor. **Evaporation** is the process by which a liquid changes into a gas. Water evaporates from oceans, lakes, and rivers every day.

## Condensation

When heat energy is removed from a gas, its particles slow down and clump together. **Condensation** is the process by which a gas changes into a liquid. Clouds form when water vapor condenses on particles of dust in the air.

_____
Liquid to solid
Energy removed

_____
Gas to liquid
_____

▶ Fill in the missing information to describe each change of state.

_____
Energy added

_____
Liquid to gas
Energy added

# Sum It Up!

When you're done, use the answer key to check and revise your work.

**Write the vocabulary term that matches each photo and caption.**

**1**

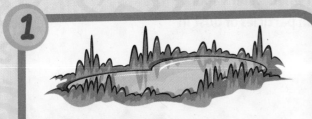

_____

The sun's heat will make this water change to a gas.

**2**

_____

These particles move very quickly and spread out in all directions.

**3**

_____

The water in this bottle has a definite volume and takes the shape of its container.

**4**

_____

This happens when water changes form.

## Summarize

**Fill in the missing words to tell about the states of matter.**

Water as a solid has a definite [5] _____ and [6] _____.

The particles vibrate in place. Liquid water does not have a definite [7] _____.

The particles [8] _____ past each other. The air around ice

has water [9] _____ in it. Since it's a gas, its particles are very far apart.

Water's changing from a liquid to a solid is [10] _____.

Adding [11] _____ can make ice melt. It also can make water change from

a liquid to a gas. This is called [12] _____. Water's changing from a gas to a

liquid is called [13] _____.

Answer Key: 1. evaporation 2. gas 3. liquid 4. change of state 5. volume/shape 6. volume/shape
7. shape 8. slide 9. vapor 10. freezing 11. heat 12. evaporation 13. condensation

# Word Play

Name _____

**1** Unscramble these words. Use the highlighted letters to find the answer below.

sag

disol

qiludi

stianodocnne

rvapnotieao

ngecha fo ttase

ttases fo tmaert

tware

povra

We can find out what state water is in by finding how fast these move. What are they?

_____

Draw a star next to each word that names a state of matter.

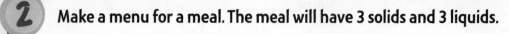

**2** Make a menu for a meal. The meal will have 3 solids and 3 liquids.

Solids                           Liquids

_____          _____

_____          _____

_____          _____

**3** Draw and label a diagram to show what happens to the particles of a substance as it changes from a solid to a liquid to a gas.

**4** Name an example of condensation.

_____

**5** Name an example of evaporation.

_____

**Take It Home!**

Make "Sunshine on a Stick"! Put an ice cube tray filled with orange juice into the freezer. When partly frozen, place a toothpick in each section. When the juice is a solid, you can eat it off the toothpicks!

# Baby, It's Cold Inside
## Refrigeration

Have you ever thought about how refrigeration has changed the way we live? We can store foods without having them rot as quickly. Spoiled foods can make people ill.

### 1920s

In the 1920s, electric refrigerators became available for home use. The inside of this refrigerator stayed cold without needing blocks of ice. It used an electric motor and a gas compressor to remove heat from its wooden or metal box.

### 1900s

By the early 1900s, many homes had iceboxes. Ice was placed in the bottom to cool the air inside the box. It became easier to cool food for longer periods of time until it could be used. These iceboxes were like coolers we use today but larger.

### 1800s

People put food on blocks of ice to keep it cold. The ice was cut from lakes or ponds, packed in straw, and stored in warehouses. This ice had to be replaced often.

## Critical Thinking

In addition to slowing food spoilage, what is another advantage of refrigerating food?

_____

_____

_____

# Make Some History

If you look closely, you will find that many of your home appliances have an *Energy Star* label. Do research to find out more about this label. Draw the Energy Star label in the space below on the timeline. Then, describe what it is and when it was first used on refrigerators.

**2010s**

Today's refrigerators are larger but use less energy. They have electronic controls that can be adjusted to set different parts of the refrigerator at different temperatures. Some modern refrigerators can alert people when a particular food supply is running low!

# Design Your Future

Think of another household appliance that helps you save time. Describe how it helps you. Then, explain what you would do to improve its design.

# Build On It!

Rise to the engineering design challenge—complete **Improvise It: Build a Rubber Band Scale** on the Inquiry Flipchart.

# Unit 7 Review

Name _____

## Vocabulary Review

Use the terms in the box to complete the sentences.

> condensation
> density
> evaporation
> law of conservation
>   of mass
> mass
> matter
> states of matter
> volume

1. Anything that takes up space and has mass

   is _____.

2. The amount of matter in an object is

   its _____.

3. The amount of space an object takes up is

   its _____.

4. The amount of matter present in a certain volume

   of a substance is its _____.

5. The idea that you cannot make or destroy matter

   is called the _____.

6. Solids, liquids, and gases are the

   three _____.

7. The process by which a liquid changes into a gas

   is _____.

8. The process by which a gas changes into a liquid

   is _____.

# Science Concepts

Fill in the letter of the choice that best answers the question.

**9.** Leila wants to describe the physical properties of an object. Which property is she describing when she determines the space taken up by the object?

(A) mass      (C) density

(B) weight      (D) volume

**10.** Tiko washes dishes and puts the clean, wet dishes on a drying rack. What causes water on these dishes to dry up?

(A) The water melts.

(B) The water condenses.

(C) The water evaporates.

(D) The water is absorbed.

**11.** Which process listed below turns solid ice into liquid water?

(A) melting      (C) condensing

(B) freezing      (D) evaporating

**12.** Which of these describes a liquid?

(A) definite shape; definite volume

(B) definite shape, no definite volume

(C) no definite shape; definite volume

(D) no definite shape; no definite volume

**13.** The diagrams below show the particles that make up a substance. Which diagram shows how the particles are arranged when the substance is solid?

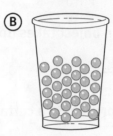 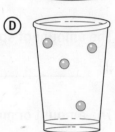

**14.** Aiden uses a balance like this one to measure the mass of an apple. He finds that it is 224 g. He then cuts up the apple into four parts of varying sizes. What can he conclude?

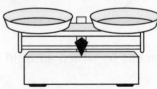

(A) The mass of each part is 56 g.

(B) The sum of the masses of the parts is 224 g.

(C) Each part has a mass that is slightly less than 56 g.

(D) Each part has a mass that is slightly greater than 56 g.

**15.** Shayna is classifying a group of objects by their physical properties. She puts a soccer ball, a blue marble, and an orange in one group. Which property did she most likely use to classify these objects?

(A) size

(B) color

(C) shape

(D) hardness

**16.** A science teacher instructs his students to make a chart identifying the physical properties of each object below.

Which of the following would be **best** to use for this chart of physical properties?

(A) age, color, length, mass

(B) hardness, mass, name, odor

(C) length, shape, name, texture

(D) color, hardness, mass, length

**17.** Which process listed below changes water vapor (a gas) into liquid water?

(A) melting

(B) freezing

(C) evaporation

(D) condensation

**18.** Amit measured the volume of the cube below. His measurements are shown on the diagram.

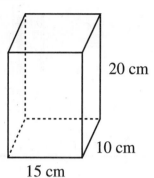

20 cm

10 cm

15 cm

What is the volume of Amit's cube?

(A) 45 cubic centimeters

(B) 180 cubic centimeters

(C) 1,500 cubic centimeters

(D) 3,000 cubic centimeters

**19.** Which set of steps would describe the changes in state of an ice cube that is left outside in the hot sun?

(A) solid→gas→liquid

(B) solid→liquid→gas

(C) liquid→solid→gas

(D) liquid→gas→solid

**20.** Cherie changed water from a liquid to a solid. What did she do to the water?

(A) She froze the water.

(B) She melted the water.

(C) She condensed the water.

(D) She evaporated the water.

# Apply Inquiry and Review the Big Idea

Write the answers to these questions.

**21.** Jason wanted to find the volume of two rocks. How could he use the tools shown below to find the volume of these irregularly shaped rocks?

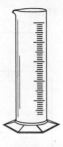 

_____

_____

_____

**22.** You have a red box and a black box that are exactly the same size. The red box is heavier than the black one. What can you conclude about the densities of the two boxes?

_____

_____

**23.** Suppose you wanted to describe an object to someone, but you could not name it.

**a.** Which properties could you include in your description if you could only share information that you can determine with your senses?

_____

_____

**b.** If you were able to use simple measuring tools, what other properties of the object could you include in your description?

_____

_____

_____

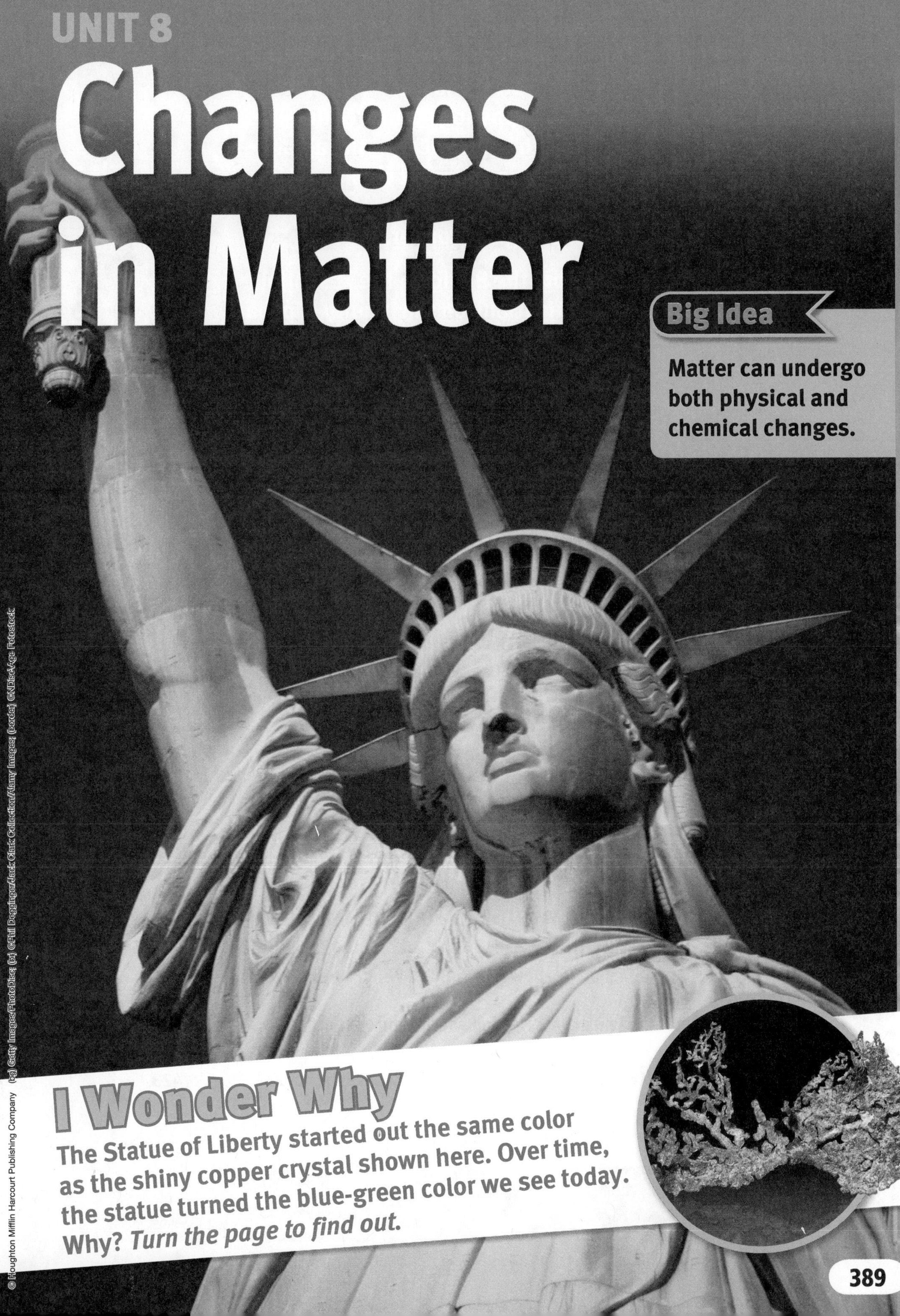

UNIT 8

# Changes in Matter

**Big Idea**

**Matter can undergo both physical and chemical changes.**

## I Wonder Why

The Statue of Liberty started out the same color as the shiny copper crystal shown here. Over time, the statue turned the blue-green color we see today. Why? *Turn the page to find out.*

**Here's Why** The Statue of Liberty is made of copper. Copper is a metal that can be hammered into different shapes. This change is a physical change. At first, the statue was the color of the copper crystal. Over time, its exposed surface reacted with substances in the air and changed color. This change is a chemical change. The substance that covers the surface of the Statue of Liberty today is different from the original copper.

In this unit, you will explore the Big Idea, the Essential Questions, and the Investigations on the Inquiry Flipchart.

Levels of Inquiry Key ■ DIRECTED ■ GUIDED ■ INDEPENDENT

Track Your Progress

**Big Idea** Matter can undergo both physical and chemical changes.

## Essential Questions

Now I Get the Big Idea!

**Science Notebook**

Before you begin each lesson, be sure to write your thoughts about the Essential Question.

**Essential Question**

# What Are Some Physical Changes?

## Engage Your Brain!

Find the answer to the following question in this lesson and record it here.

Which changes take place when melted metal is poured into a mold?

_____

_____

_____

_____

_____

_____

## Active Reading

### Lesson Vocabulary

List the terms. As you learn about each one, make notes in the Interactive Glossary.

_____

_____

_____

### Main Ideas

The main idea is the most important idea of a paragraph. The main idea may be stated in the first sentence, or it may be stated elsewhere. Active readers look for the main idea by asking themselves, What is this paragraph about?

# Physical Changes Are All Around

Matter can be changed in many ways. In how many ways can you change a piece of paper?

 **Active Reading** As you read, draw a line under the main idea of each paragraph.

## Stacked

You can describe the physical properties of this paper, such as its size and color.

## Soaked

What a mess! The paper is soggy, but it hasn't become a new substance.

## Shredded

Does shredding the paper make a new substance? No, it just changes the shape of the paper into tiny pieces.

Think of a piece of clay. Can it be changed like paper can? If you pull bits from the clay, you change its size. If you flatten the clay, you change its shape. The size or shape may be different, but it is still clay. Changing size and shape is a physical change. A **physical change** is a change in which a new substance is not formed.

You can scratch a piece of clay until it is rough. It has a new texture, but it is still clay. You can add bits to it. It is heavier, but adding clay does not make a new substance. Changing a physical property, such as size, shape, texture, or mass, is a physical change.

▶ What are some different ways that you can make a physical change to a piece of string?

_____

_____

▶ Describe the physical change.

_____

_____

_____

## Crumpled

**This paper is crinkly, but it is still the original paper.**

# So Different, yet the Same

You get a juice pop from the freezer. As you eat the pop, it begins to drip. What causes this physical change to take place in your frozen treat?

**Active Reading** As you read this page, underline its main idea.

The sticky juice dripping down your arm is caused by a change in state. A change in state is a physical change that takes place when heat energy is added or removed from matter. When you take a juice pop out of the freezer, the pop begins to warm up. As a result, the solid juice begins to melt.

Melting is a change in state from a solid to a liquid. It takes place when heat energy is added to a solid.

Evaporation is a change in state from a liquid to a gas. It takes place when heat energy is added to a liquid. When the water in a melted juice pop evaporates, sugar, syrup, and food coloring are left behind.

You can make your own pops by freezing liquid juice. Freezing is a change in state from a liquid to a solid. It takes place when heat energy is removed from liquids.

## Physical Changes

Making glass and candles are examples of physical changes. To make a glass pitcher, solid glass is heated. The glass melts and becomes a thick liquid. Then, the melted glass is molded or blown into shape. When the glass cools, it hardens into a solid.

## Melt, Pour, and Mold

To make candles, people melt, pour, and mold—all these are physical changes.

**1** When heat is added, the solid wax melts and becomes a liquid. You may add a color dye to the liquid wax.

**2** The liquid wax takes the shape of the mold. It releases heat energy as it cools.

**3** When the change in state is complete, the wax forms a solid candle.

▶ Ice cream is a solid. What happens to ice cream if it is removed from a freezer? Why? Which physical changes take place in the ice cream?

_____

_____

_____

_____

# Mix It Up!

What do a salad, the air you breathe, and coins in a piggy bank have in common? They are all mixtures.

**Active Reading** As you read these two pages, underline the main idea on each page.

Sand is a tan-colored solid. Water is a liquid. If you put sand and water into a bucket, they form a mixture because their properties do not change. A **mixture** is a combination of two or more substances that keep their identities. The sand is still a tan solid, and the water is still a liquid. Neither has become a different substance.

A salad is also a mixture. When you mix lettuce, tomatoes, carrots, and other vegetables, no new substances are made. For this reason, making a mixture is a physical change.

**This jar contains a mixture of rubber balls and marbles.**

## Mixtures

**Salad dressing is a mixture. The oil and vinegar mix when shaken. If the dressing sits, the oil and vinegar will separate.**

396

Some metals are a type of mixture called a solution. A **solution** is a mixture in which the substances are evenly mixed. To make some rings, gold and another metal, such as copper, are melted together. When the liquid metals are evenly mixed, they are poured into a mold where they cool and harden to form a solid ring.

Seawater is a solution of solids that are dissolved in a liquid. Most of the solid parts of seawater are salts. Its liquid part, water, is a solvent. A *solvent* is the larger part of a solution that dissolves other substances. A *solute* is a substance that dissolves in a solvent. Solutes are the smaller part of a solution. The dissolved salts in seawater are solutes.

## Solutions

**Lemonade is a solution made up of water, which is a solvent, and lemon juice and sugar, which are both solutes.**

# Do the Math!

## Show Percent

Air is a solution made up of gases. The table shows the percent of each gas in air. *Percent* means "out of one hundred." Use a different color pencil to shade in the correct percent of each gas in the 100-square grid.

| Gas | Percent |
|---|---|
| Nitrogen | 78 |
| Oxygen | 21 |
| Other gases | 1 |

# Clean Up an Oily Mess

Water is a solvent in many solutions. In fact, water is called the universal solvent. Water can dissolve more things than any other known solvent.

Given enough time, rocks will dissolve in water. However, something that will *not* dissolve in water is oil. When you mix oil and water, the oil forms drops or layers that float on the water.

Oil can be messy when it gets on things. Water alone can't clean up an oily mess. People need to mix water with detergent.

Soaps, such as the types used to wash our bodies, and dishwashing and laundry detergents, have ingredients that help water break up oil and wash it away.

Detergent particles form bonds with water particles and reduce their ability to bond to each other. Detergent particles also like to form bonds with oil particles. Detergent and water work together to break up oil into smaller particles that can be washed away.

Detergents can be used to clean up the environment. In 2010, an oil rig exploded in the Gulf of Mexico spilling millions of gallons of oil. The oil affected many marine plants and animals including water birds. The oil stuck to the birds' feathers, making it hard for them to swim, fly, and keep warm. To clean up the birds, wildlife scientists and volunteers used dishwashing detergent.

Detergent bonds with oil particles on the bird's feathers and helps water wash the particles away.

▶ Write the answer to each question in the space provided.

| Why can't water alone help wash away oil? | Why is using detergent and water to clean oil a physical change? |
| --- | --- |
| | |

# Sum It Up!

When you're done, use the answer key to check and revise your work.

**Use the information in the summary to complete the graphic organizer.**

## Summarize

A physical change is a change in which no new substances are formed. A mixture is a combination of two or more substances that keep their own identities. A solution is a mixture with evenly mixed substances. In a solution, a solute is the smaller part and is the substance that is dissolved. A solvent is the larger part of a solution and is the substance that dissolves the solute. Because substances in a mixture retain their identities, making a mixture is a physical change.

**1** Main Idea:

_____

_____

**2** Detail:

_____
_____
_____
_____
_____
_____

**3** Detail:

_____
_____
_____
_____
_____
_____

**4** Detail:

_____
_____
_____
_____
_____
_____

**Answer Key: 1.** A mixture is a combination of two or more substances that keep their identities. **2.–4.** (in any order) A solution is a mixture with evenly mixed substances.; Because the substances in a mixture retain their identities, making a mixture is a physical change.; In a solution, a solute is the smaller part and is the substance dissolved.

Name _____

# Word Play

**1** Use the clues to help you unscramble the letters that make up each term.

1. A change that does not result in a new substance.

   _ _ _ ◯ _ _ _     _ _ _ ◯ _ _

   y s p c l a h i   g a h c n e

2. The substance that dissolves a solute.

   _ _ _ _ _ _ ◯

   v s l t o e n

3. The change in state of a solid to a liquid.

   _ ◯ _ _ _ _

   l e m g n i t

4. A combination of two or more substances that keep their own properties.

   _ _ _ ◯ _ _ _

   t x i m r e u

5. The change in state of a liquid to a gas.

   _ _ _ _ _ _ _ ◯ _ _

   p e r o a v t a o n i

6. The change in state of a liquid to a solid.

   _ _ _ _ ◯ _ _

   e z e n g i f r

7. The substance that dissolves into a solvent.

   _ ◯ _ _ _ _

   l t o u s e

Unscramble the circled letters to reveal the answer to the joke below.

Why did the boy ask for help with his science homework?

He couldn't find the __ __ __ __ __ __ __ __.

**2** Look at the pictures below. Tell how you could make a physical change to each one.

_____    _____

_____    _____

_____    _____

**3** Circle whether each example below describes melting, freezing, or evaporating.

a. Liquid wax takes the shape of a mold as it cools. (melting, freezing, evaporating)

b. Snow changes to water and drips off a roof. (melting, freezing, evaporating)

c. Water disappears from a street puddle. (melting, freezing, evaporating)

**4** A student adds 5 g each of sand, sugar, and salt to 50 mL of water. Did he make a solution? Explain.

_____

_____

_____

_____

**Take It Home!**

With a family member, take turns making physical changes to a piece of aluminum foil and a piece of paper. How are the changes you made to the foil and paper the same? How are the changes different?

Name _____

**Essential Question**

# How Can We Make a Solution?

## Set a Purpose
What will you learn from this investigation?

_____

_____

_____

_____

## Think About the Procedure
In this investigation, which substance is a solute, and what does it do?

_____

_____

_____

_____

What are some variables in this investigation?

_____

_____

_____

_____

## Record Your Data
Draw and describe how each cup looked after Step 2.

| Before Stirring | |
|---|---|
| "Water" Cup | "Alcohol" Cup |
| | |

Now draw and describe how each cup looked after Steps 3 and 4.

| After Stirring | |
|---|---|
| "Water" Cup | "Alcohol" Cup |
| | |

## Draw Conclusions

What did the combination of sugar and water form? Explain your answer.

_____

_____

_____

_____

What did the combination of alcohol and sugar form? Explain your answer.

_____

_____

_____

_____

## Analyze and Extend

1. Why was it important to use the same amount of water and alcohol?

_____

_____

_____

_____

2. Why did stirring help dissolve the sugar in the water?

_____

_____

_____

_____

3. When you mix water and sugar together, which substance is the solvent? Explain your answer.

_____

_____

_____

_____

_____

4. Why is forming a mixture a physical change?

_____

_____

_____

_____

_____

5. What other questions would you like to ask about mixtures and solutions?

_____

_____

_____

_____

_____

_____

_____

# What Are Some Chemical Changes?

## Engage Your Brain!

Find the answer to the following question in this lesson and record it here.

Fireflies don't use electricity to produce light. Where does the light come from?

_____

_____

_____

_____

## Active Reading

### Lesson Vocabulary

List the terms. As you learn about each one, make notes in the Interactive Glossary.

_____

_____

_____

### Main Ideas and Details

Detail sentences give information about a main idea. The information may be examples, features, characteristics, or facts. Active readers stay focused when they ask themselves, What fact or information does this sentence add to the main idea?

# Chemical Properties

You place a circle of dough in a hot oven. A short time later, a delicious pizza is ready to eat. What causes this change to occur?

Copper tarnishes if left exposed; however, aluminum does not. Why? Copper and aluminum have different chemical properties. A **chemical property** is a property that describes how a substance interacts with other substances.

Quality Food

Tomato Sauce

Substances can be identified and grouped based on their chemical properties. The ability to rust is a chemical property of iron; aluminum is a substance that does not rust. The ability to burn is a chemical property of wood and gasoline. Resistance to burning is a chemical property of gold and water.

Chemical properties can help us predict how substances will change in different conditions. Think again about making a pizza. You mix flour, water, yeast, and other ingredients. When heated, these ingredients interact to form a tasty pizza. The dough will not form a pizza if you put it in a refrigerator. In the same way, wood burning in a fireplace gives off heat, light, and gases and leaves behind a pile of ash. Unless it is burned, the wood will not change into these new substances.

Both silver and copper tarnish when they react with substances in the air. The larger silver object is tarnished—it has darkened and turned black. Tarnished copper is blue-green.

The ability to burn is also a chemical property. A candle burning involves wicks and wax. Burning requires oxygen.

## Property Match-up

Draw lines from each material to match it with the properties it shows. Circle chemical properties. A property may apply to more than one material.

| Material | Property |
|----------|----------|
| glass | tarnishes |
| paper | resists burning |
| wood | folds |
| silver | burns |

Some substances react with acids. Weak acids in rain water wear away limestone and other rocks.

# Chemical Changes

If you cut a candlewick, it's still a wick. What happens if you light it with a match? It burns and gives off smoke. The smoke was not there before. It is a new substance.

**Active Reading** As you read these pages, underline the sentences that describe a chemical change.

All substances, including candlewicks, have chemical properties. Chemical properties determine how substances interact. These interactions can lead to chemical changes. A **chemical change** takes place when a substance changes into an entirely new substance. Blow out a lit candle and look at its wick. The wick is black. It is not the same substance it was before it was lit—burning has caused a chemical change.

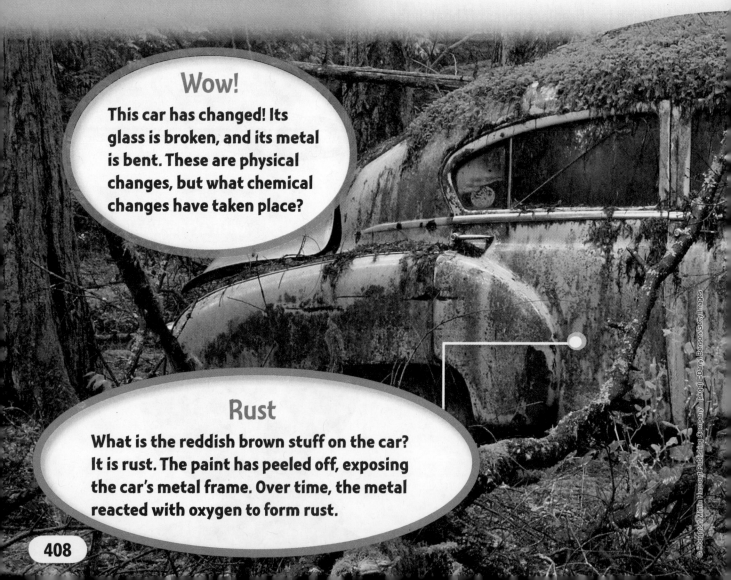

## Wow!

This car has changed! Its glass is broken, and its metal is bent. These are physical changes, but what chemical changes have taken place?

## Rust

What is the reddish brown stuff on the car? It is rust. The paint has peeled off, exposing the car's metal frame. Over time, the metal reacted with oxygen to form rust.

Where do the materials to make new substances come from? They were there all along! Look again at the car. Existing matter—oxygen and iron—combined chemically to form a new substance—rust. No new matter was created. This means that the same amount of matter, or mass, is present before and after substances react. Scientists express this idea by saying that mass is *conserved* during a chemical change.

Sometimes a chemical change results in products that are hard to see. When wood burns, smoke blows away, and invisible gases are given off. Even so, if you could collect and determine the mass of all the products—ashes, smoke, and gases—you'd find that their total mass was exactly the same as the total mass of the reactants—wood and oxygen.

▶ Fill in the table to describe two chemical changes.

| Before | After |
|---|---|
| The shiny metal car was left outside for many years. | |
| | After a candle burns, the wick is black and brittle. |

## Rubber

A chemical change happens when light and ozone in the air cause the rubber in the tire to break down.

## Rot

Have you ever smelled rotting leaves? As the leaves break down and form a new substance, they give off a gas that smells.

# Signs of Change

Clues show when a chemical change has taken place and a new substance has formed.

**Active Reading** As you read this page, find and underline clues of a chemical change.

**Y**UCK! Mold has begun to grow on an orange, causing it to rot. White fuzz appears on the orange's skin. It has a funny smell. A fungus is causing the orange to decay.

The following clues tell us that a chemical change has taken place:

- **Odor** Bacteria cause the bad smell of sour milk as they form new substances.

- **Color change** Sunlight shines on billboards, causing the colors to chemically change and fade.

- **Light** Light from a campfire or a firefly shows that chemical changes have taken place.

- **Heat** Burning is a chemical reaction. When materials burn, they give off heat.

- **Gas bubbles** Adding baking soda to vinegar causes gas bubbles to form.

## Chemical Change

You don't want to eat this orange! The mold causes a chemical change, forming new substances that are *not* safe to eat!

## Physical Change

You can take a bite of this orange! It is broken into segments, but it is still the same sweet, juicy orange. This physical change did not form a new substance.

In these fireworks, the explosion of the shell and the production of heat and light tell us that a chemical change has taken place.

Another name for a chemical change is a **chemical reaction**. Chemical reactions can take place slowly or quickly. People can control the rate of some chemical reactions. For example, you can slow the spoiling of milk by keeping it cold. On the other hand, an increase in temperature often speeds up a chemical reaction. Cutting something into smaller pieces can also speed up a reaction. If you have ever helped an adult start a campfire, you know that it is easier to get small twigs to burn than to try to set fire to a log!

Certain substances can cause some chemical reactions to speed up. For example, your stomach adds substances that help speed the breakdown of the food you eat.

▶ For each picture, identify a clue that tells you a chemical change has taken place.

# Making Pizza!

Pizza comes in many varieties: thin-crust, thick-crust, pepperoni, and veggie. Can you keep track of all the physical and chemical changes that go into making one of these pizzas?

## 1 Start with the Dough

Mix flour and water until the mixture is gooey. Next, add some yeast and a little sugar. The yeast breaks down the sugar to form new substances, including carbon dioxide gas. The gas makes bubbles in the dough, causing it to rise. The bubbles tell you that there is a chemical change. The dough is now ready to push, pull, and shape into a crust—these are physical changes.

## 2 Add the Toppings

Make the sauce by crushing tomatoes and mixing in spices. Because you can separate the spices from the tomatoes, this is a physical change. Spread the sauce, and shred some cheese on top of it. The cheese is still cheese, so this is another physical change. You can cut up some of your favorite vegetables to put on top. No new substances are formed, because cutting is a physical change.

# 3 Bake the Pizza

Now it is time to bake the pizza. The dough gets hot and turns brown. It changes from dough into a crust that is nice and crispy. You can smell the dough baking and see the change in color and texture, so you know chemical changes are happening.

# 4 Dig In!

Slice the pizza. Slicing is a physical change. Then take a big bite. As you eat the pizza, it reacts with the juices in your stomach. Your body uses it for energy. Chemical changes are taking place.

# Do the Math!
## Compare Fractions

You can cut a pizza in many different ways. Any way you slice it, pizza is a yummy treat!

1. Color the first circle to show that $\frac{4}{8}$ of the pizza has been eaten. Color the second to show $\frac{1}{4}$ has been eaten.

2. Draw a square around the pizza with the largest missing fraction.

## When you're done, use the answer key to check and revise your work.

**Read the two summaries below. Draw and describe a picture to illustrate each one. Then complete the boxes at the bottom of the page.**

**1** Substances can be described and grouped according to their chemical properties. A **chemical property** describes how a substance interacts with other substances. The ability to burn and rust are two types of chemical properties.

**2** A **chemical reaction** is another term for a chemical change. During a chemical change, an object reacts with something else. A new substance forms. Clues of a chemical change include changes in smell or color, or the release of heat or light.

**3** List three examples of chemical properties.

_____

_____

_____

_____

**4** List four clues that can tell us a chemical change has taken place.

_____

_____

_____

_____

**5** Name two factors that can affect the rate of a chemical reaction.

_____

Name _____

# Word Play

**1** Complete each sentence. Then use the answers to fill in the boxes and answer the riddle.

1. The __ __ __☐__ of a compost pile is a clue that waste is rotting to form new substances.

2. A chemical change that forms a new substance is also called a

   __ __ __ __ ☐ __ __ __  __ __ __ __ __ __ __.

3. The forming of new substances indicates that a __ __ __ __ __ __ __ __  __ __ __ ☐ __

   has happened.

4. A characteristic that describes how one substance reacts with another is a

   ☐ __ __ __ __ __ __  __ __ __ __ __ __ __ __.

5. A chemical property of iron is its ability

   to __ __ __ ☐ .

Set the answers in the boxes below to answer the riddle.

Riddle: How does a firefly read a book in the dark?

Answer:  He shines a __ __ __ __ __ on it.

| chemical change* | chemical property* | smell |
| chemical reaction* | rust | |

\* Key Lesson Vocabulary

# Apply Concepts

**2** Read the steps in the recipe for scrambled eggs. Circle the step where the chemical change takes place. Then describe how you know.

Step 1: Break 2 eggs into a bowl.

Step 2: Beat the eggs until they are smooth.

Step 3: Pour the eggs into a hot pan.

Step 4: Stir as you cook until eggs are fluffy.

Step 5: ENJOY!

_____

_____

**3** Look at the matches. Circle the match that shows a chemical change has taken place, and describe how you know.

_____

_____

_____

**4** A friend tells you that after a candle burns, there is less matter than before the flame was lit. Is your friend correct? Explain why or why not.

_____

_____

_____

**Take It Home!**

One sign of a chemical change is heat. Use the Internet to research how vinegar and steel wool can be used to observe a chemical reaction that gives off heat. Report your findings to the class.

# What's It Made Of?

## Body Armor

Do you skate? Play football? Or play catcher for a softball team? If so, then you know how hard, bulky, and heavy sports safety gear can be. Not to worry—change is coming. Members of the U.S. Olympic ski team have worn suits with safety pads made of a new kind of body armor!

These light-weight, flexible, shock-absorbing safety pads mold to the wearer's body. Long chains of carbon and hydrogen particles make up the pads.

Before an impact, these particles are loosely connected, which gives the armor its gel-like flexibility.

On impact, the particles quickly absorb the energy produced. They "lock" together, and the pad hardens to protect the wearer. Then, just as quickly as before, the particles unlock, and the pad returns to its gel-like state!

## Troubleshooting

Over time, sunlight can make the new safety pads hard and breakable. Suppose safety gear made from this material will be worn in full sun. How would you change its design?

_____

_____

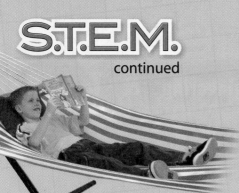

# What Else Could It Do?

Think about the properties of this new material. What other uses could it have? Suppose it was used to make a hammock. How would it work?

_____

_____

_____

_____

## Design Your Future

What are some other uses of this type of material? Draw a picture of your idea. Include labels to show when the material is flexible and when it is hard. Then, describe how your idea works.

_____

_____

_____

## Build On It!

Rise to the engineering design challenge—complete **Build in Some Science: Making Carbon Dioxide** on the Inquiry Flipchart.

Name _____

Essential Question

# How Can You Tell When a New Substance Forms?

## Set a Purpose
**What will you learn from this experiment?**

_____

_____

_____

_____

_____

## Think About the Procedure
**What does each sample test?**

_____

_____

_____

_____

_____

_____

## Record Your Data
**Make a chart to record your observations.**

## Draw Conclusions

What two factors tell you that a chemical change has occurred?

_____

_____

_____

_____

_____

_____

Could a scientist use your samples as evidence that a chemical change has occurred? Explain.

_____

_____

_____

_____

_____

_____

_____

_____

## Analyze and Extend

1. Given what you have learned, what kind of warning might you place on a box of steel wool pads?

_____

_____

_____

_____

_____

2. From what you have learned, describe two uses for steel wool—one that won't cause it to rust, and one that will cause it to rust.

_____

_____

_____

_____

_____

3. Think of other questions that you would like to ask about rusting.

_____

_____

_____

_____

# Meet the Chemists

Benerito invented wash-and-wear cotton. It doesn't need ironing.

## Ruth Rogan Benerito

Ruth Rogan Benerito's work as a chemist gave us wash-and-wear cotton clothing. Before the 1950s, clothing made from cotton wrinkled after washing. So, many people switched to synthetic cloth. The cotton farmers began to suffer. Benerito discovered a way to treat the cotton particles so that they were chemically joined. In doing so, she made a cloth that had few wrinkles. Benerito taught college classes for many years .

## Héctor Abruña

Dr. Héctor Abruña is a chemist. He studies fuel cells. A fuel cell makes electricity from chemical changes. Unlike energy from burning fossil fuels, there is very little pollution from a fuel cell. Fuel cells can provide energy for cars, buildings, and even cell phones. Abruña has taught chemistry at Cornell University for nearly 30 years. He works to help more women and minorities become scientists.

Dr. Abruña studies ethanol as a possible fuel source for fuel cells. Ethanol is a made from corn or other plants.

# Chemistry Is All Around You!

Read the chemistry clues. Then **label** each item with the number of the matching clue.

**1** It can make things stick almost instantly. A chemical change creates the bond.

**2** It is lightweight. Garbage bags and water pipes are some of the many things made from this.

**3** A chemical change makes milk into this tangy food.

**4** This synthetic fabric is used to make clothing and tents. It is made from a chemical change.

**5** Without it, you would be in the dark. A gas-filled tube uses a chemical change to make light.

**6** A chemical change lets us see pictures on a screen.

**7** A chemical change inside of this object makes electricity so objects can turn on or move.

LCD monitor

batteries

super glue

nylon

yogurt

plastic

fluorescent bulb

## Think About It!

You may find some or all of the items above in your home. Name five other things in your home that chemistry helped make.

_____

_____

_____

Name _____

## Vocabulary Review

Use the terms in the box to complete the sentences.

chemical change
chemical property
chemical reaction
mixture
physical change
solution

1. A change in matter in which a new substance is not formed

   is a _____.

2. A mixture that has the same composition throughout because all the parts are mixed evenly is called

   a(n) _____.

3. A characteristic that describes how a substance will interact with

   another substance is a _____.

4. The picture of the salad shows a combination of two or more different substances in which the substances keep their own properties.

   This salad is an example of a _____.

5. Any change in matter in which a new and different substance

   forms is called a _____.

6. Another name for a chemical change is

   a _____.

# Science Concepts

Fill in the letter of the choice that best answers the question.

**7.** Mrs. Green wants to cook rice for dinner. She puts some water into a pot and turns on the stove. After about 5 minutes, the pot looks like the one shown here.

Which of these statements is **true**?

(A) The stove chemically changes the pot.

(B) The water undergoes a physical change.

(C) The water and the pot form a solution.

(D) The water and the pot react chemically.

**8.** Naveen puts some ice cubes in a glass of water. He leaves his glass on the counter. When he returns, the ice is gone.

Before        After

Which statement is **true**?

(A) Naveen observes a mixture form.

(B) Naveen observes a solution form.

(C) Naveen observes a chemical reaction.

(D) Naveen observes a physical change.

**9.** Physical changes happen when a substance changes, but its composition doesn't. Which of the following is a physical change?

(A) burning          (C) freezing

(B) decaying         (D) rusting

**10.** Miguel buys a ring made of gold and silver. After a few weeks, the silver part of the ring looks black and dull. The gold part stays shiny. What can you conclude about Miguel's ring?

(A) The silver is really steel.

(B) Silver reacts with the air but gold does not.

(C) The gold and silver undergo physical changes.

(D) The gold and silver have the same chemical properties.

**11.** Ms. Royce's students are having an end-of-the-year party. They go to a nearby park on a sunny day. Which party activity describes a chemical change?

(A) climbing the monkey bars

(B) cooking hamburgers on a grill

(C) playing hide-and-seek

(D) putting a hot dog and mustard on a bun

**12.** Solutions are special types of mixtures. Which of the items below is a solution?

(A) carbonated water

(B) gelatin with bananas

(C) spicy salad dressing

(D) orange juice with pulp

**13.** Trina and Josh mix a liquid and a solid in a test tube. In the pictures below, Test Tube *A* shows what the content of the tube looks like after they shake it. Test Tube *B* shows what the content of the tube looks like after it is heated.

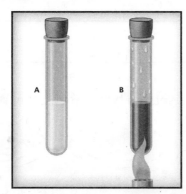

Based on the pictures, which of these statements is a valid conclusion?

(A) A chemical change takes place when the substances are heated.

(B) The solid does not dissolve when it is mixed with the liquid.

(C) The liquid changes color when it is mixed with the solid.

(D) A physical change takes place when the test tube is heated.

**14.** Carlos is making caramel apples. He heats sugar, stirring it in a pan on a stove. As he stirs, the sugar turns brown. He puts a stick into an apple and swirls the apple through the caramel. Then Carlos waits for the caramel to harden.

Which of the following is a chemical change?

(A) the heat dissolving the sugar

(B) the sugar becoming caramel

(C) the caramel hardening

(D) the sugar melting

**15.** A scientist doing an experiment follows the procedure below.

Step 1: Find the mass of two substances.

Step 2: Mix the substances in a test tube.

Step 3: Heat the substances in a special chamber that collects all of the gases given off.

Step 4: Measure the mass of the materials left in the test tube and the gases gathered in the chamber.

How will the total mass of the substances in this experiment change?

(A) The mass will increase.

(B) The mass will decrease.

(C) The mass will stay the same.

(D) The new material will have no mass.

**16.** After mowing the lawn, Jenna collects the grass clippings and adds them to a compost pile. In a few weeks, these clippings will decompose. She finishes up by sweeping bits of grass off of the sidewalk. Which statement is **true**?

(A) Composting is a physical change.

(B) Cutting the grass is a chemical change.

(C) Sweeping the sidewalk is a physical change.

(D) Dumping the clippings is a chemical change.

**17.** At the beach, Lauren feels the warm sand and smells the sea salt in the air. She finds a broken shell and a brownish nail. Which one of her observations is the result of a chemical change?

(A) warm sand

(B) sea salt smell

(C) brownish nail

(D) broken shell

# Apply Inquiry and Review the Big Idea

Write the answers to these questions.

**18.** Linea's teacher gives her two beakers of water, some table salt, and some pepper. Her teacher tells her to use the materials to make one mixture and one solution. Describe what Linea should do.

_____

_____

_____

**19.** Franco wants to test the effects of water on steel wool. He sets up two plates. Steel Wool J is dry and exposed to air. Steel Wool K is wet and exposed to air.

J

Dry Steel Wool
on Plate

K

Wet Steel Wool
on Plate

**a.** Franco makes some observations about the steel wool before he starts the test. What are two observations that he can make and what tools should he use to make those observations?

_____

_____

_____

**b.** What changes is Franco likely to observe after one week? Are these changes chemical or physical? Tell how you know.

_____

_____

_____

**20.** Kate and Henry are making bread. They mix water, flour, and a little sugar to make dough. They stir some yeast into a cup of warm water and add it to the dough to make the bread rise. Finally, they add cinnamon and raisins to the dough and bake it. The bread comes out of the oven and is golden brown. Identify the physical and chemical changes that take place as they make the bread.

_____

_____

_____

# Energy

## Big Idea

**Heat is a form of energy that can be transferred between objects.**

## I Wonder Why

This surfer lets many waves go by him before choosing one to ride. Why? *Turn the page to find out.*

**Here's Why** The best waves have a lot of energy. Surfers use the energy from these waves to get a nice, long ride to shore.

In this unit, you will explore the Big Idea, the Essential Questions, and the Investigations on the Inquiry Flipchart.

Levels of Inquiry Key ■ DIRECTED ■ GUIDED ■ INDEPENDENT

**Big Idea** Heat is a form of energy that can be transferred between objects.

## Essential Questions

Now I Get the Big Idea!

Track Your Progress

**Science Notebook**

Before you begin each lesson, be sure to write your thoughts about the Essential Question.

**Essential Question**

# What Are Some Forms of Energy?

## Engage Your Brain!

Find the answer to the following question in this lesson and record it here.

How does this person use energy to ride the river's rapids?

_____

_____

_____

_____

## Active Reading

### Lesson Vocabulary

List the terms. As you learn about each one, make notes in the Interactive Glossary.

_____  _____

_____  _____

_____  _____

### Main Idea and Details

In this lesson, you'll read about different kinds of energy. Active readers look for main ideas before they read to give their reading a purpose. Often, the headings in a lesson state the main ideas. Preview the headings in this lesson to give your reading a purpose.

# What Is Energy?

All the lights in your house need energy. So do the refrigerator and washing machine. Can you name three other things in your home or school that use energy?

**Active Reading** As you read these two pages, find and underline a definition of *energy*. Then circle two sources of energy.

What do you and a car have in common? You both need energy. Gasoline is the car's source of energy. This car won't go anywhere if it runs out of gas.

▶ Draw lines to match each item on the left with its source of energy.

Name something that uses electricity as a source of energy.

_____

_____

M aking an object move is a change. **Energy** is the ability to cause change in matter. So, everything that moves has energy.

Where does energy come from? You can see some sources of energy on these two pages. What sources of energy have you used today?

Where does this toy get its energy?

_____

_____

This man needs energy to run. Where do you think he gets it? Runners eat healthful foods such as trail mix so they will have plenty of energy.

# Get Moving!

Have you ever been on a roller coaster? When roller coaster cars climb a hill, they seem to stop at the top for just a moment. Then they speed down to the bottom. How does energy make this happen?

**Active Reading** As you read these two pages, find and underline the definition of *mechanical energy*. Then draw circles around the two parts of mechanical energy.

Something in motion, such as the girl on the pogo stick, has kinetic energy. **Kinetic energy** is the energy of motion. Something at the top of a hill, such as a roller coaster car, has potential energy. **Potential energy** is the energy something has because of its position or condition.

**Mechanical energy** is the total potential energy and kinetic energy of an object.

▶ Everything in the left column has potential energy. Tell what happens when the potential energy of each object is changed to kinetic energy.

| | |
|---|---|
| A ball sits on top of a hill | |
| A person stretches back a rubber band | |
| Someone gets ready to throw a paper airplane | |

The girl pushes the pogo stick's spring down. The spring now has potential energy. When the spring spreads out, the pogo stick goes up and has kinetic energy.

As the roller coaster cars climb to the top of a hill, they gain potential energy. The higher the cars go, the more potential energy they have.

As the cars go down a hill, their potential energy decreases because it changes to kinetic energy. The roller coaster cars have more kinetic energy when they move faster. At each point along the ride, the mechanical energy of the cars is the sum of their potential and kinetic energies.

This roller coaster goes fast because of mechanical energy. That's good, because a slow roller coaster isn't much fun!

# Flash and Boom!

You see lightning flash across the sky. Then you hear a boom that's so loud, it makes your heart pound. These are two forms of energy.

Light energy is produced and used in different ways. Light is a form of energy that can travel through space. Plants use light from the sun to make food. The same energy from the sun allows us to see. Another source of light energy is electricity. If we couldn't use electricity to produce light energy, it would be difficult to work or play in the evening.

Another form of energy is sound. Sound is made when something moves back and forth. This back-and-forth motion is called vibration. Sound can be described in different ways. For example, pitch describes how high or low a sound is. Loud sounds have more energy than quiet sounds. Can you think of an example of a loud, high-pitched sound?

## Do the Math!
### Solve Real-World Problems

How far away was that lightning strike? As soon as you see a flash of lightning, count the seconds until you hear thunder. Then divide the number of seconds by 5. This gives you the approximate distance in miles.

35 seconds _____

20 seconds _____

40 seconds _____

Lightning can be hotter than the surface of the sun. It makes the air around it rapidly expand. This causes the boom of thunder.

▶ Describe how each member of this musical group produces sound. Write your answers in the spaces provided.

# Energy Is All Around Us

Do you think you could do without energy for one day? Without chemical energy, you couldn't mow the lawn. Without electrical energy, you couldn't power your MP3 player.

**Active Reading** As you read these two pages, draw a circle around a use of chemical energy. Draw a box around a use of electrical energy.

Many things use chemical energy and electrical energy. **Chemical energy** is energy than can be released by a chemical change. Chemical energy from food gives us energy. Most cars run on gasoline, a source of chemical energy. Have you ever warmed yourself by a campfire? Fire is the release of chemical energy.

Electrical energy provides the energy for most of the devices you use, like computers and televisions. **Electrical energy** is energy that comes from electric current. Anything plugged into a wall outlet uses electrical energy.

Where does electricity come from? In most cities, electricity is generated using the chemical energy released during the burning of fossil fuels such as coal and natural gas. The sun and wind can also be used to generate electricity.

▶ Identify the things in this scene that use chemical energy and those that use electrical energy. Write your answers in the spaces provided.

# Energy Can Change Forms

Can you read by the light of chemical energy? Can you use electrical energy to make something move? You can do both of these things, and more.

**Active Reading** As you read these two pages, draw a line under two examples of energy changing forms.

Chemical energy changes into light energy in a glow stick.

Energy can change from one form to another. Electrical energy changes to light energy when you turn on a light switch. You may also feel the heat energy given off by some light bulbs. Chemical energy in gasoline changes to mechanical energy when a driver presses the gas pedal to drive.

Glow sticks have a glass tube inside them. The glass tube has chemicals inside it. When you bend the glow stick, the tube breaks. The chemicals in the tube mix with other chemicals in the glow stick. When they mix, light energy is given off.

A remote control sends radio waves to the remote-controlled car. Radio waves are another form of energy, similar to light energy. The radio waves change to electrical energy to tell the motor what to do—start, stop, or go faster. The car also has batteries inside it. The batteries change chemical energy to electrical energy to move the car.

This plant changes light energy from the sun into chemical energy in food.

## Changing Energy

Draw a picture that shows another way that energy can change form.

# Sum It Up!

When you're done, use the answer key to check and revise your work.

**Use information in the summary to complete the graphic organizer.**

## Summarize

Energy is the ability to cause change in matter. Making an object move is a change. So, everything that moves has energy. Kinetic energy is the energy of motion. Potential energy is the energy something has because of its position. The mechanical energy of an object is the sum of its kinetic and potential energies. Light energy enables plants to make food and helps us see. Sound energy is caused by a vibrating object. Energy can change from one form to another.

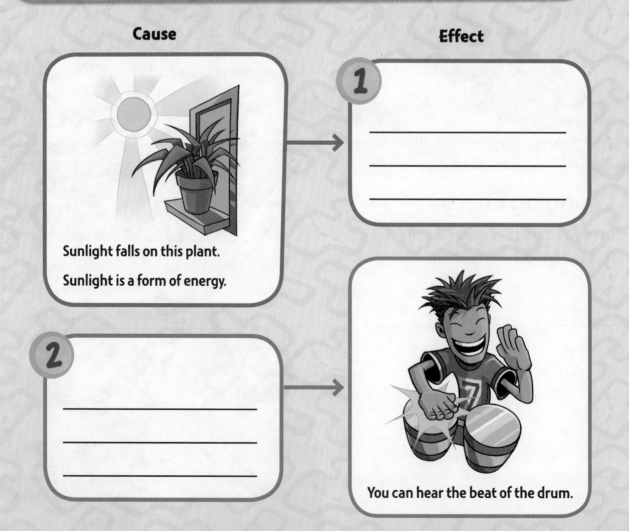

**Cause**

Sunlight falls on this plant.

Sunlight is a form of energy.

**Effect**

1 _____

2 _____

You can hear the beat of the drum.

440

Answer Key: 1. The plant captures light energy from the sun and uses it to make food.
2. The drum heads vibrate to make sound.

Name _____

## Word Play

**1** Choose words from the box to complete the Forms of Energy word web.

### Forms of Energy

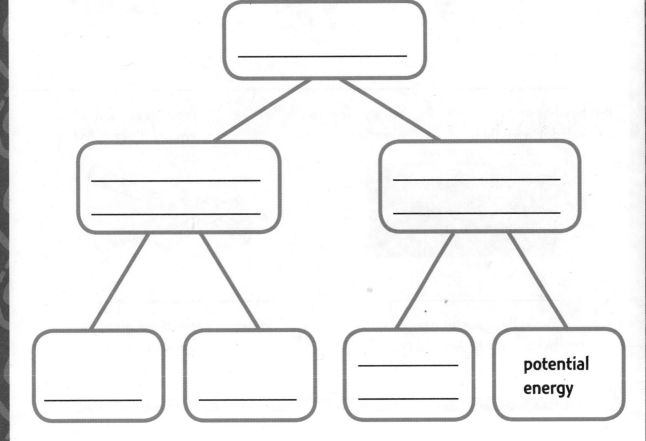

potential energy

| energy* | chemical energy* | mechanical energy* |
|---|---|---|
| kinetic energy | food | gasoline |

* Key Lesson Vocabulary

# Apply Concepts

2 Use the words from the box to label each picture. Each term will be used once.

| chemical energy | kinetic energy | potential energy |
|---|---|---|
| sound | light | |

_____

This boy has an up-and-down motion.

_____

You can feel the cello's vibrations.

_____

Food gives this bird the energy it needs to live.

_____

The roller coaster cars go to the top of the hill and stop for a moment.

_____

You can carry these glow sticks in the dark so people can see you.

3 A light bulb changes electrical energy into two other forms of energy. What are they?

_____

_____

442

**4** **Which of these objects has potential energy? How do you know?**

_____
_____
_____
_____

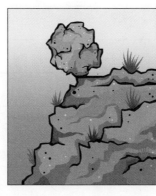

**5** **Describe how sound energy is produced when you strike the top of a drum.**

_____
_____
_____
_____
_____

**6** Many forms of energy are around us and within us. Write three paragraphs in the form of an e-mail to a friend or family member describing some ways you use energy in a typical day. Tell your reader where the energy comes from and how it transforms into other forms of energy.

_____

_____

_____

_____

_____

_____

_____

_____

_____

_____

_____

_____

_____

_____

_____

**Take It Home!**

Share what you have learned about forms of energy with your family. With a family member, discuss how you use different forms of energy around your house.

Name _____

Essential Question

# Where Does Energy Come From?

## Set a Purpose
**What will you learn from this experiment?**

_____

_____

_____

_____

## Think About the Procedure
**Why did you repeat Step 3 four times?**

_____

_____

_____

_____

## Record Your Data
**In the space below, make a table in which you record your results.**

## Draw Conclusions

What did you observe in this investigation?

_____

_____

_____

_____

## Analyze and Extend

1. Why do you think the ball traveled farther when it was pushed by the fully compressed spring?

_____

_____

_____

_____

2. When you compressed the spring, it gained potential energy. What was the source of this energy?

_____

_____

_____

3. What happened to the spring's potential energy when you let go of the ball?

_____

_____

_____

4. Explain why squeezing the spring halfway affects the distance the ball travels.

_____

_____

_____

_____

5. Did each group in the class have the same results from the investigation? Why or why not?

_____

_____

_____

_____

_____

6. Think of other questions you would like to ask about energy and how it changes form.

_____

_____

_____

_____

_____

**Essential Question**

# What Is Heat?

**Find the answer to the following question in this lesson and record it here.**

Most photographs show people and objects as we see them. What do you think this photograph shows?

_____

_____

_____

## Active Reading

### Lesson Vocabulary
List the terms. As you learn about each one, make notes in the Interactive Glossary.

_____

_____

_____

_____

### Signal Words: Contrast
Signal words show connections between ideas. Words that signal contrasts include *unlike, different from, but,* and *on the other hand.* Active readers remember what they read because they are alert to signal words that identify contrasts.

# The Energy of Heat

It takes heat to shape glass or to make tea. But what is heat, exactly? Think about it for a moment. How would you define *heat*?

**Active Reading** As you read these two pages, find and underline the definition of *heat*.

Temperature measures how hot or cold something is. Energy moves between objects that have different temperatures. You've already learned about many kinds of energy. **Heat** is the energy that moves between objects of different temperatures. The difference in temperature makes the energy move.

You sense heat as a warming feeling. More precisely, you feel the change in temperature as you gain energy. Heat moves naturally from an object with a high temperature to one with a lower temperature. In other words, heat moves from a warmer object to a cooler object.

## Super Hot
You can see and feel heat moving from the flame to the glass. This melted glass is about 1,500 °C/2,732 °F!

## Incredibly Cold
This is dry ice—frozen carbon dioxide. It is really cold—about –80 °C/–112 °F.

# Do the Math!
## Use Temperature Scales

Temperature is measured in different scales. The two scales on this thermometer are Celsius and Fahrenheit. Write the letter of each picture at the appropriate place on the thermometer.

This girl's clothes trap heat near her body. Her jacket slows down energy transfer to the cold air. This girl stays warm while playing in the snow in temperatures as low as 0 °C/32 °F.

The water coming from this shower head is hotter than the air around it. The average temperature of shower water is 42 °C/108 °F.

Heat moves from the burner to the kettle, from the kettle to the water, and then from the water vapor to the air. Water boils at 100 °C/212 °F.

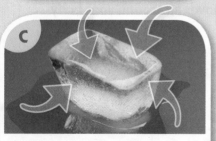

Ice cubes melt as heat transfers to them from the warm air. The puddle of water is about 20 °C/68 °F.

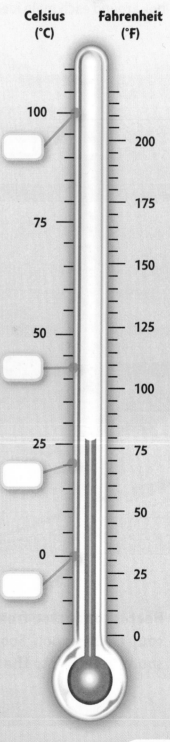

Celsius (°C) / Fahrenheit (°F)

| Celsius (°C) | Fahrenheit (°F) |
|---|---|
| 100 | 200 |
| 75 | 175 |
| | 150 |
| 50 | 125 |
| | 100 |
| 25 | 75 |
| | 50 |
| 0 | 25 |
| | 0 |

# Heat on the Move!

Heat can move in different ways.

**Active Reading** As you read these two pages, draw a box around each main idea.

Heat is conducted from your hand into the snow. The snow melts. Your hand feels cold.

## Conduction

**Conduction** is the transfer, or movement, of heat between two objects that are touching. It can also occur *within* an object. Heat moves from inside your body to warm your skin. Your feet and hands stay warm because heat moves all around your body.

Heat is conducted from the soup to the spoon. Soon the spoon feels hot to the touch.

1. Heat is conducted from the burner to the pot to the water.

2. Heated water travels up, warming the cooler water above.

3. Cooler water sinks to the bottom, where it gets heated. The cycle repeats. This movement is called a *convection current*.

## Convection

**Convection** is the transfer of heat within a liquid or a gas. Particles in liquids and gases move easily, and they take heat with them. Heat from a campfire warms the air around it by convection. Warmer air is always buoyed upward. In this case, the fire is the source of heat for convection.

Hot air rises above cooler air. That's what keeps a hot-air balloon in flight.

▶ Write the kind of heat transfer that takes place in the following situations.

| An eruption of lava on the ocean floor | Winds blowing in from a warmer part of the country | Feet touching a cold floor |
| --- | --- | --- |
| | | |

# Feeling Radiant!

Heat moves by conduction between solids that are touching. Heat moves by convection through gases and liquids. But can heat travel without moving through matter? Find out.

As you read the next page, draw boxes around the clue words or phrases that signal one thing is being contrasted with another.

Heat travels from the campfire by convection and radiation.

The third way heat can move is radiation. **Radiation** is the transfer of heat without matter to carry it. Heat simply leaves one object and goes directly to another. Suppose you're standing near a campfire. You can feel the heat from the fire because it warms the air. But you can also feel the heat because it warms you directly through radiation.

In some ways, radiation may be the most important way heat can move. Life on Earth needs heat from the sun. But space is a vacuum. How does heat travel through the emptiness of space? By radiation.

The room is cool and air-conditioned. On the other hand, heat radiating from this light keeps the young chickens warm.

▶ Circle the objects that are radiating heat.

Heat from the sun radiates through space and through the atmosphere before it warms this girl's face.

# Sum It Up!

When you're done, use the answer key to check and revise your work.

**Fill in the missing words to complete the conversation.**

## Summarize

**Rebecca:** Ow! How did my cell phone get so hot?

**Abdullah:** Well, there are (1) _____ ways that heat could have moved into your phone.

**Rebecca:** I know. If it had been sitting in sunlight, I'd know it was heated through (2) _____ . But it was in the shade.

**Abdullah:** Well, there's also convection.

**Rebecca:** Yeah, but that only happens within (3) _____ and (4) _____ . My phone's a solid.

**Abdullah:** Then it must have been the third way: (5) _____ .

**Rebecca:** But that only happens when two things are (6) _____ each other. My phone was sitting by itself.

**Abdullah:** Where?

**Rebecca:** On top of my laptop.

**Abdullah:** In that case, heat traveled into your phone through (7) _____ .

**Rebecca:** Really? How does it do that?

**Abdullah:** Heat moves from warm objects to (8) _____ objects. Your laptop was probably much warmer than your cell phone.

**Rebecca:** Maybe I'll leave it on my wooden desk from now on!

454

Name _____

# Word Play

**1** **Unscramble each word and write it in the boxes.**

How heat moves from one end of a solid to the other

C C N O T N O I U D

☐ ☐ ☐ ◯ ☐ ◯ ☐ ☐ ☐ ☐

The topic of this lesson

T H E A

☐ ◯ ◯ ☐

What heat does during convection or conduction

S R T F N R A E S

☐ ◯ ☐ ☐ ☐ ◯ ☐ ☐ ☐

How heat moves through a liquid

T N E V C O I N C O

☐ ☐ ☐ ☐ ◯ ☐ ☐ ☐ ☐ ☐

Heat moves from this source by convection and radiation

F I R M P A C E

☐ ☐ ◯ ◯ ☐ ☐ ☐

How heat travels through empty space

D O T A I R N I A

◯ ☐ ☐ ☐ ◯ ☐ ☐ ☐ ☐

**Unscramble the letters in the circles to form a word that is related to this lesson.**

_____

# Apply Concepts

**2** A transfer of heat happens between objects of different temperatures. Draw an arrow between each pair of objects to show the direction heat would travel between them.

**3** Label each part of the drawing as an example of conduction, convection, or radiation.

A. _____

B. _____

C. _____

**4** Label each of the following as examples of conduction, convection, or radiation.

hot water added to bath

_____

space heater

_____

iron-on decal

_____

clothes dryer

_____

sunlight through a window

_____

sandwich press

_____

**5** In this pizza restaurant, heat is traveling in different ways. Label the examples of conduction, convection, and radiation in the spaces provided.

_____

_____

_____

_____

With your family, find three devices that give off heat in your home. For each device you find, discuss where the heat comes from and the way in which the heat is transferred.

© Houghton Mifflin Harcourt Publishing Company

Name _____

Essential Question

# How Is Heat Produced?

## Set a Purpose
What do you think you will learn from this experiment?

_____

_____

_____

## State Your Hypothesis
Write your hypothesis, or testable statement.

_____

_____

_____

## Think About the Procedure
How does the paper spiral test for the presence of heat?

_____

_____

_____

_____

_____

## Why would you use the spiral instead of your hand?

_____

_____

_____

_____

## Record Your Data
In the space below, make a table in which you record your observations.

## Draw Conclusions

Was your hypothesis supported? Why or why not?

_____
_____
_____
_____
_____

What conclusions can you draw about light sources and heat?

_____
_____
_____
_____
_____

## Analyze and Extend

1. What did you learn from this procedure about the difference between compact fluorescent bulbs and ordinary light bulbs?

_____
_____
_____
_____
_____

2. Ordinary light bulbs use more electrical energy than compact fluorescent bulbs do. Why do you think this is so?

_____
_____
_____
_____
_____

3. What other materials could you test in this way to see if they produce heat?

_____
_____
_____
_____
_____
_____
_____

4. What other questions do you have about heat transfer?

_____
_____
_____
_____
_____

# 8 THINGS YOU SHOULD KNOW ABOUT Geothermal Technicians

**1** *Geothermal* means heat from inside of Earth. Volcanoes, geysers, and hot springs are all sources of geothermal energy.

**2** Geothermal energy is a *green energy*, which means that it is renewable, and it does not pollute the environment.

**3** At geothermal energy stations, machines called *generators* convert geothermal energy into electrical energy.

**4** Geothermal technicians may work inside, using computers to monitor energy production.

**5** They may work outside, installing and repairing equipment used to capture geothermal energy.

**6** Geothermal technicians read blueprints and technical drawings as part of their work.

**7** They work with geothermal engineers to design and install geothermal systems.

**8** To be a geothermal technician, you must complete high school and a special set of training courses.

## Show What You Know About Geothermal Technicians

Answer the five questions about geothermal technicians.

**1** What type of energy do these technicians work with, and where does it come from?

_____

_____

_____

_____

**2** What do geothermal technicians do when they work outside?

_____

_____

_____

**3** Why is geothermal energy green energy?

_____

_____

_____

**4** What are some natural sources of geothermal energy?

_____

_____

_____

_____

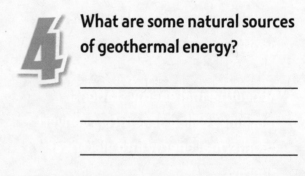

**5** Would you like to work as a geothermal technician? Why or why not?

_____

_____

_____

## Think About It!

Would you want to heat your home using geothermal energy? Explain.

_____

_____

_____

# Essential Question

# What Are Conductors and Insulators?

## Engage Your Brain!

Find the answer to the following question in this lesson and record it here.

How can these dogs stay warm in such cold weather?

_____

_____

_____

_____

_____

## Active Reading

### Lesson Vocabulary

List the terms. As you learn about each one, make notes in the Interactive Glossary.

_____

_____

_____

_____

### Cause and Effect

Some ideas in this lesson are connected by a cause-and-effect relationship. Why something happens is a cause. What happens as a result of something else is an effect. Active readers look for effects by asking themselves, What happened? They look for causes by asking, Why did it happen?

# Go with the Flow... of Heat

A pan in the oven gets very hot. But if you pick it up with an oven mitt, your hand stays cool. Why?

**Active Reading** As you read these two pages, circle lesson vocabulary each time it is used.

Heat moves through some materials very easily. In the example above, heat from the oven moved easily into the pan. But heat from the pan did not pass through the oven mitt. A material that allows heat to move through it easily is called a **conductor**. Many heat conductors also conduct electricity well.

For the most part, solids are better conductors of heat than liquids or gases are. That's because the particles that make up a solid are packed closely together. They vibrate, but don't move apart much. Heat can move quickly from one particle to another.

### Glass
Glass does not conduct heat well. If you pour boiling water into a metal bowl, the outside of the bowl quickly gets hot. A glass bowl gets warm more slowly.

### Stone
Marble does not conduct heat as well as metals do. But it can still conduct heat away from your body. That's why marble feels cool when you touch it.

### Metal
Metals are great heat conductors. Some metals conduct heat better than others do.

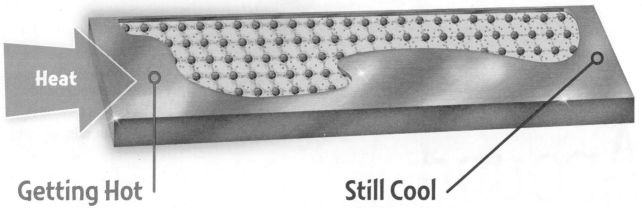

**Heat**

## Getting Hot

This diagram shows the particles of a metal bar. The particles on this end are hot. This end was placed over a flame, but the other end wasn't.

## Still Cool

The particles on this end aren't hot yet, but they will be soon. In metals, heat moves from particle to particle very easily.

▶ Imagine you touched the handles of all four spoons. Circle the spoon handle that would be the hottest. Then explain your choice.

_____

_____

_____

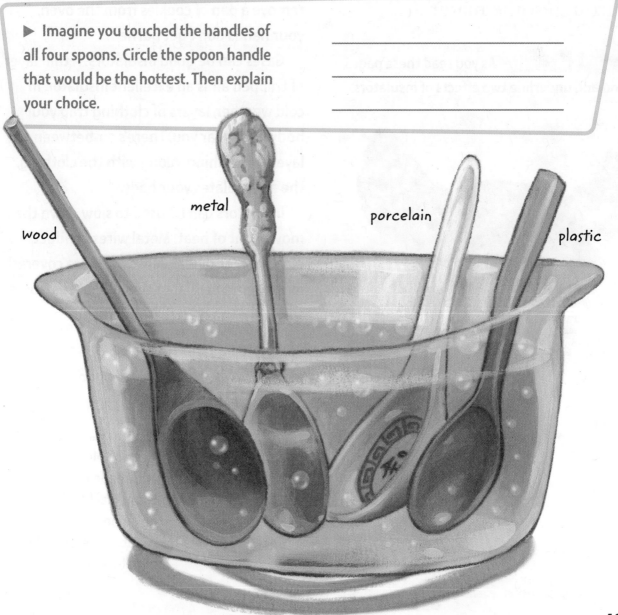

wood

metal

porcelain

plastic

# Turn the Heat Around

Not all materials are conductors. Heat does not move easily—or at all—through some materials.

**Active Reading** As you read these pages, find and underline two effects of insulators.

Wearing gloves insulates your hands. The gloves trap heat near your skin.

**M**aterials that do not conduct heat well are called **insulators**. Oven mitts are insulators. They are made of materials that are poor conductors of heat. When you remove a pan of cookies from the oven, your hands don't get burned.

Gases can be good insulators. A thin layer of trapped air is an excellent insulator. In cold weather, layers of clothing trap your body heat near you. There's air between the layers of clothing. Along with the clothing, the air insulates your body.

Insulators can be used to slow down the movement of heat. Metal wires conduct electricity and heat. Most wires are covered in rubber to insulate them and keep people safe from the electricity and heat.

## Hair as an Insulator

Most furry animals stay warm in cold weather. Fur is made of thick hairs. Around each hair is air. The air and the fur act as insulators, keeping the animal warm.

# Why Does a Thermos Work?

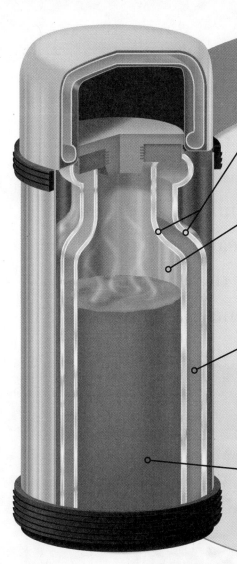

### Glass lining
A layer of glass holds the tea. Glass does not conduct heat very well.

### Reflection
Even in a vacuum, radiation can move energy. The facing sides of the layers are coated in silver, which act like a mirror. It reflects some heat back.

### Vacuum
There is a vacuum between the inner and outer glass layers of the bottle. The vacuum keeps conduction or convection from taking place.

### Still Hot
With the conduction, convection, and radiation slowed down, the tea stays hot for a long time!

▶ Although the straw house is not the sturdiest, a straw house can be well insulated. Why?

# Heat Proofing a Home

All across the United States, people are trying to conserve, or save, energy. It's good for the environment, and it saves money. Heat proofing a home is one way that people can conserve energy.

When the weather is hot, you want to keep heat from coming into your home. When the weather is cold, you want to keep heat from leaving your home. It costs money to cool and heat a home! There are different ways to slow the flow of heat into or out of a house. Some things need to be done while the house is being built. Others can be done to an existing home. Insulating a home saves money. It also helps conserve energy.

## 1 Insulation

Insulation is blown inside the walls of a house. Insulation keeps heat from traveling through to the attic.

2 glass panes

## 2 Windows

These windows have two panes of glass to limit conduction. They also have a coating that limits heat radiation.

## 3 Pipes

Hot pipes radiate heat from water into the air. Wrapping them keeps the heat from escaping.

## 4 Soil

Soil is a great insulator. Basements are usually cool, even in the summer.

# Do the Math!
## Solve Real-World Problems

The Ogburn family wants to heat proof their house. They can save about $800 a year by adding insulation. Wrapping the water pipes will save an additional $5 each month. Buying new, energy-efficient windows will save them about $2,000 every year.

1. How much money will wrapping the water pipes save the Ogburns in a year?

_____

2. About how much more money will replacing the windows save each year than wrapping the water pipes?

_____

3. Write an equation to calculate how much all three things will save the Ogburns in a year.

_____

## Bonus!

If new windows cost $10,500, pipe insulation costs $100, and adding insulation costs $400, in how many years will the savings pay for the cost of these home improvements?

_____

_____

_____

When you're done, use the answer key to check and revise your work.

**Write the vocabulary term that describes each material.**

**1**
metal cube

_____

**2**
a knit hat

_____

**3**
rubber bands

_____

**Draw a box around the correct answer or answers.**

| | | | |
|---|---|---|---|
| [4] Heat moves easily through it. | insulator | conductor | |
| [5] Heat does not move easily through it. | insulator | conductor | |
| [6] Solids often do this to heat. | insulate | conduct | |
| [7] A thin layer of trapped air can do this to heat. | insulate | conduct | |
| [8] Which forms of heat transfer do insulated bottles prevent? | conduction | convection | radiation |
| [9] Wrapping hot water pipes prevents which form of heat transfer? | conduction | convection | radiation |

**Answer Key: 1.** conductor **2.** insulator **3.** insulator **4.** conductor **5.** conductor **6.** insulate **7.** insulate **8.** conduction, convection, and radiation **9.** radiation

## Word Play

**1** Use the clues to help you write the correct word in each row. Some boxes have been filled in for you.

A. | | I | N | | | | |
B. | | I | N | | | | | | |
C. | | I | N | | | | |
D. | | | | | | C | | |
E. | | | | | | C | |
F. | | | | M | | |
G. | | | | M | | | |
H. | | | | M | | | |
I. | | | | | | M | |

A. Some of them have two panes of glass.

B. It can be blown inside walls.

C. It slows the transfer of heat.

D. It's the opposite of answer C.

E. The silver layer of an insulated bottle does this to radiated heat.

F. Because of natural insulation, it's often the coolest part of a house.

G. It's an excellent conductor.

H. It does not conduct as well as metals do.

I. It makes conduction and convection impossible.

# Apply Concepts

**2** You are going to make a kitchen spoon. It will be used to stir hot liquids. Circle the material that will be warmest when you touch its handle.

cotton

metal

plastic

wood

**3** Many people are building "green" houses, which use very little energy. Some of these houses are partially or completely underground. Why?

_____

_____

_____

**4** How would you design a lunchbox that could keep hot food hot or cold food cold? Sketch a diagram of the box.

Take It Home!

Look around your kitchen with your family. Find two things that conduct heat and two things that are heat insulators.

Name _____

# Which Materials Are Conductors?

## Set a Purpose
**What do you think you will learn from this experiment?**

_____

_____

_____

_____

_____

## State Your Hypothesis
**Write your hypothesis, or testable statement.**

_____

_____

_____

_____

_____

## Think About the Procedure
**What is the tested variable?**

_____

_____

_____

_____

_____

**What things must be the same in each setup?**

_____

_____

_____

_____

_____

_____

## Record Your Observations

Record your results in the chart below.

## Draw Conclusions

Which material did heat move through more quickly?

_____

_____

Which material is a conductor? Which is an insulator? How do you know?

_____

_____

_____

_____

## Analyze and Extend

1. On which knife did the butter melt faster? On that knife, which pat of butter melted faster?

_____

_____

_____

2. Write a hypothesis about which knife would lose heat faster. Then plan an experiment to test your hypothesis.

_____

_____

_____

_____

_____

_____

_____

3. What other materials could you test this way?

_____

_____

_____

4. What other questions would you like to ask about conductors and insulators?

_____

_____

_____

# How It Works:
## Piezoelectricity

This gas lantern has a tool that changes kinetic energy from an impact into electrical energy. Electrical energy produced this way is called *piezoelectricity*, or electricity from pressure!

Quartz is a piezoelectric material.

**Gas Chamber**

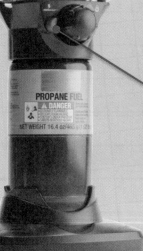

You don't need a match to light this lantern! It has a piezoelectric igniter. The igniter is a tool made up of a small, spring-loaded bar and a piezoelectric material.

**Piezoelectric Igniter**

When this red button is pushed, the bar strikes, or impacts, the piezoelectric material.

PROPANE FUEL
DANGER
NET WEIGHT 16.4 oz/465 g (1 lb.)

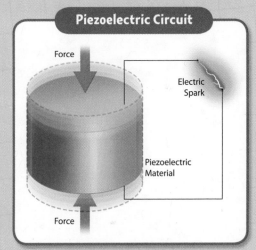

**Piezoelectric Circuit**

Force

Electric Spark

Piezoelectric Material

Force

The bar's force squeezes the piezoelectric material, producing electric charges that flow as an electric current. Inside the lantern's gas chamber, the current jumps between two conductors, causing an electric spark. The spark ignites the gas. *Voilà!* Light and heat are produced.

## Troubleshooting

Why might a lantern not light up when a piezo igniter is pushed?

_____

_____

_____

These solar cells transform, or change, solar energy into electrical energy. Electrical energy is changed into heat and light inside the home.

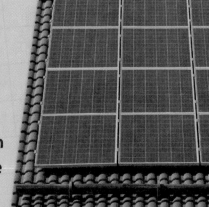

# Show How It Works

The gas lantern shows some ways energy changes take place. Kinetic energy changed into electrical energy, which ignited the natural gas. Chemical energy stored in the gas changed into heat and light. Identify different kinds of energy and their sources in your classroom or home. In the space below, draw and describe how energy from one of these sources is transformed.

_____

_____

_____

_____

_____

_____

_____

_____

Suppose that popcorn kernels are being cooked over a campfire. Describe the kinds of energy being used and how they are being transformed.

_____

_____

## Build On It!

Rise to the engineering design challenge—complete **Design It: Solar Water Heater** on the Inquiry Flipchart.

# Unit 9 Review

## Vocabulary Review

Use the terms in the box to complete the sentences.

> conduction
> conductor
> convection
> heat
> insulator
> kinetic energy
> potential energy
> radiation

1. The energy of motion is _____.

2. The energy something has because of its position or condition
   is _____.

3. The energy that moves between objects of different temperatures
   is _____.

4. The transfer or movement of heat between two objects that are
   touching is _____.

5. The transfer of heat within a liquid or a gas is
   _____.

6. The movement of heat without matter to carry it is
   _____.

7. A material that allows heat to move through it easily is
   a(n) _____.

8. A material that does not let heat move through it easily is
   a(n) _____.

# Science Concepts

Fill in the letter of the choice that best answers the question.

**9.** Objects that vibrate make energy. Which type of energy results from vibrations that travel through the air?

(A) sound     (C) potential

(B) chemical     (D) electrical

**10.** Niko jumps on a trampoline. The pictures below show him at different points during jumping.

1     2     3     4

At which point does Niko have the most potential energy?

(A) Point 1     (C) Point 3

(B) Point 2     (D) Point 4

**11.** Energy can change form. Which picture shows electrical energy changing into heat energy?

(A)     (C)

(B)     (D)

**12.** Ang has a pogo stick like the one shown. When he jumps on it, the spring squeezes toward the ground and then moves back to its starting position.

The potential and kinetic energies of the spring are forms of which type of energy?

(A) chemical energy

(B) electrical energy

(C) magnetic energy

(D) mechanical energy

**13.** The **total** energy of water as it falls from a waterfall is which type of energy?

(A) heat     (C) kinetic

(B) potential     (D) mechanical

**14.** Rachel tests how quickly different materials change temperature. Rachel heats each one the same way. The table shows the change in temperature.

| Material | Starting Temperature (°C) | Temperature After Five Minutes (°C) |
|---|---|---|
| 1 | 19 | 37 |
| 2 | 19 | 48 |
| 3 | 19 | 31 |
| 4 | 19 | 42 |

Which material is the best insulator?

(A) Material 1     (C) Material 3

(B) Material 2     (D) Material 4

**15.** What type of energy change takes place as a car burns fuel to race down a track?

Ⓐ electrical energy to light energy

Ⓑ kinetic energy to potential energy

Ⓒ chemical energy to kinetic energy

Ⓓ mechanical energy to kinetic energy

**16.** Rondell knows that radiation is a form of heat transfer. Which example describes a transfer of heat through radiation?

Ⓐ A cup of hot tea warms a hand.

Ⓑ A flame warms air in a hot air balloon.

Ⓒ A puddle of water warms under the sun.

Ⓓ A pot of boiling water warms on a gas burner.

**17.** Trey holds an ice cube in his hand. After some time passes, the ice cube begins to melt. Which term describes the process of heat transfer?

Ⓐ radiation

Ⓑ insulation

Ⓒ conduction

Ⓓ convection

**18.** A scientist measures the movement of energy between a pot of hot water and a cold metal spoon. What is he measuring?

Ⓐ heat          Ⓒ insulation

Ⓑ current      Ⓓ temperature

**19.** Jaden has many things on his desk at home as shown in the picture below.

Which material was **most** likely used because it is a good insulator?

Ⓐ copper used for the coins

Ⓑ metal used for the computer

Ⓒ steel used for the paper clips

Ⓓ rubber used for the lamp cord

**20.** This picture shows a pot of water heating on a stovetop.

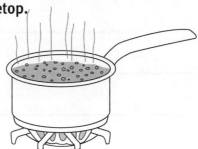

Which statement explains what happens to the water in the pot?

Ⓐ The water temperature decreases inside the pot.

Ⓑ The water will freeze when it gathers enough heat.

Ⓒ Heat energy travels from the water in the pot to the burner.

Ⓓ Heat energy travels from the burner to the pot and then to the water.

# Apply Inquiry and Review the Big Idea

**Write the answers to these questions.**

**21.** Luis is studying motion. He is using two balls—Ball 1 and Ball 2. The picture shows the equipment he is using. To shoot each ball, Luis pulls back on the stick (5), which compresses the spring (4). When he releases the stick, the ball shoots forward.

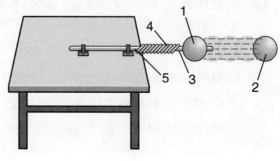

Suppose Ball 1 and Ball 2 are shot from the table with the same force. How does the potential and kinetic energy of Ball 1 compare to that of Ball 2?

_____

_____

_____

**22.** Paula is camping with her family. After their parents light a fire, Paula and her sister stand nearby to warm their hands. Her sister thinks that conduction warms their hands. Paula disagrees. Explain all methods of heat transfer taking place as they warm their hands.

_____

_____

_____

**23.** Misa puts thermometers in four boxes that are exactly alike. She covers each box with a top made of a different kind of material. Then, Misa leaves the boxes outside on a hot, sunny day. Explain which thermometer should show the highest temperature after two hours.

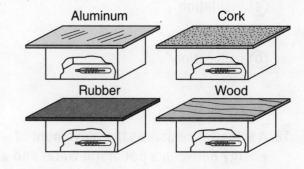

_____

_____

_____

_____

# Electricity

## Big Idea

Electric currents and magnets can be used for many purposes.

## I Wonder Why

Electrical energy is important to modern society. How does electricity reach homes and businesses? *Turn the page to find out.*

**UNIT 10**

Here's Why Generating stations transform potential and kinetic energy into electrical energy. Electrical energy travels over the electric grid. This grid is a system of steel towers, conductors, and insulators that carries electricity from generating stations to our homes and businesses.

In this unit, you will explore the Big Idea, the Essential Questions, and the Investigations on the Inquiry Flipchart.

Levels of Inquiry Key ■ DIRECTED ■ GUIDED ■ INDEPENDENT

**Track Your Progress**

**Big Idea** Electric currents and magnets can be used for many purposes.

## Essential Questions

Now I Get the Big Idea!

**Science Notebook**

Before you begin each lesson, be sure to write your thoughts about the Essential Question.

© Houghton Mifflin Harcourt Publishing Company   (b) ©Corbis; (inset) ©Charlie Brewton/Alamy Images/Corbis (border) ©NDisc/Age Fotostock

Essential Question

# What Is Electricity?

## Engage Your Brain!

Find the answer to the following question in this lesson and record it here.

What causes the girl's hair to stand out from her head?

_____

_____

_____

_____

## Active Reading

### Lesson Vocabulary

List the terms. As you learn about each one, make notes in the Interactive Glossary.

_____

_____

### Main Ideas

The main idea of a paragraph is the most important idea. The main idea may be stated in the first sentence, or it may be stated elsewhere. Active readers look for the main idea by asking themselves, What is this section mostly about?

# All Charged UP

You can charge a battery. A football player can charge downfield. How is an electric charge different?

**Active Reading** As you read these two pages, underline the main idea on each page.

What do you, this book, and your desk all have in common? You are all made of atoms. *Atoms* are the building blocks of all matter. Atoms are so small that you cannot even see them without a special microscope. Atoms are made up of even smaller particles called protons, neutrons, and electrons.

The main difference between protons, electrons, and neutrons is their electric charge. *Electric charge* is a property of a particle that affects how it behaves around other particles.

- Protons have a positive charge (+1).

- Electrons have a negative charge (−1).

- Neutrons are neutral. They have no charge.

When an atom has equal numbers of protons and electrons, the positive charges and negative charges cancel each other. The atom itself has no charge.

Protons and neutrons are found in a region of the atom called the nucleus. Electrons are found in a region of mostly empty space called the electron cloud.

## Legend

 = neutron   = proton  ● = electron

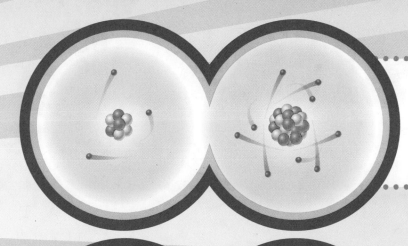

Each of these atoms has the same number of protons and electrons. Both atoms are neutral.

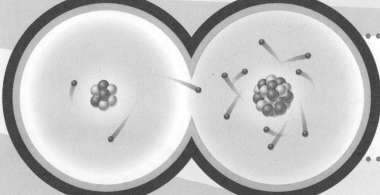

An electron from the atom on the left moves to the atom on the right.

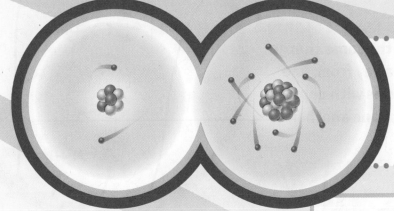

The atom on the left now has a charge of +1. The atom on the right has a charge of –1.

Atoms sometimes gain or lose electrons. This gain or loss causes an atom to have an unequal number of positive and negative charges. For example, if an atom with nine protons and nine electrons gains an electron, the atom will have a charge of –1.

If a neutral atom loses an electron, the number of protons will no longer balance the number of electrons. The atom will have a charge of +1.

▶ Draw an atom with three protons, four neutrons, and two electrons.

What is the charge of this atom?

# Opposites Attract

Have you ever had a "bad hair day"? Your hair sticks out in every direction and won't lie flat. What causes that?

**Active Reading** As you read this page, circle the definitions of *repel* and *attract*. On the next page, draw a box around the sentence with the main idea.

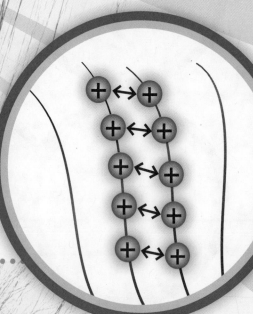

Particles with the same charge repel, or push away from, one another. Particles with opposite charges attract one another, or pull together.

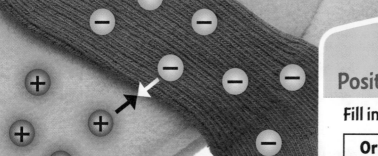

## Do the Math!
### Positive and Negative Numbers

Fill in the missing squares in the table.

| Original charge on an object | Electrons gained or lost | Final charge on the object |
|---|---|---|
| +300 | Gains 270 | |
| −300 | Loses 525 | |
| −270 | | −500 |

In the dryer, atoms in clothing gain and lose electrons. Each piece of clothing becomes charged. The positively charged surfaces attract the negatively charged surfaces. As a result, the clothes stick together.

Electric charges can build up on objects. This buildup is **static electricity**. *Static* means "not moving." Objects with opposite electric charges attract each other. Objects with the same charge repel each other.

When you brush your hair, electrons move from each strand of hair to the brush. Soon, all the strands are positively charged. All the strands having the same charge causes them to repel one another and stick out.

A charged object can attract a neutral object. If you rub a balloon on your hair, the balloon picks up extra electrons that give it a negative charge. When you bring the balloon near a wall, electrons in a small part of the wall are repelled and move away, leaving a positive charge at the wall surface. As a result, the balloon sticks to the wall.

# Lightning Strikes

Thunderstorms can be scary. Lightning can be dangerous. What is lightning? How can you stay safe during a thunderstorm?

**Active Reading** As you read these two pages, underline the main idea on each page.

Static electricity is a buildup of charges on an object. Charges stay on an object until it comes close to an object that has a different charge.

As you walk across a carpet, electrons move from the carpet to you. Because electrons repel each other, they spread out all over your body. When you touch something, the electrons jump from your finger to the object. This jumping is called an electrostatic discharge. You feel it as a tiny shock.

Zap! Electrons jump from a person with a negative charge.

▶ Complete this cause-and-effect graphic organizer.

Cause: An object with a negative charge is placed near an object with a positive charge. → Effect: _____ _____ _____

Not all electrostatic discharges cause small shocks. Some result in huge shocks. During a thunderstorm, tiny raindrops or ice particles bump into each other. These collisions cause an electric charge to build in the clouds. Positive charges form at the top of a cloud and on the ground. Negative charges form near the bottom of a cloud.

When the difference in charge between a cloud and the ground is great enough, there is a huge electrostatic discharge that we call lightning. A lightning spark can jump between two clouds, between a cloud and the air, or between a cloud and the ground. The temperature inside a lightning bolt can reach 27,760 °C (50,000 °F), which is hotter than the surface of the sun!

## Lightning Safety

- Stay inside during thunderstorms.

- Turn off electrical appliances and stay away from windows.

- If you can't get inside a safe structure, wait in a car with a metal top for the storm to pass.

- Know the weather forecast. If you will be outside, have a plan in case a thunderstorm develops.

When lightning strikes, it can catch objects on fire. A tree struck by lightning may split.

▶ Draw a cloud in the sky. Then, draw positive and negative charges to show what causes lightning to form.

# Current Events

Electrostatic discharges may be exciting to watch, but flowing charges are more useful.

**Active Reading** As you read these two pages, draw a box around the sentence that contains the main idea.

When electric charges have a path to follow, as they do in the wire below, they move in a steady flow. This flow of charges is called an **electric current**.

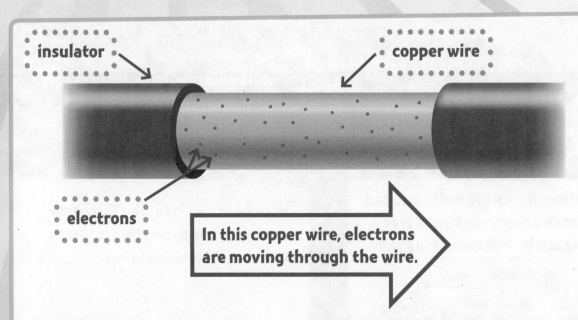

insulator

copper wire

electrons

In this copper wire, electrons are moving through the wire.

An insulator is a material that resists the flow of electrons. Electric currents can flow easily through a copper wire.

▶ What do the blue dots on this wire represent? What is the flow of these blue dots called?

_____

_____

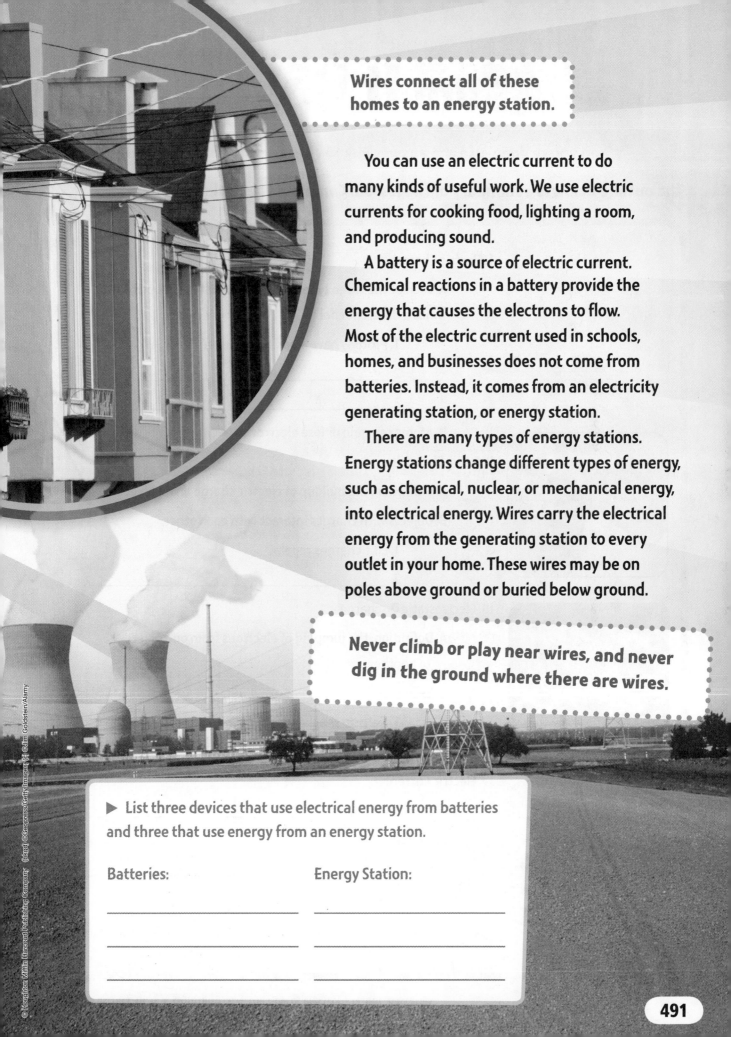

Wires connect all of these homes to an energy station.

You can use an electric current to do many kinds of useful work. We use electric currents for cooking food, lighting a room, and producing sound.

A battery is a source of electric current. Chemical reactions in a battery provide the energy that causes the electrons to flow. Most of the electric current used in schools, homes, and businesses does not come from batteries. Instead, it comes from an electricity generating station, or energy station.

There are many types of energy stations. Energy stations change different types of energy, such as chemical, nuclear, or mechanical energy, into electrical energy. Wires carry the electrical energy from the generating station to every outlet in your home. These wires may be on poles above ground or buried below ground.

Never climb or play near wires, and never dig in the ground where there are wires.

▶ List three devices that use electrical energy from batteries and three that use energy from an energy station.

Batteries:                    Energy Station:

_____    _____

_____    _____

_____    _____

When you're done, use the answer key to check and revise your work.

**The outline below is a summary of the lesson. Complete the outline.**

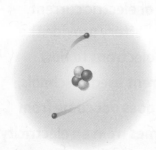

**I. Electric Charges**

    **A.** Each of the three types of particles that make up atoms has a different charge.

        **1. Protons have a positive charge.**

        **2.** _____

        **3.** _____

    **B.** Atoms can gain or lose electrons.

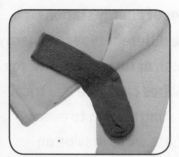

**II. Static Electricity**

    **A. Definition:** the buildup of electric charge on an object.

    **B.** Objects with charges interact with each other.

        **1. Like charges repel.**

        **2.** _____

**III. Electrostatic Discharge**

    **A. Definition:** the jumping of electrons from one object to another.

    **B. Examples**

        **1. Getting shocked after walking across a rug**

        **2.** _____

**IV. Electric Current**

    **A. Definition:** _____

    **B. Sources**

        **1.** _____

        **2. Generating stations**

Answer Key: I. A. 2. Electrons have a negative charge. I. A. 3. Neutrons have no charge. II. B. 2. Opposite charges attract. III. B. 2. Lightning IV. A. the flow of electrons IV. B. 1. Batteries

 **Brain Check**

Name _____

# Word Play

**1** Fill in the blank in each sentence. Then, find the words in the blanks in the word search below.

a. Two positive charges _____ each other.

b. A positive charge and a negative charge _____ each other.

c. The buildup of electric charge on an object is _____ electricity.

d. The flow of electric charges along a path is electric _____.

e. A proton has a _____ charge.

f. A neutron is _____ because it has no charge.

g. An electron has a _____ charge.

h. Electricity is produced at a generating _____.

| | | | | | | | |
|---|---|---|---|---|---|---|---|
| C | N | E | G | A | T | I | V | E |
| U | F | R | E | P | E | L | R | V |
| R | I | G | H | T | E | N | I | I |
| R | N | A | T | T | R | A | C | T |
| E | G | C | I | T | A | T | S | I |
| N | E | U | T | R | A | L | L | S |
| T | I | G | H | T | N | I | N | O |
| S | T | A | T | I | O | N | G | P |

Find the letters you didn't circle in the word search. Write them in order from left to right in the blanks below.

Riddle: What do you call a very scary electrostatic discharge?

_____  _____

# Apply Concepts

**2** List the three particles that make up an atom. Describe the charge of each particle.

| Parts of an Atom | |
|---|---|
| Particle | Charge |
| | |
| | |
| | |

Where are these particles found in an atom?

_____

_____

**3** Explain why the balloons are sticking to this cat.

_____

_____

_____

_____

_____

**4** List three ways you can use an electric current. Describe the energy change that takes place.

_____

_____

_____

_____

_____

Name ______________________________



**5** Fill in the blanks to complete the sequence graphic organizer.

A wool sock and a cotton shirt ________________ against each other in a dryer.

↓

Electrons move from the wool to the ______________ .

↓

The two pieces of clothing have ________________ charges and they ________________ each other.

**6** Explain why the event in the picture takes place.

_______________________________________________

_______________________________________________

_______________________________________________

_______________________________________________

_______________________________________________

_______________________________________________

_______________________________________________

_______________________________________________

_______________________________________________

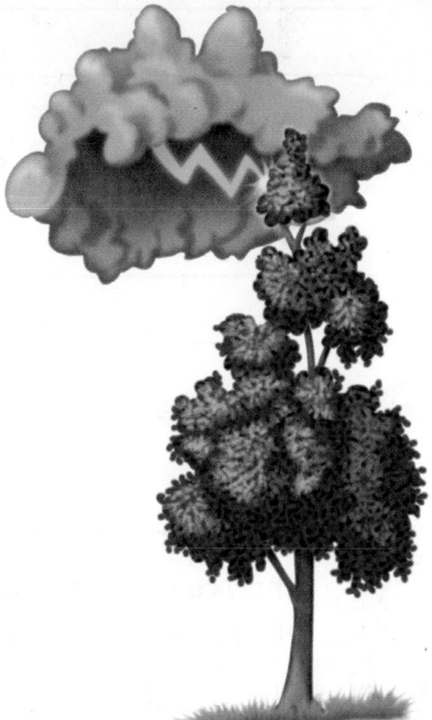

**7** Draw a line from each picture to its description. Circle the pictures that show sources of current used by people every day.

| | | | |
|---|---|---|---|
| electric current | static electricity | electrostatic discharge | battery |

**8** Suppose you are playing soccer at a park, and you hear thunder that sounds far away. Describe some things you should and should not do to stay safe.

_____

_____

_____

_____

_____

_____

**Take It Home!**

Do your clothes stick together when they come out of the dryer? If so, how could you prevent this from happening? Use Internet resources to learn how dryer sheets work to reduce static electricity in your clothes.

Name _____

**Essential Question**

# How Do Electric Charges Interact?

## Set a Purpose
**What do you think you will observe during this activity?**

_____

_____

_____

_____

## Think About the Procedure
**Why do you rub only one balloon in Step 2?**

_____

_____

_____

_____

**Why do you rub both balloons in Step 3?**

_____

_____

_____

_____

**Why is this activity not an experiment?**

_____

_____

_____

_____

## Record Your Observations
**Draw and label diagrams to show what happened during Steps 2 and 3.**

## Draw Conclusions

What caused the balloons to act the way they did in Steps 2 and 3?

_____

_____

_____

_____

_____

_____

## Analyze and Extend

1. What do you think happens when you rub a balloon with a wool cloth?

_____

_____

_____

_____

2. What happens when objects with opposite charges are near one another? Give an example that you have seen in your everyday activities.

_____

_____

_____

_____

_____

3. What happens when objects with similar charges are near each other? Give an example that you have seen.

_____

_____

_____

4. Look at the pictures of balloons below. Each picture shows the charges on one balloon. Look at the way the pairs of balloons are interacting, and draw the charges on the second balloon.

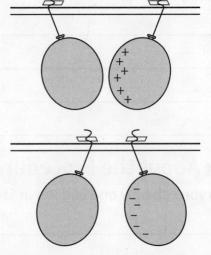

5. What other questions would you like to ask about using electric charges? What investigations could you do to answer your questions?

_____

_____

_____

_____

_____

_____

Name _____

# What Is an Electric Circuit?

## Set a Purpose
**What will you learn from this investigation?**

_____

_____

_____

_____

## Think About the Procedure
**Did the order in which you arranged the parts make a difference? Explain.**

_____

_____

_____

_____

**Was the procedure an experiment? Why or why not?**

_____

_____

_____

_____

## Record Your Data
In the space below, draw your circuit that worked. Label each part, and describe how the parts were connected.

┌─────────────────────────┐
│                         │
│                         │
│                         │
│                         │
│                         │
│                         │
│                         │
│                         │
└─────────────────────────┘

Place a check mark next to the materials that enabled the bulb to light up.

**Paper clip** _____

**Wood craft stick** _____

**Pencil lead** _____

## Draw Conclusions

How can you build a circuit?

_____

_____

_____

_____

_____

_____

## Analyze and Extend

1. Why is it helpful to have a switch in a circuit?

_____

_____

_____

_____

_____

2. Why would a circuit not work when a wire is replaced with a cotton string?

_____

_____

_____

_____

3. Look at the first part of the word *circuit*. Why do you think what you built is called a circuit?

_____

_____

_____

4. Look at the picture below. Draw lines to show how three wires could be connected to make the bulbs light up.

5. Each part of a circuit has a different job. Write the name of each part that performs the jobs listed below.

- Source of current          _____

- Carries current            _____

- Turns circuit
  on and off                 _____

- Changes electrical
  energy to light             _____

6. What other questions would you like to ask about electric circuits? What investigations could you do to answer the questions?

_____

_____

_____

_____

_____

_____

_____

500

**Essential Question**

# What Are Electric Circuits, Conductors, and Insulators?

## Engage Your Brain!

Find the answer to the following question and record it here.

This picture shows the inside of a robot. What do the dark lines have to do with the robot's operation?

_____

_____

_____

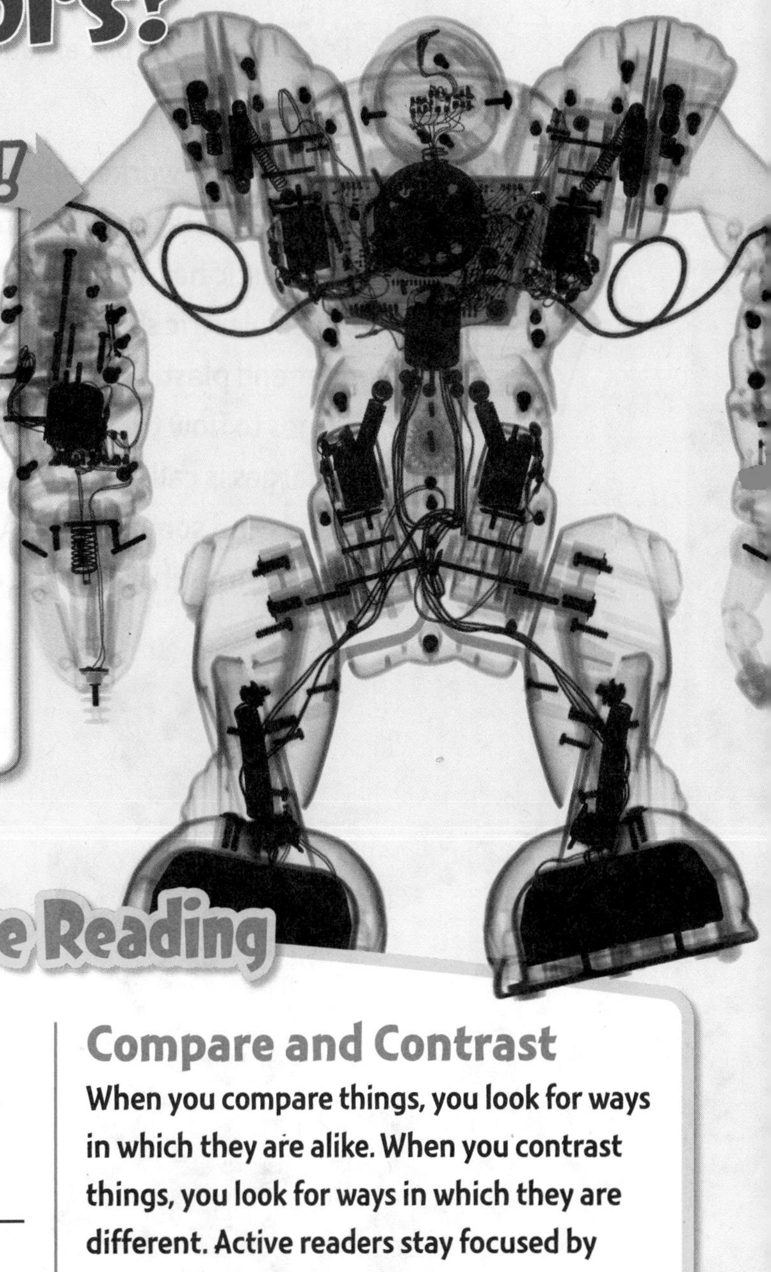

## Active Reading

### Lesson Vocabulary

List the terms. As you learn about each one, make notes in the Interactive Glossary.

_____    _____

_____    _____

_____

### Compare and Contrast

When you compare things, you look for ways in which they are alike. When you contrast things, you look for ways in which they are different. Active readers stay focused by asking themselves, How are these things alike? How are these things different?

# It's Shocking!

Working around electric utility lines is dangerous! How does a line worker stay safe?

**Active Reading**  Draw a box around the sentences that contrast conductors and insulators.

**E**ven on a hot day, a worker who repairs electric utility lines must be bundled up in protective clothing. The thick gloves, the bulky boots, and the hard plastic hat are heavy; however, these clothes protect the worker from an electric shock!

The rubber and plastic used in the protective clothing do not allow electric charges to flow through them. A material that resists the flow of electric charges is called an **insulator**. Electric charges flow easily through metals and some liquids. A material that readily allows electric charges to pass through it is called a **conductor**.

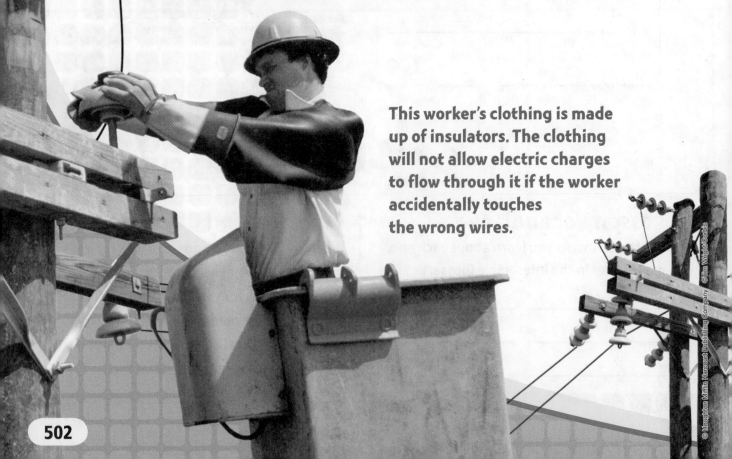

This worker's clothing is made up of insulators. The clothing will not allow electric charges to flow through it if the worker accidentally touches the wrong wires.

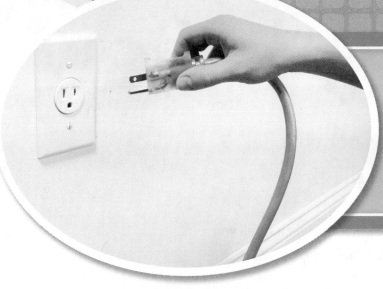

The parts of a plug that you hold and the covering on the wire are insulators. The metal prongs that go into the outlet are good conductors.

Electrical appliances work when electric charges flow through them. The parts that carry electric charges are made from conductors. Insulators are wrapped around the conductors to make appliances safe to handle.

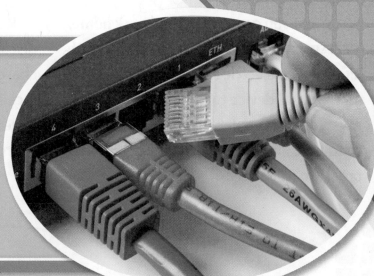

▶ Label the parts of the wire as a conductor or an insulator.

_____

_____

▶ Why are insulators used?

_____
_____
_____
_____
_____
_____
_____

# A Path to Follow

If the wiring in a lamp does not change,
why isn't the lamp on all of the time?

Draw a box around the sentences that tell you
how a closed circuit and an open circuit are different.

When you go to school and back home,
your path is a loop. A **circuit** is a path
along which electric charges can flow. For
an electrical device to work, the circuit
must form a complete loop. This type of
circuit is called a *closed circuit*. There are no
breaks in its path.

What happens if a loose wire gets
disconnected? The path is broken, and
charges cannot flow. This type of circuit
is called an *open circuit*. Many circuits
have a switch. A switch controls the flow of
charges by opening and closing the circuit.

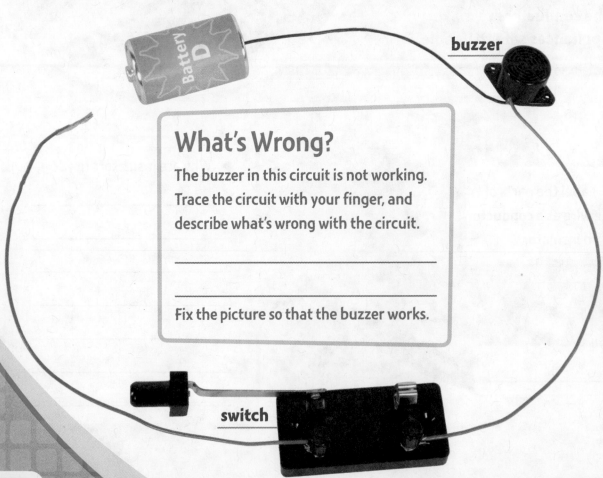

buzzer

## What's Wrong?

The buzzer in this circuit is not working.
Trace the circuit with your finger, and
describe what's wrong with the circuit.

_____

_____

Fix the picture so that the buzzer works.

switch

## Open Circuit

When the switch in a circuit is open, the circuit is not complete. Electric charges cannot flow, so the light stays off.

## Closed Circuit

When the switch is closed, the circuit is complete. Electric charges can flow through it to light up the bulb.

▶ The filament in a light bulb is a tiny wire. It is part of the circuit. If the filament breaks, the circuit will be _____.

filament

# Who Needs a Map?

To travel from point A to point B, you usually take the shortest route. What if one of the roads on that route is blocked? Simple! You just take another road. What would happen if there were only one road between point A and point B?

**Active Reading** Underline the sentences that compare series circuits and parallel circuits.

## Series Circuits

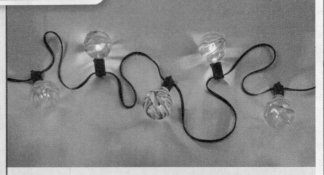

**If one light bulb in a series circuit burns out, all of the lights go out, because the circuit is broken.**

In a series circuit, electric charges must follow a single path. The charged particles move from the battery's positive terminal to its negative terminal.

▶ Draw arrows to show how charges flow in this circuit.

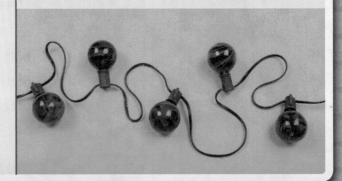

Suppose that the television and all the lights in a room are part of the same circuit. What would happen if one of the light bulbs burned out? It would depend on how the circuit is wired.

A **series circuit** has only one path for electric charges to follow. If any part of the path breaks, the circuit is open. Nothing works!

A circuit with several different paths for the charges to follow is called a **parallel circuit**. If one part of the circuit breaks, the charges can still flow along the other parts.

## Color a Complex Circuit

1. Look at the circuit below. Color the bulb or bulbs that should be lit.
2. Draw an *X* on the switch that is open. Draw an arrow above the closed switch.

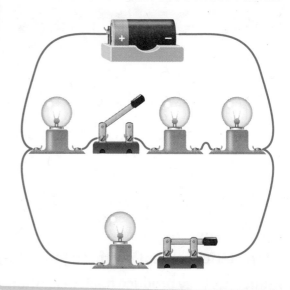

## Parallel Circuits

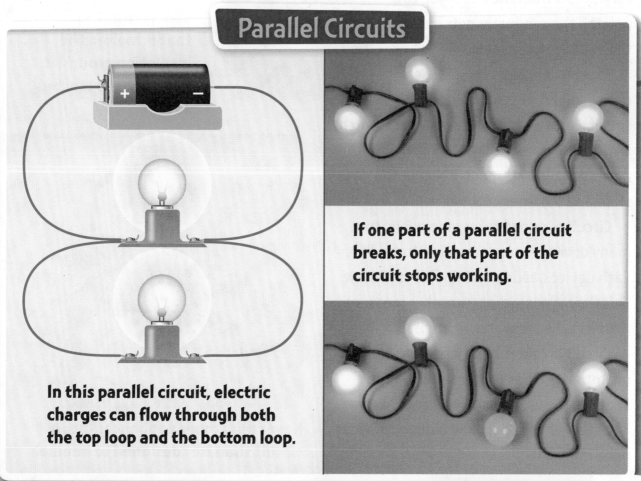

In this parallel circuit, electric charges can flow through both the top loop and the bottom loop.

If one part of a parallel circuit breaks, only that part of the circuit stops working.

**507**

# Circuit Overload!

Some house fires are caused by overloaded electrical wiring. How can you use electrical appliances safely?

television
3 amps

hair dryer
12.5 amps

As electric charges flow through conductors, they produce heat. Insulation protects the materials around these conductors from the heat—up to a point! If the conductor gets too hot, the insulation can melt.

WOW!

This wire got so hot that it melted the insulation around it. It could have started a fire.

To protect against fires, a fuse or a circuit breaker is added to each circuit. Fuses and circuit breakers are switches that work automatically. They open if charge flows too quickly through a circuit. The flow stops and the wires cool, which prevents a fire.

Circuit overload takes place when too many devices in one circuit are turned on. Each device needs a certain flow of charge. This flow of charge, or current, is measured in units called *amperes*, or amps.

Circuit breakers open when the number of amps is greater than a certain value. Suppose the value for a breaker is 15 amps. The breaker will open if all plugged devices draw more than 15 amps.

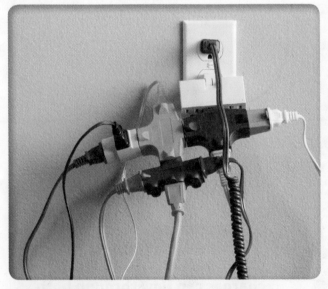

Never plug more appliances into a circuit than it is designed to handle!

With power strips like this one, it's possible to plug many devices into a single wall outlet. **That could be a big mistake!**

## Should You Plug It In?

Draw a line connecting the hair dryer to one of the outlets in the power strip. Then connect the other devices you could use at the same time without overloading a 15-amp circuit breaker.

**lava lamp**
**0.5 amp**

**laptop computer**
**1.5 amps**

**clothes dryer**
**42 amps**

This panel contains circuit breakers. Each breaker allows a certain number of amps of electric current to pass through one circuit.

## Do the Math!
### Solve Word Problems

1. How many times as much current does a television need than a lava lamp?

   _____

2. Circuit breakers are made in increments of 5 amps. What size breaker would you need for a circuit with a television, two laptops, and a lava lamp?

   _____

# Sum It Up!

When you're done, use the answer key to check and revise your work.

**On each numbered line, fill in the vocabulary term that matches the description.**

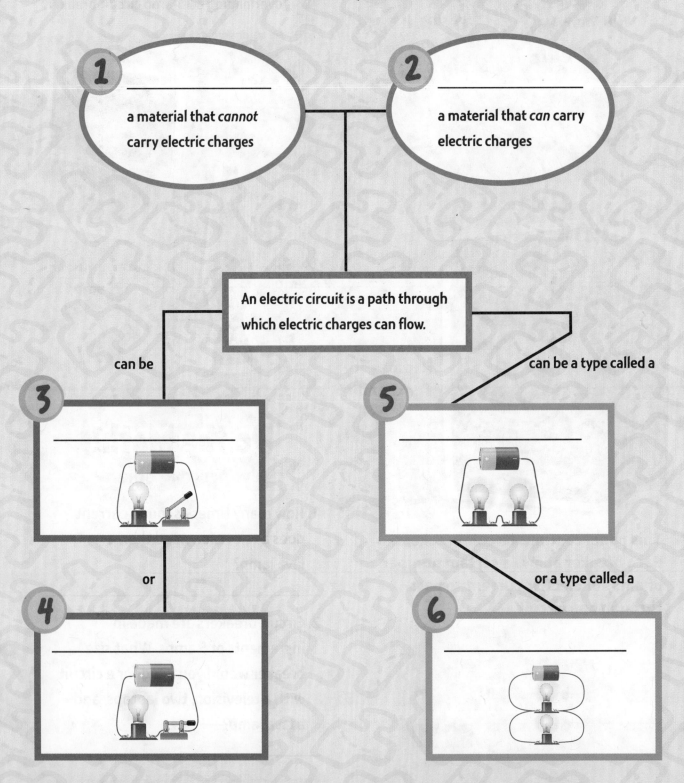

**1** _____
a material that *cannot* carry electric charges

**2** _____
a material that *can* carry electric charges

An electric circuit is a path through which electric charges can flow.

can be

**3** _____

can be a type called a

**5** _____

or

**4** _____

or a type called a

**6** _____

Name _____

## Word Play

**1** Unscramble the scrambled word in each sentence. Write the unscrambled word after the sentence. The first one is done for you.

| | |
|---|---|
| A. In some circuits, electrical energy is transformed into light energy by a light **lubb**. | Ⓑ U L B<br>6 |
| B. The wires in a circuit are made of a material that is a **doortuccn**. | _ _ _ _ _ _ _ _ _ ◯<br>10 |
| C. A path that an electric current can follow is an electric **icurict**. | _ _ _ _ ◯ _ ◯<br>4   5 |
| D. A circuit in which electric charges can follow several different paths is called a **rallpale** circuit. | _ ◯ _ _ _ _ _<br>8 |
| E. If a wire is disconnected, the circuit is an **enop** circuit. | _ _ ◯ _<br>9 |
| F. The covering on electric plugs and around wires is made of an **rainulost**. | ◯ _ _ _ _ _ _ _ ◯<br>2                          7 |
| G. A circuit in which all the devices are connected in a single path is a **ressie** circuit. | _ _ ◯ _ _<br>3 |
| H. When a light is on, it is part of a **scolde** circuit. | ◯ _ _ _ _ _<br>1 |

Solve the riddle by writing the circled letters above in the correct spaces below.

**Riddle:** What is another name for a clumsy electrician?

A _ _ _ C _ I _     B_ E _ K _ _ _
  1  2  3   4   5      6 7   8   9 10

# Apply Concepts

**2** Draw a closed series circuit with two light bulbs, a battery, and a switch. What would happen if one of the light bulbs blows out?

_____

_____

_____

_____

**3** Explain what causes an overloaded circuit. How can you prevent an overloaded circuit?

_____

_____

_____

_____

_____

**4** Write the word _conductor_ or _insulator_ on each of the lines. Then infer which type of material is inside the holes in the outlet. Explain your answer.

**5** Suppose you are building a series circuit using a small battery and a small light bulb, and you run out of wire. What everyday objects could you use to connect the battery to the light bulb? Explain.

_____

_____

_____

**6** Identify each lettered part of the circuit, and explain what each part does.

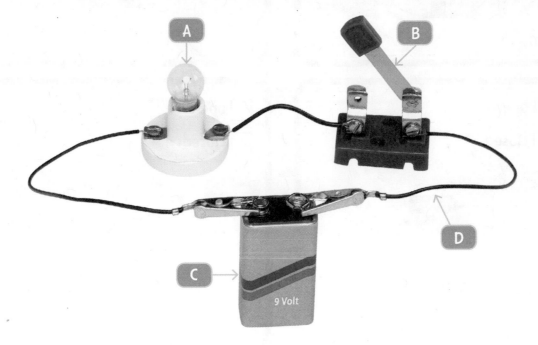

A _____

B _____

C _____

D _____

**7** Study each of the following circuits.

- Make a check mark to show whether the circuit is open or closed.
- Draw the missing parts needed to make the open circuits work.
- Label each circuit as a series circuit or a parallel circuit.

☐ open
☐ closed

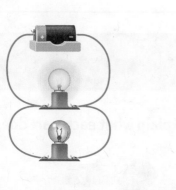

☐ open
☐ closed

☐ open
☐ closed

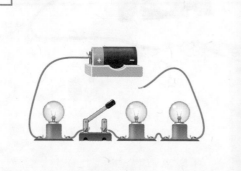

☐ open
☐ closed

**Take It Home!**

Discuss with your family what you have learned about circuits. Gather some electrical devices and explain how they use electricity. Try flipping some switches in your home, and explain whether they are series circuits or parallel circuits.

# Ask an Electrician

**Q.** Do electricians make electricity?

**A.** No. Electricity is produced in energy stations and carried to buildings through wires. Electricians work with wires to make sure the electricity moves safely.

**Q.** Don't electricians worry about electric shocks when they work?

**A.** Electricians must always turn off electricity to the wires they are working on. Electricity can be dangerous and safety is an important part of the job.

**Q.** What kind of training do you need to be an electrician?

**A.** Most electricians learn from experienced electricians while they are attending classes. During this period, they are called an apprentice.

## Now It's Your Turn!

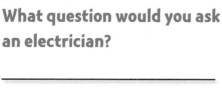

What question would you ask an electrician?

_____

_____

_____

_____

# Untangle the Wires!

For each circuit, explain what would happen
when the switch at the bottom is closed.

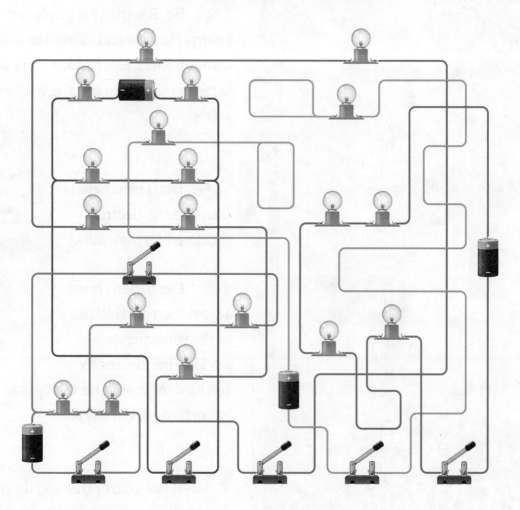

**Red:** _____

**Purple:** _____

**Green:** _____

**Orange:** _____

**Blue:** _____

**Essential Question**

# How Do We Use Electricity?

## Engage Your Brain!

Find the answer to the following question in this lesson and record it here.

What types of energy is electricity being changed into in this picture?

_____

_____

_____

## Active Reading

### Lesson Vocabulary

List the terms. As you learn about each one, make notes in the Interactive Glossary.

_____

_____

_____

_____

### Cause and Effect

Some ideas in this lesson are connected by a cause-and-effect relationship. Why something happens is a cause. What happens as a result of something else is an effect. Active readers look for effects by asking themselves, What happened? They look for causes by asking, Why did it happen?

# Electricity
## Has Many Uses

How did your day start? Did an alarm clock wake you? Did you turn on a light? Did you eat something out of the refrigerator? Yes? Then you used electricity!

As you read these two pages, draw a box around the sentence that contains the main idea.

Think of all the things in your home or school that use electricity. What do they do? Devices that use electricity change electrical energy into other types of energy, such as light or heat. We use electricity to heat our homes and cook our food. We also use it to light our rooms and to keep foods cold.

A computer changes electrical energy into light, sound, and heat. When you turn on a computer, you see pictures and hear sounds. You feel heat coming off of it. A computer can be plugged into an electrical outlet. It can also run on batteries. How do the objects on these pages change electrical energy?

a ceiling fan

a television and a video game system

Many electrical devices have electric motors. An **electric motor** is a machine that changes electrical energy into energy of motion. An electric fan uses an electric motor to move air. A refrigerator uses an electric motor to keep foods cold. What other objects in your home have electric motors? Any electric device that makes motion probably does.

an electric stove

a hair dryer and a light

## Making a Better Change

A light bulb produces heat and light. Why would an engineer want to reduce the amount of heat a light bulb produces?

_____

_____

_____

# Magnets and Magnetism

You can feel the force between two magnets. You feel magnets pull together, and you feel them push apart. How do magnets work?

**Active Reading** As you read these two pages, underline words or phrases that describe what causes magnets to push or pull.

Each flat surface on a ring magnet is either an *N* pole or an *S* pole.

Magnets have been used for thousands of years. A **magnet** is an object that attracts iron and a few other metals. People make magnets, but they are also found in nature. Magnets are found in many common things.

*Magnetism* is a physical property of matter. Magnets push and pull because of their magnetic field. A *magnetic field* is the space around the magnet where the force of the magnet acts.

Each magnet has two ends, or *poles*. A magnetic pole is the part of a magnet where its magnetic field is the strongest. One end is called the *south-seeking* pole, or *S* pole. The other is the *north-seeking* pole, or *N* pole.

Two *N* poles or two *S* poles are similar, or like, poles. If you place the *N* poles of two magnets near each other, they repel, or push away. Two *S* poles push away, too. Like poles repel each other.

An *N* pole and an *S* pole are unlike poles. If you place unlike poles of two magnets near each other, they attract, or pull toward each other.

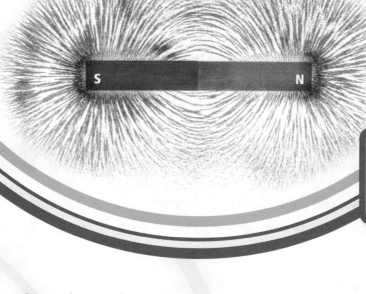

The picture above shows a bar magnet. The iron filings around the magnet show the shape of the magnetic field. Where do you see the most iron filings? They are at the *S* and *N* poles of the magnet, which are where the magnetic field is strongest. Where do you see fewer iron filings? The middle of the magnet has fewer iron filings. The magnetic field is weakest there. The size and the type of material used to make a magnet affect its strength.

These magnets have magnetic fields that are strong enough to attract each other through a person's hand!

▶ Why are some magnets floating around the pencil in the picture on the left?

_____

_____

_____

_____

_____

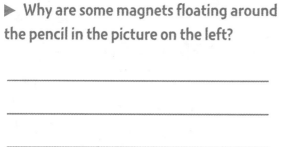

# Electromagnets

Electricity and magnetism are related.
One can produce the other.

As you read this page, circle the sentence that explains how magnetism produces an electric current.

Suppose you slide a coil of wire back and forth around a bar magnet. When the ends of the wire are attached to a light bulb, the bulb lights! Moving a magnet and a wire near each other produces an electric current.

Turning the handle on the device below turns a coil of wire inside three U-shaped magnets. Electric charges flow through the wire and the bulb lights. On the picture on the right, an electric current is used to make a magnet.

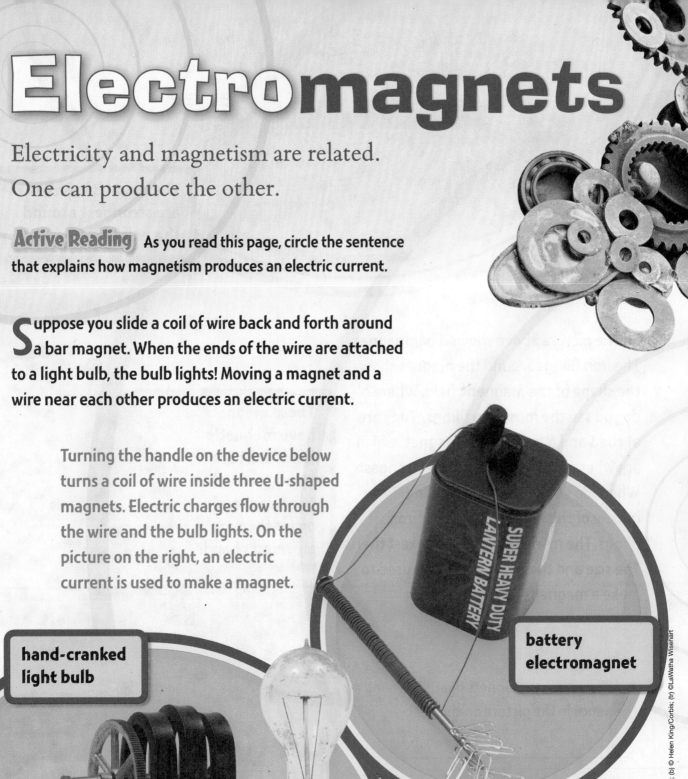

hand-cranked
light bulb

battery
electromagnet

If magnets produce electricity, can electricity make magnets? Yes! Wrapping a coil of current-carrying wire around an iron coil such as a nail makes a magnet. You can use this magnet to pick up small iron objects such as paper clips. A device in which current produces magnetism is called an **electromagnet**.

Huge electromagnets are used in junkyards. They separate iron and steel objects from other objects. The operator swings the electromagnet over a pile of junk. He turns on the current. All the iron pieces are attracted to the magnet. The operator then swings the magnet over a container and turns off the current. The magnetism stops, and the iron drops into the container.

Electromagnets have become very important and useful. Today, every electric motor contains at least one electromagnet. You can also find electromagnets in telephones, doorbells, speakers, and computers. Doctors can use electromagnets to take pictures of the inside of the body.

junkyard electromagnet

## What Are the Parts of an Electromagnet?

List the parts of an electromagnet. Then draw an electromagnet in the space provided.

_____

_____

_____

_____

_____

# Generating Electricity

We use electricity every day. How does it get to our homes and schools?

**Active Reading** As you read, circle the resources used to make electricity.

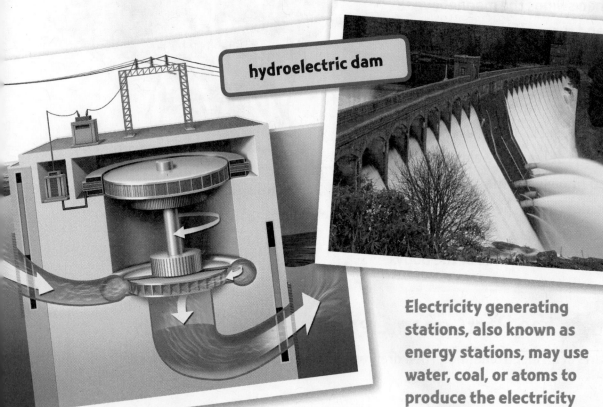

hydroelectric dam

Electricity generating stations, also known as energy stations, may use water, coal, or atoms to produce the electricity you use.

Inside a hydroelectric [hy•droh•ee•LEK•trik] dam, the mechanical energy of falling water is used to turn generators, which change mechanical energy into electrical energy.

windmills

Windmills have been used to grind grain or pump water. Today, wind turbines generate electricity.

Suppose you spin a magnet inside a coil of wire. A current begins to flow through the wire. You've made a **generator**, a device that converts mechanical energy to electrical energy. Huge generators in energy stations produce electricity that travels through wires to homes, schools, and businesses.

Some energy stations use falling water or wind to turn generators. Other stations convert sunlight, or solar energy, into electrical energy. These resources are called renewable resources, because they can be replaced quickly.

Most energy stations burn coal or other fuels to heat water. The water rises as steam, which turns the generators. Coal is a nonrenewable resource that will eventually run out. That's why it's important for us to conserve, or use less, electricity.

# Do the Math!
## Solve a Problem

Sam's electric bill was $200 for the month of June. The air conditioner accounts for $\frac{1}{2}$ of the bill, and the water heater accounts for $\frac{1}{5}$ of the bill. How much did it cost to run each appliance in June?

When you're done, use the answer key to check and revise your work.

**Use information in the summary to complete the graphic organizer.**

## Summarize

Electricity is used and produced in many ways. Electrical devices change electrical energy into other types of energy, such as heat, light, and sound. Many devices, including fans and refrigerators, have electric motors that change electrical energy into energy of motion. Electricity and magnetism are related. Magnets produce a magentic field. A magnetic field can be used to produce an electric current. An electric current may also be used to make an electromagnet. An electromagnet can be used in a generator at an energy station. A generator changes energy of motion into electrical energy. Energy stations produce the electrical energy we use. We need to conserve electricity because some resources used by energy stations will run out.

**1 Main Idea:**

_____

_____

**2 Detail:** Electrical devices convert

_____

_____

_____

_____

**3 Detail:** Magnetism and electricty are related because

_____

_____

_____

_____

**4 Detail:** An electromagnet can be used in a generator at an energy station to produce

_____

_____

_____

Name _____

# Word Play

**1** Unscramble each of the clues to form a word or a phrase from the word bank. Copy each letter in a numbered cell to the cell below with the same number.

TECGARLOETNEM [ ][ ][ ][ ][ ][ ][ ][ ][5][ ][ ][ ]

RECLICTE ROOTM [ ][ ][8][ ][ ][ ][3][ ][ ]  [ ][ ][ ][ ][ ][ ]

TORRAGEEN [ ][4][ ][ ][ ][ ][ ][ ][ ]

ONECREVS [ ][ ][ ][2][ ][ ][ ][ ]

REECUSROS [ ][ ][ ][ ][1][ ][ ][ ][ ]

GANETM [ ][10][7][ ][ ][ ]

CICLETERTIY [6][ ][ ][ ][ ][9][ ][ ][ ][ ][11][ ]

**Word Bank**
conserve
electricity
electric motor
electromagnet
generator
magnet
resources

This lesson is about [1][2][3][4][5]  [6][7][8][9][10][11] .

# Apply Concepts

**2** Draw a common electrical appliance. Then explain how it changes electrical energy to other forms of energy.

_____

_____

_____

_____

# Apply Concepts

**3** Draw an *X* over each appliance that changes electrical energy to mechanical energy. You may use an appliance more than once.

Circle each appliance that is designed to change electrical energy into heat energy.

Draw a square around each appliance that changes electrical energy to sound energy.

Draw a triangle around each appliance that changes electrical energy to light energy.

**4** What is the device in the picture to the right called? What would happen if you put this device near a pile of iron nails?

_____

_____

_____

**5** A. What are some resources used to generate electrical energy at energy stations?

_____

_____

_____

_____

B. Describe three ways that you can conserve electrical energy.

_____

_____

_____

_____

**Take It Home!**

Discuss with your family ways that you could conserve electrical energy. You might talk about ways to use less energy or about things you can do by hand instead of using electrical appliances.

# How It Works:

## The Electric Grid

At home, you flip a switch and a light comes on. The electricity to power the light comes from generating stations. Generating stations are a part of a larger system know as the *electric grid*. Generators, high voltage steel towers, conductors, insulators, and your home appliances are all parts of this system.

At generating stations, generators transform kinetic energy into electrical energy.

From the generating stations, electrical energy travels over electrical lines on tall steel towers. These lines are made up of a conductor and an insulator.

Coal is a fossil fuel. There is plenty of it in the United States. Most of our electricity comes from burning coal.

Wind turbines are large generators. Turbines use energy from wind to generate electricity.

## Troubleshooting

During prolonged hot weather, many people use air conditioning units to remain cool. How could this affect the electric grid and the environment?

_____

_____

## continued

# Show How It Works

Water falling through a turbine can generate electricity. Most hydroelectric generating stations have a dam that blocks a river. A lake forms behind the dam and provides a constant source of falling water. The dam also floods areas that were once dry land. Draw a picture that shows what you think the area behind the dam looked like before the dam was built.

A hydroelectric dam uses energy from moving water to generate electricity.

Research the benefits and risks for each of the first three sources of electrical energy listed below. Fill out the chart. Then, identify the energy source described in the last entry.

| Electrical energy source | Benefits | Risks |
|---|---|---|
| Wind turbines | do not pollute air, land, or water | |
| Coal-burning generating stations | | Coal mines change the landscape; they can cause land, air, and water pollution. |
| Hydroelectric dams | use water, a renewable resource | |
| | do not pollute air, land, or water | These produce toxic wastes that must be stored for a very long time. |

# Build On It!

Rise to the engineering design challenge—complete **Build in Some Science: An Attractive Option** on the Inquiry Flipchart.

# Unit 10 Review

## Vocabulary Review

Use the terms in the box to complete the sentences.

> circuit
> conductor
> electric current
> electric motor
> generator
> insulator
> magnet
> static electricity

1. A path along which electric charges flow is called

   a(n) _____.

2. An object that attracts iron and a few other metals is called

   a(n) _____.

3. A device that changes electrical energy into mechanical energy

   is a(n) _____.

4. A material through which electricity travels easily is

   called a(n) _____.

5. The buildup of electric charges on an object is

   called _____.

6. A material that resists the movement of electricity through

   it is called a(n) _____.

7. A device that produces an electric current by
   converting mechanical energy to electrical energy is

   a(n) _____.

8. The flow of electric charges along a path is called

   a(n) _____.

# Science Concepts

Fill in the letter of the choice that best answers the question.

9. Carlita hangs two balloons from a desk. When they hang normally, they are close together but do not touch. Carlita rubs both balloons with a wool cloth. What happens when she lets the balloons hang near one another?

Ⓐ They push each other away.

Ⓑ They touch each other and pop.

Ⓒ They touch each other and stick together.

Ⓓ They are close together but do not touch.

10. Ari is combing his hair. After a while, he notices that the comb attracts the hairs on his head as shown below.

Which explanation **best** describes why the hairs are attracted to the comb?

Ⓐ Combing the hairs caused them to lose their static charge.

Ⓑ Combing the hairs caused the comb to lose its static charge.

Ⓒ Combing the hairs gave them a charge that is opposite the charge on the comb.

Ⓓ Combing the hairs gave them a charge that is the same as the charge on the comb.

11. Identify the parts of an electromagnet.

Ⓐ battery, battery holder, nail, copper wire

Ⓑ battery, battery holder, bulb, copper wire

Ⓒ battery, battery holder, nail, bulb

Ⓓ battery, battery holder, switch, copper wire

12. When an electric current runs through a doorbell buzzer, a mechanism inside vibrates back and forth to make the buzzer work. When someone pushes the button on a doorbell, how does energy transform?

Ⓐ Electrical energy transforms into heat, then sound.

Ⓑ Electrical energy transforms into motion, then sound.

Ⓒ Motion energy transforms into electrical energy, then back to motion.

Ⓓ Sound energy transforms into motion, then back to sound.

13. Jayden uses various objects to complete a circuit. He compares how brightly a bulb glows using each object. His results are shown below.

| Object | Glow |
|---|---|
| nail | very bright |
| crayon | dim |
| eraser | very dim |
| pencil lead | bright |

Which object is the **best** electrical conductor?

Ⓐ nail

Ⓑ eraser

Ⓒ crayon

Ⓓ pencil lead

14. While planning an investigation, Harini draws four ways she could connect a battery, a paper clip, a light bulb, and some wire. Which arrangement below would light the bulb?

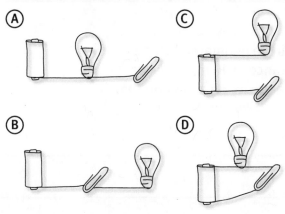

15. You rub a balloon on your hair on a dry day. Then, you bring a second balloon near the first one. How would you describe what happens to the balloons?

(A) They repel each other.

(B) They attract each other.

(C) They neither attract nor repel each other.

(D) Opposite charges make one balloon become larger and one smaller.

16. People use many sources of mechanical energy to generate electricity. Which frequently used source will eventually run out?

(A) wind

(B) coal

(C) solar energy

(D) running water

17. The picture below shows a large dam used to produce electricity. Water flows from the lake behind the dam to the river below it. Water passes through turbines connected to electric generators.

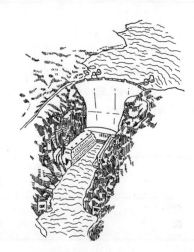

Which energy transformation takes place in the hydroelectric power plant?

(A) heat energy into electrical energy

(B) energy of motion into electrical energy

(C) electrical energy into energy of motion

(D) energy of motion and sound energy into electrical energy

18. When Tony left the room, he flipped the light switch. The light bulb stopped giving off light. What caused it to go out?

(A) The tiny wires inside the bulb stopped moving, so it could not make light.

(B) The electric current stopped, so no more electrical energy was changed into light.

(C) The bulb became cooler, so the light bulb stopped changing heat energy into light.

(D) The electric current stopped, so light could not be changed into electrical energy.

# Apply Inquiry and Review the Big Idea

Write the answers to these questions.

**19.** Explain how a magnet and some wire can be used to generate electricity.

_____

_____

**20.** The amount of static electricity on a balloon can be estimated by how many pieces of confetti the balloon picks up at a distance of 1 cm. Yuma wants to find out if a dryer sheet produces less static electricity on a balloon than a piece of wool. Describe an investigation she can carry out.

_____

_____

_____

_____

**21.** Eshe builds two circuits. After checking that all the bulbs work, she removes one bulb from each circuit, as shown below.

Circuit A

Circuit B

Explain why the bulb goes out in Circuit B but stays lighted in Circuit A.

_____

_____

_____

# Motion

© Houghton Mifflin Harcourt Publishing Company (bg) ©Angelo Cavalli/Getty Images; (inset) ©Angelo Cavalli/Getty Images; (border) ©NIbc-Age Fotostock

**Big Idea**

Motion can be
measured and
described. It is
influenced by forces
such as friction.

## I Wonder Why

Rides at a state fair move in many different
directions and at many different speeds.
Why is this so? *Turn the page to find out.*

**Here's Why** Forces make objects move in straight lines, in curves, or back and forth. A force can change the speed or direction of an object.

In this unit, you will explore the Big Idea, the Essential Questions, and the Investigations on the Inquiry Flipchart.

Levels of Inquiry Key ■ DIRECTED ■ GUIDED ■ INDEPENDENT

Track Your Progress

**Big Idea** Motion can be measured and described. It is influenced by forces such as friction.

## Essential Questions

Now I Get the Big Idea!

**Science Notebook**
Before you begin each lesson, be sure to write your thoughts about the Essential Question.

**Essential Question**

# What Is Motion?

## Engage Your Brain!

As you read the lesson, figure out the answer to the following question. Write the answer here.

How would you describe the motion of the hummingbird in this picture?

_____

_____

_____

_____

_____

_____

_____

## Active Reading

### Lesson Vocabulary

List the terms. As you learn about each one, make notes in the Interactive Glossary.

_____  _____

_____  _____

_____  _____

### Main Idea and Details

Detail sentences give information about a main idea. The details may be examples, features, characteristics, or facts. Active readers stay focused on the topic when they ask, What fact or other information does this detail add to the main idea?

What tells you that the person in the picture is moving? Is it possible for a person to move in more than one direction at a time? You can find out!

## Active Reading

As you read the next page, find and circle details about how this girl can move.

## Curve

The boy's body moves in a curved path around the bar.

The blurry lines show you the directions in which the girl is moving.

## Straight Line

As the girl flips down the balance beam, she moves in a straight line.

ow would you describe where your left hand is right now? Is it on top of this book, or is it touching your chin? Can you describe where it is without naming something else that is close by? No! **Position** is the location of an object in relation to a nearby object or place. The second object or place is called the *reference point.*

Now put your left hand in a different place. This change in position is **motion**. To describe your hand's motion, you'd tell in what direction it moved from its earlier position as well as how fast it moved.

The girl in the picture is in motion. Parts of her body move up and down, back and forth, in circles, and in a straight line. Her feet move in a straight line down the beam and then up and down as she flips forward.

## Back and Forth

Draw a picture of something that vibrates, or moves back and forth.

▶ Name a part of the girl's body that is moving in several ways as she flips.

_____

# 10 Where Is It?

How can you tell that the penguin is moving?

**Active Reading** As you read the next page, underline the words that describe specific reference points.

1. The penguin has just jumped from the top of the ice.

2. The penguin is between the top of the ice and the water.

3. The penguin is entering the water.

**Y**ou know something is moving if its position changes against a background. The background is called the *frame of reference.*

The picture of the penguin shows three images taken as the penguin jumped off the ice. Notice that each image of the penguin has the same frame of reference. You can choose any part of that background as a reference point. The words *top of the ice* describe the reference point for Image 1. Both *top of the ice* and *the water* describe reference points for Image 2. Only *the water* describes a reference point for Image 3.

What if the images of the penguin had been in the wrong order? Could you put them in the correct order? Sure! You know that things don't fall up, so you could use the water as the reference point for each image. The image of the penguin highest above the water must be first. The image of the penguin closest to the water is last.

Look at the pictures of the horse race. In the pictures, what can you use for reference points? How can you use the reference points to put the pictures in order?

> ▶ Put these pictures in order by writing numbers in the circles. Then explain how you decided on the order.
>
> _____
>
> _____
>
> _____
>
> _____

**5 meters**

| 0 | 5 | 10 | 15 | 20 | 25 | 30 | 35 | 40 | 45 |

## Ready! Set! Go!

**00:00** → **00:10**

The turtle, cat, and rabbit start running at the same time. How far does each of them go in 10 seconds?

# Fast or Slow?

Could a turtle beat a rabbit in a race? It depends on each animal's speed.

**Active Reading** As you read this page, underline the definitions of *speed* and *velocity*.

One way to describe motion is to find speed, or how fast or slow something is moving. **Speed** tells you how the position of an object changes during a certain amount of time. You can measure time in hours (hr), minutes (min), or seconds (sec).

To find an object's speed, you divide how far it goes by the time it takes to get there. So if you walk 30 meters (m) in 15 seconds (sec), your speed is 2 m/sec.

$$30 \text{ m} \div 15 \text{ sec} = 2 \text{ m/sec}$$

How is velocity different from speed? **Velocity** is the speed of an object in a particular direction. Suppose you walk toward the east. If your speed is 2 m/sec, then your velocity is 2 m/sec, east.

In a race on a straight track, all the runners move in the same direction. Their velocities differ only because their speeds differ. Could a turtle win a race against a rabbit? Sure! The rabbit might run at a very slow speed—or in the wrong direction!

© Houghton Mifflin Harcourt Publishing Company   (l) ©Martin Harvey/Alamy; (r) ©Getty Images/PhotoDisc

**80 meters**

**100 meters**

| 50 | 55 | 60 | 65 | 70 | 75 | 80 | 85 | 90 | 95 | 100 |

# Do the Math!
## Calculate Speed

1. What is the speed of the rabbit during the race?

_____

2. What is the speed of the turtle during the race?

_____

3. A chicken joins the race and runs at 4 m/sec. On the distance line, draw the chicken where it would be after 10 seconds.

_____

_____

_____

_____

# Pushes and Pulls

**Gravity**
Gravity pulls down with a force that keeps the truck on the road.

Sand

What causes objects to start moving? What causes objects to stop moving once they are in motion?

**Active Reading** As you read these two pages, draw circles around two words that name types of forces.

What have you pushed or pulled today? Maybe you pushed open a door or pulled on your shoes. A push or a pull is a **force**. Suppose you want to change the way something is moving. A force can change an object's speed or direction.

Many forces act on you. *Gravity* is a force that pulls objects down to Earth. Gravity keeps you on the ground or on a chair.

*Friction* is a force that acts directly against the direction of motion. Friction can slow things down or make them stop.

▶ Why do you think workers spread sand on icy, snow-covered roads?

_____

## Force
The force of the road on the truck pushes the truck forward.

## Friction
The snow exerts a force of friction that pushes backward against the truck and slows it down.

▶ Look at the girl on the sled. Draw arrows and label *gravity*, *force*, and *friction*.

# Changing It Up

The gas pedal on a car is called an accelerator. Did you know that the brakes and steering wheel are also accelerators?

**Active Reading** As you read these pages, circle three phrases that tell how an object can accelerate.

You may hear people say that a car is accelerating when it speeds up. That's only partly correct. **Acceleration** is any change in velocity. Remember that velocity tells both the speed and the direction of motion. So matter accelerates if it speeds up, slows down, or changes direction.

Acceleration of any kind is caused by forces. Forces can push and pull on matter from all directions. If a force pushing against an object in one direction is greater than a force pushing in the opposite direction, the object will accelerate.

Look at the path of the fly. The fly accelerates each time it changes either its speed or its direction. Sometimes it changes both its speed and its direction at the same time!

## Turn and Speed Up

In this section, the fly accelerates because it changes both its direction and its speed.

## Slow Down

Here, the fly is traveling in a straight line while slowing down. This is also acceleration.

## Speed Up

In this section of its path, the fly travels in a straight line. It accelerates because it is speeding up.

## Stop and Start

The fly lands on the wall and stops moving. Its body doesn't accelerate. When it starts moving again, it speeds up. So it accelerates.

## Change Direction

The fly's speed stays the same as it changes direction. Because its velocity changes, it accelerates.

▶ Fill in the missing parts of the table.

| Item | Speed | What happens? | Acceleration? |
|------|-------|---------------|---------------|
| Mouse | 1 m/sec | suddenly chased by a cat | |
| Runner | 8 m/sec | runs at the same speed around a circular track | |
| Train | 80 km/hr | moves along a straight track | |
| Jet plane | 300 km/hr | | Yes, slows down. |

# Sum It Up!

When you're done, use the answer key to check and revise your work.

**Read the summary statements below. Each statement is incorrect.**
**Change the part of the statement in blue to make it correct.**

**1** You know that something is in
motion when it speeds up.

_____

_____

**2** Before you describe how an object
in a picture moved, you have to
choose a type of motion.

_____

_____

**3** To measure the speed of an object,
you need to know how far it traveled
and in what direction it traveled.

_____

_____

**4** Gravity and friction are two types of
motion that an object can have.

_____

_____

**5** An object accelerates when it
moves left or moves right.

_____

_____

**548**

Name _____

## Word Play

**1** Important words from this lesson are scrambled in the following box.
Unscramble the words. Place each word in a set of squares.

| lcaoeciranet | despe | eerrfcnee | oitmon |
|---|---|---|---|
| hups | crefo | vatgiyr | ovltyiec |

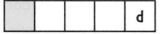

[ ][ ][ ][ c ][ ]

[ ][ r ][ ][ ][ ]

[ ][ ][ ][ o ][ ]

[ ][ ][ c ][ ][ ][ ][ ][ ][ ][ ][ ]

[ ][ ][ s ][ ]

[ ][ ][ ][ r ][ ][ ][ ]

[ ][ ][ ][ d ][ ]

[ ][ ][ ][ o ][ ][ ][ ]

Rearrange the letters in the colored boxes to form
a word that describes the location of an object.

[ ][ ][ ][ ][ ][ ][ ][ ][ ]

Put a star next to two words that describe
how fast something moves.

# Apply Concepts

**2** Describe the motion and path of the diver. Use the words *position*, *speed*, *velocity*, and *acceleration* in your description.

_____

_____

_____

_____

_____

_____

_____

_____

_____

_____

_____

**3** You are riding in a bus. Your friend is standing on the street corner as the bus goes by. How would you describe the way your friend seems to move? How would your friend describe your motion? Why do the descriptions differ?

_____

_____

_____

_____

_____

4

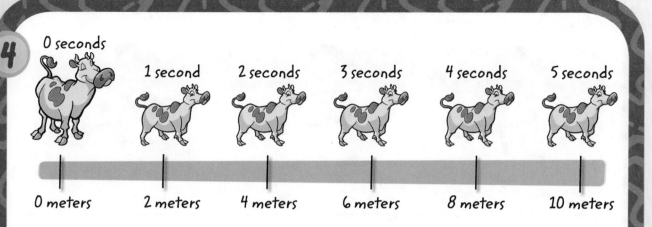

0 seconds    1 second    2 seconds    3 seconds    4 seconds    5 seconds

0 meters    2 meters    4 meters    6 meters    8 meters    10 meters

**The diagram represents the motion of a cow walking in a straight line across a field. Use it to answer these questions.**

**a. Is the cow accelerating? Why or why not?**

_____

_____

_____

_____

_____

_____

**b. Calculate the speed of the cow.**

_____

_____

_____

_____

**c. How long will it take the cow to travel 24 meters? Describe how you found the correct answer.**

_____

_____

_____

_____

**d. How far will the cow travel in 35 seconds? Describe how you found the correct answer.**

_____

_____

_____

_____

_____

**5** Describe three different forces that act on you as you walk. Draw an arrow on each picture to show the direction of a force. Be sure to include gravity and friction.

_____    _____    _____

_____    _____    _____

_____    _____    _____

_____    _____    _____

**6** In each box, draw a picture that shows an object moving in the way described by the label at the top of the box.

curve

back and forth and curve

**Take It Home!**

Choose three places in your community. With a family member, visit each place and look for things that move. Record what you observe in a chart. Can you identify the forces causing the motion?

Name _____

**Essential Question**

# What Is Speed?

## Set a Purpose
What do you think you will learn from this experiment?

_____

_____

_____

_____

## State Your Hypothesis
Write your hypothesis, or testable statement.

_____

_____

_____

_____

## Think About the Procedure
How can you figure out the speed at which the ball is moving?

_____

_____

_____

_____

As you pull the ball back farther each time, what happens to the force with which the ball is launched?

_____

_____

## Record Your Data
In the space below, draw a table in which to record your observations.

## Draw Conclusions

**What conclusion can you draw from this investigation?**

_____

_____

_____

## Analyze and Extend

1. **How can the same object move at different speeds?**

_____

_____

_____

_____

2. **What other factors might have affected the speed at which the ball moved?**

_____

_____

_____

3. Are there limits to how much force you could apply to the ball in this inquiry? If so, what are they?

_____

_____

_____

_____

_____

4. What would you expect to happen if you were to use a larger rubber band?

_____

_____

_____

_____

_____

5. Think of other questions you would like to ask about speed and motion.

_____

_____

_____

_____

_____

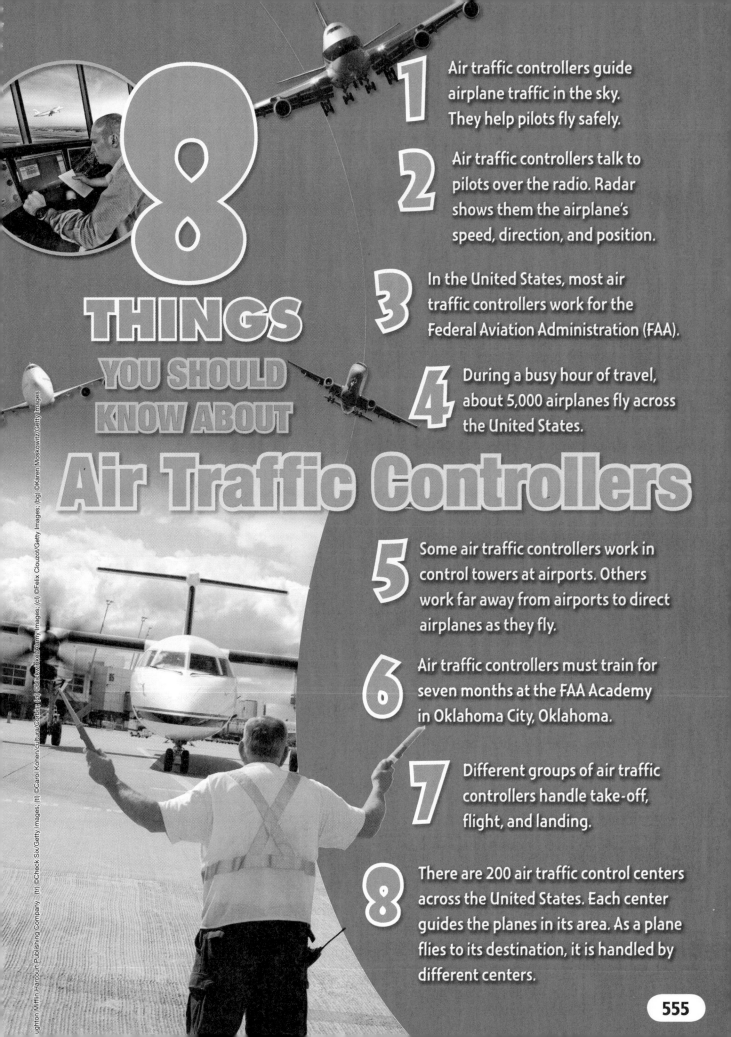

# 8 THINGS
## YOU SHOULD KNOW ABOUT
# Air Traffic Controllers

**1** Air traffic controllers guide airplane traffic in the sky. They help pilots fly safely.

**2** Air traffic controllers talk to pilots over the radio. Radar shows them the airplane's speed, direction, and position.

**3** In the United States, most air traffic controllers work for the Federal Aviation Administration (FAA).

**4** During a busy hour of travel, about 5,000 airplanes fly across the United States.

**5** Some air traffic controllers work in control towers at airports. Others work far away from airports to direct airplanes as they fly.

**6** Air traffic controllers must train for seven months at the FAA Academy in Oklahoma City, Oklahoma.

**7** Different groups of air traffic controllers handle take-off, flight, and landing.

**8** There are 200 air traffic control centers across the United States. Each center guides the planes in its area. As a plane flies to its destination, it is handled by different centers.

# You Be an Air Traffic Controller

This radar screen shows four airplanes flying near an airport. The screen shows the position of each airplane and the direction of travel. Use the key to help you answer the questions below.

## Key

| ✈ Flight 423 | ✈ Flight 893 | ✈ Flight 781 | ✈ Flight 672 |
|---|---|---|---|
| Speed: 480 km/hr | Speed: 480 km/hr | Speed: 480km/hr | Speed: 910 km/hr |
| Altitude: 3,000 m | Altitude: 3,000 m | Altitude: 3,000 m | Altitude: 12,000 m |

1. Find flights 423 and 893. How are these airplanes moving relative to each other?

2. Which airplane is flight 781 approaching? What instructions would keep these airplanes apart?

3. Will flight 672 come close to any of the other airplanes on the screen? Explain.

1. _____
   _____

2. _____
   _____

3. _____
   _____

## Think About It!

Name three ways that an airplane can change its motion in flight.

_____
_____

# How It Works:

## Gyroscopes

Have you ever played with a top? A top can balance on a point as it spins around its axis. The spinning motion keeps the top standing up. When the top begins to slow down, gravity makes it wobble and fall over. A gyroscope behaves like a top.

When a force acts on the gyroscope, the disk's spinning motion makes the central ring resist changing position. The rest of the gyroscope turns around the fixed central ring.

Central ring

Disk and Axle

This gyroscope has a disk and axle and a central ring that swivels on an outer ring, or gimbal.

The axle is attached to the central ring. There is little friction where these parts connect, so the disk spins rapidly on the axle.

Gimbal

## Troubleshooting

Suppose that the disk of a gyroscope spins for a very short time before coming to a quick stop. What could be wrong? How would you fix it?

_____

_____

_____

_____

# S.T.E.M.
continued

## Show How It Works

Gyroscopes are used in airplanes, boats, and spacecraft. Electronic sensors around a gyroscope tell how the vehicle has moved. Think about how data from a gyroscope might help keep a spacecraft from veering off course. In the space below, make a list of the vehicle's systems that may use data from the gyroscope.

On Earth, a magnetic compass tells us which direction we are facing. A space telescope cannot use a magnetic compass. These compasses do not work in space. So, the Hubble Space Telescope uses gyroscopes to maintain direction.

_____

_____

_____

Design a toy, tool, or any device that uses a built-in gyroscope. Draw a picture of your device. Then, answer the questions.

Exlain what your toy, tool, or device does and how it works.

_____

_____

_____

Why does your invention need a gyroscope?

_____

_____

_____

_____

_____

## Build On It!

Rise to the engineering design challenge—complete **Improvise It: A Game of Skill and Motion** on the Inquiry Flipchart.

Name _____

## Vocabulary Review

Use the terms in the box to complete the sentences.

acceleration
force
friction
gravity
motion
position
speed
velocity

1. Any change in the speed or direction of an object's motion

   is _____.

2. A measure of an object's change in position during a certain

   amount of time is _____.

3. A push or a pull is a(n) _____.

4. The location of an object in relation to another object or place

   describes _____.

5. The force that acts to pull all objects down to Earth

   is _____.

6. An object that is changing its position is

   in _____.

7. A force that acts against the direction of an object's motion and

   causes it to slow or stop is _____.

8. The speed of an object in a particular direction is

   its _____.

# Science Concepts

Fill in the letter of the choice that best answers the question.

9. Cars, bicycles, and people are all objects that can be in motion. What is true about motion?

   Ⓐ An object in motion is accelerating.

   Ⓑ Motion is the change in position of an object.

   Ⓒ Gravity and friction are responsible for all motion.

   Ⓓ An object in motion has no speed, but it does have velocity.

10. The picture shows a boy as he rolls straight down a hill at a constant speed.

   What is changing as the boy rolls?

   Ⓐ position

   Ⓑ acceleration

   Ⓒ speed

   Ⓓ velocity

11. To make sure your measurements are clear, it is important to use appropriate units. Which of these is a unit of speed?

   Ⓐ seconds per gram (sec/g)

   Ⓑ meters per second (m/sec)

   Ⓒ grams per milliliter (g/mL)

   Ⓓ milliliters per second (mL/sec)

12. The line graph below shows an object's speed over time.

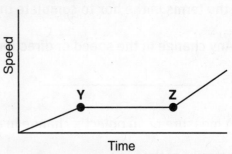

   What is happening to the object between Point Y and Point Z?

   Ⓐ The object is speeding up.

   Ⓑ The object has no velocity.

   Ⓒ The object is slowing down.

   Ⓓ The object's acceleration is zero.

13. Renee is throwing a ball high into the air and then catching it. What force is responsible for the ball's coming back to the ground?

   Ⓐ acceleration

   Ⓑ friction

   Ⓒ gravity

   Ⓓ speed

14. In which example is a force causing an object to accelerate?

   Ⓐ a soccer ball sitting on the ground

   Ⓑ a rock sitting on a ledge at the top of a mountain

   Ⓒ a train moving at constant speed around a curve in a track

   Ⓓ a girl riding a bicycle at a constant speed along a straight path

**15.** Jamal lives 2 km from his school. When he walks to school, the entire trip takes half an hour. What is Jamal's average speed during his walk?

(A) 0.5 km/h

(B) 1 km/h

(C) 2 km/h

(D) 4 km/h

**16.** An object moves from Point A to Point B in 2 minutes at a constant rate. What is the speed of the object?

**A** ●————— 18 meters —————● **B**

(A) 2 min/m

(B) 9 m/min

(C) 9 min/m

(D) 18 m/min

**17.** A car is stopped at a red light. The light turns green and the car turns right around a corner. What property of the car is changing?

(A) position only

(B) speed only

(C) direction only

(D) acceleration

**18.** Jen is walking her dog at a constant rate. They keep a constant rate as they turn a corner. Why has their velocity changed?

(A) because their speed changed

(B) because their direction changed

(C) because their position changed

(D) because their force changed

**19.** A roller coaster speeds up as it travels downhill and then slows as it enters a curve. Which statement best describes the motion of the roller coaster during this trip?

(A) Velocity changes, but acceleration remains constant.

(B) The velocity of the roller coaster remains constant.

(C) The roller coaster accelerates throughout the trip.

(D) The speed of the roller coaster remains constant.

# Apply Inquiry and Review the Big Idea

Write the answers to these questions.

20. Liu and Simone conduct an experiment about speed and velocity. They lay out two tracks that start from a raised platform and then flatten out into a straight, flat track. They send a different car down each track. The chart contains the data from their experiment.

| Car | Distance traveled (m) | Time taken (sec) | Direction of motion |
|-----|-----|-----|-----|
| red | 10 | 5 | west |
| blue | 20 | 10 | east |

a. Describe the velocity of both cars. _____

_____

b. Liu decides to raise the platform of the blue car's track even higher. How will this

change the speed of the car? _____

21. A boy uses a rope to pull a box across the ground. Explain how gravity and friction act on the box.

_____

_____

_____

22. A truck, a car, and a bicycle are stopped at a light. The light turns green and all three begin to move. The truck uses a big engine for this acceleration while a car uses a smaller engine. The bicycle rider uses the force of his own muscles.

a. Why does each vehicle require a different amount of force to accelerate?

_____

_____

b. Suppose each vehicle is pushed forward with a force of the same size. Which vehicle

will be moving faster after one minute? Why? _____

_____

23. Can an object moving at a constant speed accelerate? Explain your answer.

_____

_____

# Interactive Glossary

As you learn about each term, add notes, drawings, or sentences in the extra space. This will help you remember what the terms mean. Here are some examples.

**Fungi** [FUHN•jeye]  A kingdom of organisms that have a nucleus and get nutrients by decomposing other organisms

A mushroom is from the kingdom Fungi.

**physical change** [FIZ•ih•kuhl CHAYNJ] Change in the size, shape, or state of matter with no new substance being formed

When I cut paper, the paper has a physical change.

## Glossary Pronunciation Key

With every glossary term, there is also a phonetic respelling. A phonetic respelling writes the word the way it sounds, which can help you pronounce new or unfamiliar words. Use this key to help you understand the respellings.

| Sound | As in | Phonetic Respelling | Sound | As in | Phonetic Respelling |
|---|---|---|---|---|---|
| a | bat | (BAT) | oh | over | (OH•ver) |
| ah | lock | (LAHK) | oo | pool | (POOL) |
| air | rare | (RAIR) | ow | out | (OWT) |
| ar | argue | (AR•gyoo) | oy | foil | (FOYL) |
| aw | law | (LAW) | s | cell | (SEL) |
| ay | face | (FAYS) | | sit | (SIT) |
| ch | chapel | (CHAP•uhl) | sh | sheep | (SHEEP) |
| e | test | (TEST) | th | that | (THAT) |
| | metric | (MEH•trik) | | thin | (THIN) |
| ee | eat | (EET) | u | pull | (PUL) |
| | feet | (FEET) | uh | medal | (MED•uhl) |
| | ski | (SKEE) | | talent | (TAL•uhnt) |
| er | paper | (PAY•per) | | pencil | (PEN•suhl) |
| | fern | (FERN) | | onion | (UHN•yuhn) |
| eye | idea | (eye•DEE•uh) | | playful | (PLAY•fuhl) |
| i | bit | (BIT) | | dull | (DUHL) |
| ing | going | (GOH•ing) | y | yes | (YES) |
| k | card | (KARD) | | ripe | (RYP) |
| | kite | (KYT) | z | bags | (BAGZ) |
| ngk | bank | (BANGK) | zh | treasure | (TREZH•er) |

# Interactive Glossary

## A

**acceleration** [ak•sel•er•AY•shuhn] Any change in the speed or direction of an object's motion (p. 544)

**adaptation** [ad•uhp•TAY•shuhn] A trait or characteristic that helps an organism survive (p. 154)

**air mass** [AIR MAS] A large body of air that has the same temperature and humidity throughout (p. 276)

**air pressure** [AIR PRESH•er] The weight of the atmosphere pressing down on Earth (p. 261)

**atmosphere** [AT•muhs•feer] The mixture of gases that surround Earth (p. 247)

**axis** [AK•sis] The imaginary line around which Earth rotates (p. 298)

## B

**behavioral adaptation** [bih•HAYV•yu•ruhl ad•uhp•TAY•shuhn] Something an animal does that helps it survive (p. 159)

## C

**carnivore** [KAHR•nuh•vawr]  An animal that eats only other animals (p. 192)

**change of state** [CHAYNJ uhv STAYT]  A physical change that occurs when matter changes from one state to another, such as from a liquid to a gas (p. 378)

**chemical change** [KEM•ih•kuhl CHAYNJ]  A change in one or more substances, caused by a reaction, that forms new and different substances (p. 408)

**chemical energy** [KEM•ih•kuhl EN•er•jee]  Energy that can be released by a chemical reaction (p. 437)

**chemical property** [KEM•ih•kuhl PRAHP•er•tee]  A property that involves how a substance interacts with other substances (p. 406)

**chemical reaction** [KEM•ih•kuhl ree•AK•shuhn]  A chemical change (p. 411)

**chlorophyll** [KLAWR•uh•fihl]  A green pigment in plants that allows plant cells to make food using sunlight (p. 110)

**circuit** [SER•kuht]  A path along which electric charges can flow (p. 504)

# Interactive Glossary

**community** [kuh•MYOO•nih•tee]  All of the organisms that live in the same place (p. 176)

**conduction** [kuhn•DUK•shuhn]  The movement of heat between two materials that are touching (p. 450)

**complete metamorphosis** [kuhm•PLEET met•uh•MAWR•fuh•sis]  A complex change that most insects undergo that includes larva and pupa stages (p. 141)

**conductor** [kuhn•DUK•ter]  A material that lets heat or electricity travel through it easily (pp. 464, 502)

**computer model** [kuhm•PYOO•ter MOD•l]  A computer program that models an event or object (p. 49)

**conservation** [kahn•ser•VAY•shuhn]  The use of less of something to make its supply last longer (p. 228)

**condensation** [kahn•duhn•SAY•shuhn]  The process by which a gas changes into a liquid (pp. 248, 379)

**constellation** [kahn•stuh•LAY•shuhn]  A pattern of stars that form an imaginary picture or design in the sky (p. 304)

**R4**

© Houghton Mifflin Harcourt Publishing Company   HMH Credits

**consumer** [kuhn•SOOM•er]  Animals that eat plants or other animals to get energy (p. 181)

**density** [DEN•suh•tee]  The amount of matter present in a certain volume of a substance (p. 358)

**convection** [kuhn•VEK•shuhn]  The transfer of heat within a liquid or a gas (p. 451)

**design** [dih•ZYN]  To conceive something and to prepare the plans and drawings for it to be built (p. 66)

**D**

**E**

**data** [DEY•tuh]  Individual facts, statistics, and items of information (p. 35)

**ecosystem** [EE•koh•sis•tuhm]  A community of organisms and the physical environment in which they live (p. 174)

**decomposer** [dee•kuhm•POHZ•er]  A living thing that gets energy by breaking down wastes and the remains of plants and animals (p. 181)

**electric current** [ee•LEK•trik KER•uhnt]  The flow of electric charges along a path (p. 490)

# Interactive Glossary

**electric motor** [ee•LEK•trik MOHT•er] A device that changes electrical energy into mechanical energy (p. 519)

**energy** [EN•er•jee] The ability to cause changes in matter (p. 431)

**electrical energy** [ee•LEK•trih•kuhl EN•er•jee] Energy that comes from electric current (p. 437)

**engineering** [en•juh•NIR•ing] The use of scientific and mathematical principles to develop something practical (p. 65)

**electromagnet** [ee•lek•troh•MAG•nit] A temporary magnet caused by an electric current (p. 523)

**environment** [en•VY•ruhn•muhnt] All the living and nonliving things that surround and affect an organism (p. 152)

**endangered species** [en•DAYN•jerd SPEE•sheez] Organisms whose whole population is at risk of dying out (p. 228)

**evaporation** [ee•vap•uh•RAY•shuhn] The process by which a liquid changes into a gas (pp. 247, 379)

© Houghton Mifflin Harcourt Publishing Company   HMH Credits

## F

**fertilization** [fur•tl•i•ZAY•shuhn] The joining together of a sperm and an egg cell (p. 120)

**front** [FRUHNT] The boundary between two air masses (p. 276)

**food chain** [FOOD CHAYN] The transfer of food energy in a sequence of living things (p. 190)

## G

**gas** [GAS] The state of matter that does not have a definite shape or volume (p. 374)

**food web** [FOOD WEB] A diagram that shows the relationships among different food chains in an ecosystem (p. 196)

**generator** [JEN•er•ayt•er] A device that makes an electric current by converting mechanical energy to electrical energy (p. 525)

**force** [FAWRS] A push or a pull (p. 544)

**germination** [jer•muh•NAY•shuhn] The sprouting of a seed (p. 118)

# Interactive Glossary

**groundwater** [GROWND•waw•ter]  Water located within the gaps and pores in rocks below Earth's surface (p. 250)

**humidity** [hyoo•MID•uh•tee]  The amount of water vapor in the air (p. 261)

H

**habitat** [HAB•ih•tat]  The part of an ecosystem that meets the needs of an organism (p. 179)

**hypothesis** [hy•PAHTH•uh•sis]  A possible explanation or answer to a question; a testable statement (p. 9)

I

**heat** [HEET]  The energy that moves between objects of different temperatures (p. 448)

**incomplete metamorphosis** [in•kuhm•PLEET met•uh•MAWR•fuh•sis]  Developmental change in some insects in which a nymph hatches from an egg and gradually develops into an adult (p. 143)

**herbivore** [HER•buh•vawr]  An animal that eats only plants or other producers (p. 192)

**inference** [IN•fer•uhns]  An untested conclusion based on observations (p. 19)

**instinct** [IN•stinkt] A behavior an animal knows how to do without having to learn it (p. 159)

**insulator** [IN•suh•layt•er] A material that does not let heat or electricity move through it easily (pp. 466, 502)

**investigation** [in•ves•tuh•GAY•shuhn] A procedure carried out to gather data about an object or an event (p. 7)

### K

**kinetic energy** [kih•NET•ik EN•er•jee] The energy of motion (p. 432)

### L

**law of conservation of mass** [LAW UHV kahn•ser•VAY•shuhn UHV MAS] The idea that you cannot make or destroy matter (p. 370)

**leaf** [LEEF] The part of a plant that makes food, using air, light, and water (p. 108)

**liquid** [LIK•wid] The state of matter that has a definite volume but no definite shape (p. 374)

# Interactive Glossary

M

**magnet** [MAG•nit]  An object that attracts iron and a few other—but not all—metals (p. 520)

**mass** [MAS]  The amount of matter in an object (p. 352)

**matter** [MAT•er]  Anything that has mass and takes up space (p. 352)

**maturity** [muh•TYOOR•ih•tee]  The stage at which organisms can reproduce (p. 118)

**mechanical energy** [muh•KAN•ih•kuhl EN•er•jee]  The total potential and kinetic energy of an object (p. 432)

**microscope** [MY•kruh•skohp]  A tool that makes an object look several times bigger than it is (p. 31)

**mixture** [MIKS•cher]  A combination of two or more different substances that retain their identities (p. 396)

**model** [MOD•l]  A representation of something real that is too big, too small, or has too many parts to investigate directly (p. 47)

© Houghton Mifflin Harcourt Publishing Company  HMH Credits

**moon phase** [MOON FAYZ]  A change in the appearance of the moon's shape as it orbits Earth (p. 319)

**nonrenewable resource** [nahn•rih•NOO•uh•buhl REE•sawrs] A natural resource that cannot be replaced in a reasonable amount of time (p. 210)

**motion** [MOH•shuhn]  A change of position of an object (p. 539)

**nymph** [NIMF]  An immature form of an insect that undergoes incomplete metamorphosis (p. 143)

N

O

**natural resource** [NACH•er•uhl REE•sawrs] Materials found in nature that people and other living things use (p. 208)

**observation** [ahb•zuhr•VAY•shuhn] Information collected by using the five senses (p. 7)

**niche** [NIHCH]  The role a plant or an animal plays in its habitat (p. 179)

**omnivore** [AHM•nih•vawr]  An animal that eats both plants and other animals (p. 192)

# Interactive Glossary

**orbit** [AWR•bit] The path of one object in space around another object (p. 300)

**physical adaptation** [FIZ•ih•kuhl ad•uhp•TAY•shuhn] An adaptation to a body part. (p. 155)

**P**

**pan balance** [PAN BAL•uhns] A tool that measures mass (p. 32)

**physical change** [FIZ•ih•kuhl CHAYNJ] A change in which a new substance is not formed (p. 393)

**parallel circuit** [PAIR•uh•lel SER•kit] An electric circuit that has more than one path for the electric charges to follow (p. 507)

**physical property** [FIZ•ih•kuhl PRAHP•er•tee] A characteristic of matter that you can observe or measure directly (p. 352)

**planet** [PLAN•it] A large, round body that revolves around a star in a clear orbit (p. 328)

**photosynthesis** [foht•oh•SIHN•thuh•sis] The process in which plants use energy from the sun to change carbon dioxide and water into sugar and oxygen (p. 110)

**pollination** [pol•uh•NEY•shuhn]
The transfer of pollen from the male parts
to the female parts of seed plants (p. 122)

**potential energy** [poh•TEN•shuhl
EN•er•jee]  Energy that an object has
because of its position or its condition
(p. 432)

**pollution** [puh•LOO•shuhn]  Harmful
substances mixed with water, air, or soil
(p. 226)

**precipitation** [pree•sip•uh•TAY•shuhn]
Water that falls from clouds to Earth's surface
(p. 249)

**population** [pahp•yuh•LAY•shuhn]  A group
made up of the same type of individuals in an
ecosystem (p. 177)

**producer** [pruh•DOOS•er]  A living thing,
such as a plant, that can make its own food
(p. 181)

**position** [puh•ZISH•uhn]  The location of
an object in relation to a nearby object or
place (p. 539)

**prototype** [PROH•tuh•typ]  The original or
model on which something is based (p. 67)

# Interactive Glossary

**radiation** [ray•dee•AY•shuhn] The movement of heat without matter to carry it (p. 453)

**renewable resource** [rih•NOO•uh•buhl REE•sawrs] A natural resource that can be replaced within a reasonable amount of time (p. 209)

**root** [ROOT] A plant part that is usually underground and absorbs water and minerals from the soil (p. 106)

**rotate** [ROH•tayt] To turn about an axis (p. 298)

**runoff** [RUN•awf] Water that does not soak into the ground and instead flows across Earth's surface (p. 251)

**science** [SY•uhns] The study of the natural world (p. 5)

**scientist** [SY•uhn•tist] A person who asks questions about the natural world (p. 5)

**series circuit** [SIR•eez SER•kit] An electric circuit in which the electrical charges have only one path to follow (p. 507)

**solar system** [SOH•ler SIS•tuhm]  A star and all the planets and other objects that revolve around it (p. 328)

**spore** [SPAWR]  A reproductive structure of some plants, such as mosses and ferns, that can form a new plant (p. 126)

**solid** [SAHL•id]  The state of matter that has a definite shape and a definite volume (p. 374)

**spring scale** [SPRING SKAYL]  A tool that measures forces, such as weight (p. 32)

**solution** [suh•LOO•shuhn]  A mixture that has the same composition throughout because all the parts are mixed evenly (p. 397)

**states of matter** [STAYTS uhv MAT•er]  The physical forms (such as solid, liquid, and gas) that matter can exist in (p. 374)

**speed** [SPEED]  The measure of an object's change in position during a certain amount of time (p. 542)

**static electricity** [STAT•ik ee•lek•TRIS•uh•tee]  The buildup of electric charges on an object (p. 487)

# Interactive Glossary

**stem** [STEM]  The part of a plant that holds it up and has tubes that carry water, minerals, and nutrients through the plant (p. 107)

**two-dimensional model** [TOO-di•MEN•shuh•nuhl MOD•l]  A model that has the dimensions of length and width only (p. 47)

## T

**technology** [tek•NOL•uh•jee]  Any designed system, product, or process used to solve problems (p. 81)

## V

**velocity** [vuh•LAHS•uh•tee]  The speed of an object in a particular direction (p. 542)

**three-dimensional model** [THREE-di•MEN•shuh•nuhl MOD•l]  A model that has the dimension of height as well as width and length (p. 49)

**volume** [VAHL•yoom]  The amount of space an object takes up (p. 356)

**tool** [TOOL]  Anything used to help people shape, build, or produce things to meet their needs (p. 80)

W

**water cycle** [WAWT•er SY•kuhl] The process in which water continuously moves from Earth's surface into the atmosphere and back again (p. 247)

**weather** [WETH•er] What is happening in the atmosphere at a certain place and time (p. 260)

# Index

# Index

# Index

# Index

predicting, 20
prey, 194–195
producers, 181, 190
protons, 484–485
prototypes, 67–68
pupa, 142–143

# Index

as natural resource, 214–217,
    252–253
pollination and, 123
states of, 376–379
treatment facilities, 229
as universal solvent, 398
**water cycle,** 246–251
**water irrigation system,** 85,
    115–116
**watershed,** 215
**water vapor,** 247–248, 266, 377
**weather,** 260–269
    air masses, 276–277
    air pressure and, 261–263
    clouds and, 248, 266–267
    factors affecting, 260–261

forecasting, 278–281
fronts, 276–277
mapping, 278–279
models, 50–51
precipitation, 249, 261,
    268–269
reporters, 51
storms and hurricanes,
    280–281
tracking, 274–275
wind and, 264–265
**Why It Matters,** 50–51, 88–89,
    144–145, 182–183, 198–199,
    216–217, 252–253, 280–281,
    306–307, 320–321, 336–337,
    360–361, 398–399, 412–413,

468–469, 488–489, 508–509,
    524–525
**wind**
    global and local winds,
        264–265
    measurement, 264, 285–286
    pollination and, 122–123
    weather and, 264–265
**windmills,** 525
**wind vane,** 264
**winter,** 302–303

**Yellowstone National Park,** 199